Y0-BZU-362

GUTS

The Anatomy of

THE WALKING DEAD

PAUL VIGNA

HarperCollins books may be purchased for educational, business, or sales promotional use. For information, please email the Special Markets Department at SPsales@harpercollins.com.

A hardcover edition of this book was published in 2017 by Dey Street Books, an imprint of William Morrow.

FIRST DEY STREET BOOKS PAPERBACK EDITION PUBLISHED 2018.

Designed by William Ruoto

Shutterstock art credits: zombie herd by Pavel Chagochkin; zombies outside farmhouse by IfH; blood splatter puddle by jannoon028; zombie head by DM7; bloody hands by Plateresca; blood splatter by Mrspopman1985.

Library of Congress Cataloging-in-Publication Data has been applied for.

ISBN 978-0-06-266612-3

18 19 20 21 22 RS/LSC 10 9 8 7 6 5 4 3 2 1

TO MY SON, ROBERT,
MY REASON TO KEEP FIGHTING

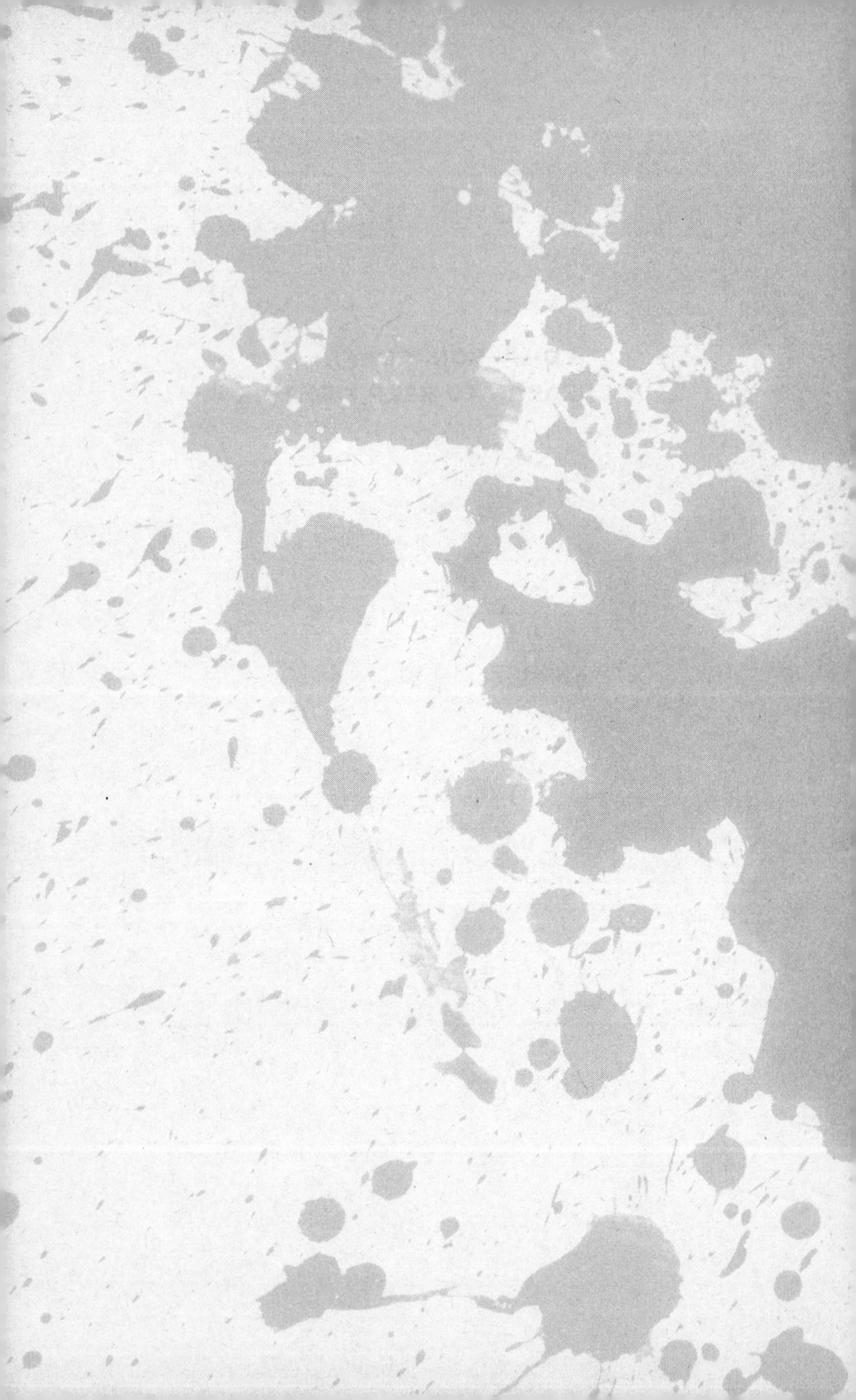

CONTENTS

AUTHOR'S NOTE . . . IX

INTRODUCTION: THE BEATING HEART OF *THE WALKING DEAD* . . . 1

RECAP: SEASON 1 . . . 9

CHAPTER 1: THE GERM . . . 17

CHAPTER 2: THE MAGIC TRICK . . . 33

RECAP: SEASON 2 . . . 45

CHAPTER 3: PATHOLOGY . . . 51

CHAPTER 4: BRINGING THE DEAD TO LIFE . . . 67

GUT-WRENCHING MOMENTS . . . 81

RECAP: SEASON 3 . . . 93

CHAPTER 5: HEART . . . 99

CHAPTER 6: RUPTURE . . . 119

MINOR CHARACTERS . . . 133

RECAP: SEASON 4 . . . 143

CONTENTS

CHAPTER 7: EXPANSION . . . 151
CHAPTER 8: MARCUS AURELIUS AND ZOMBIES . . . 167

TOP TEN EPISODES . . . 185

RECAP: SEASON 5 . . . 195

CHAPTER 9: *THE WALKING DEAD*'S GREATEST MOMENT . . . 203
CHAPTER 10: FOUR WALLS AND A ROOF IN CHARLOTTE, NC . . . 215

WEAPONS . . . 229

RECAP: SEASON 6 . . . 237

CHAPTER 11: DISSECTION . . . 245
CHAPTER 12: WAR AND PIECES . . . 255

RECAP: SEASON 7 . . . 269

CHAPTER 13: SANITY AND MORALITY . . . 277
CHAPTER 14: THE FIRST DAY OF THE REST OF YOUR LIFE . . . 289
AFTERWORD: THE END . . . 297

BIBLIOGRAPHY . . . 303
ACKNOWLEDGMENTS . . . 317

AUTHOR'S NOTE

In some ways, this book is an extension of the recaps of *The Walking Dead* that I write for the *Wall Street Journal,* and because of that, I figured it'd be worth carrying over the ground rules I've used there in writing about the show. First off, this is your one blanket spoiler alert: this book discusses everything on the TV show through season 7. For that matter, it also references *The Walking Dead* graphic novels, *Fear the Walking Dead, The Walking Dead: Rise of the Governor* novels, *Night of the Living Dead, The Odyssey, Mad Men, Cheers, The Sopranos,* an Edgar Allan Poe story about zombies, and *Historia rerum Anglicarum,* a thirteenth-century book that contains the first recognizable zombie story. Do not read on if you care about spoilers. Second, while we will explore the concept of internal logic and story consistency, we are not going to waste time on nitpicking critiques (except for when we get to Glenn in the alley, when we will nitpick quite a lot). Lastly, this book is about the TV show called *The Walking Dead,* and while that is based on graphic novels, we are primarily interested here in the show, not the comics. Also, as a follower of the show first, I make a point of never reading ahead in the comics, so I don't really know what happens in that universe anyway. Don't spoil it for me.

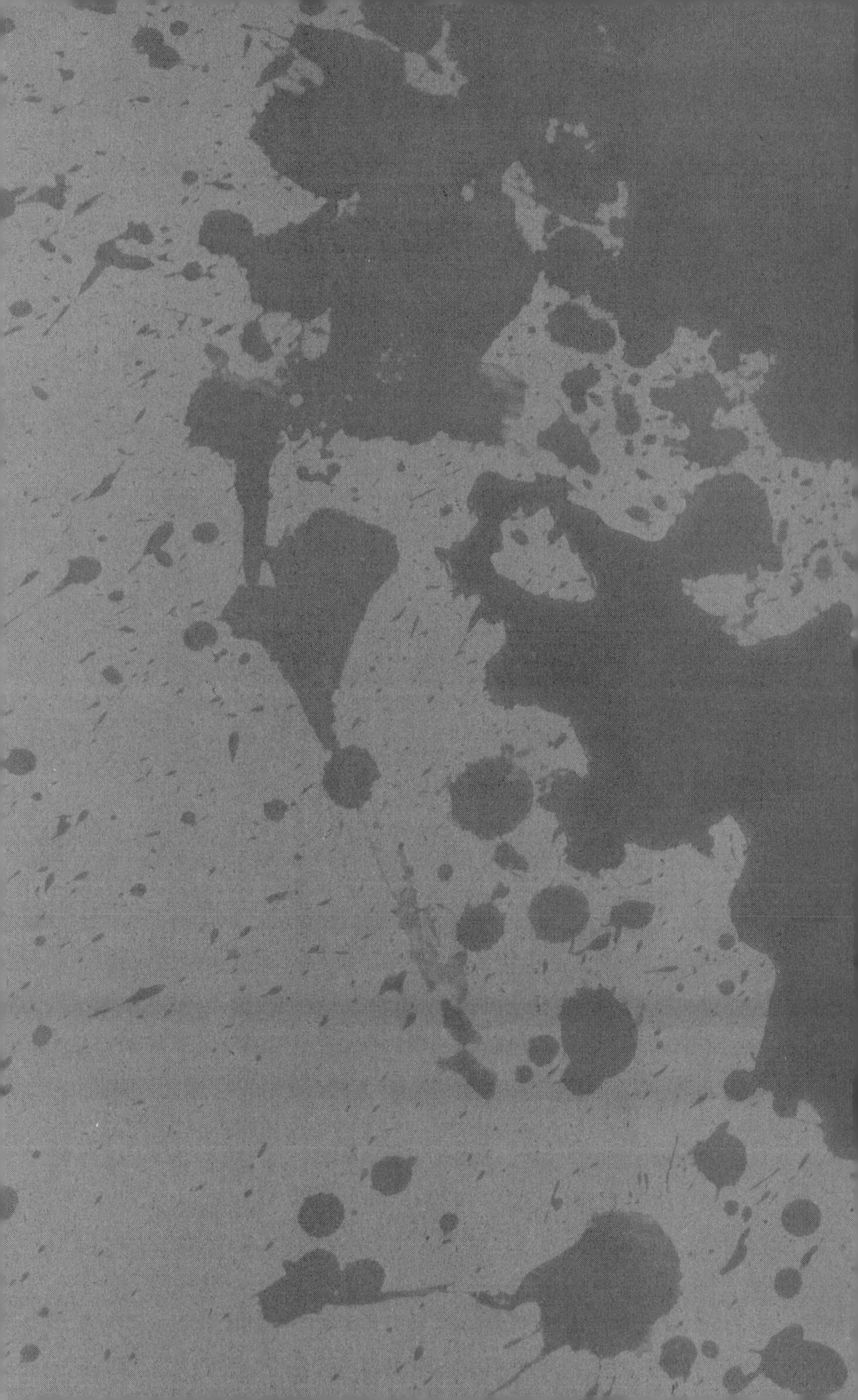

GUTS

INTRODUCTION

THE BEATING HEART OF *THE WALKING DEAD*

It was a cold, rainy October night in New York City, and the wet pavement along Eighth Avenue, always a crowded spot in the heart of busy Midtown, was packed with people standing in a line waiting to get into what bills itself as the world's most famous arena. It isn't an unusual occurrence, of course: The Garden has played host to Stanley Cup championships, the NBA Finals, the "Fight of the Century" between Muhammad Ali and Joe Frazier, and both the Democratic and Republican National Conventions. The Stones, Springsteen, Clapton, and Dylan have all walked its stage. However, the people excitedly milling around in the rain that October night weren't there for a basketball game, or a concert, or politics. They weren't there to see the pope, either; His Holiness had delivered a mass at the Garden two weeks earlier and charmed the city, but was long gone.

The crowds flocking outside the arena that night, October 9, 2015, were there to see *The Walking Dead*.

The executives behind AMC's wildly popular show about a group of zombie fighters surviving an apocalypse rented out the Garden for a special viewing party in the middle of the annual New York Comic Con, ahead of the show's season 6 premiere.

Doing something at Comic Con was routine for a show like *The Walking Dead,* which was, after all, based on a graphic novel of the same name by Robert Kirkman (who also produces the show). But that night at the Garden was different, and the show's fans were giddy. Nobody had ever commandeered a setting as big and prestigious as Madison Square Garden for a TV show. Roughly fifteen thousand people had shown up for it. A stage was erected on the arena floor and designed to look like Alexandria, the fictional town where the series was set at the time (and still is as of this writing). Kirkman was there, as were producer Gale Anne Hurd, director Greg Nicotero, showrunner Scott Gimple, and the other executives. The hundreds of people in the crew were all there, seated on the floor to the right of the stage and occupying a dozen or so rows. And, of course, the entire cast was there, as well as actors whose characters had died over the show's run. Plenty of them were on hand.

Three massive screens hung from the rafters for an early premiere of the first episode of season 6, "First Time Again," in which the Alexandrians discover an old quarry that's become a bottomless pit of "walkers." Rick Grimes (Andrew Lincoln), the former sheriff's deputy who is the show's star and de facto leader of the town, develops a plan to draw them away. There were hundreds, maybe thousands, of zombies in that pit—three hundred extras were dressed to look like the living dead (the rest were CGI effects), more than the show had ever used at one time. The premiere represented a new level of complexity for the show, and the fans absolutely loved it.

The fanfare extended well past the screens and stage. The lobby had props from the show on display, like the notorious fish tanks of the villain called the Governor (hint: they didn't hold fish) and the hospital cafeteria doors with DON'T OPEN DEAD INSIDE written on them. The concession stands sold "Apocalyptic Popcorn," "The Walking Bread," "The Governor's Nuts," and "Sgt. Abraham's Macho Nachos." People in zombie makeup roamed around—good makeup, too, show quality; these zombies looked like extras from a taping, not your friends at a Halloween party. The undead posed for selfies, scared unsuspecting people in the lobby, and lumbered around the seats during the show. The entire Garden had been transformed; it was like Christmas night for zombie fans.

The thousands of fans who attended had come enthusiastically, and in costume. There were plenty of Rick Grimeses in the audience, and Michonnes, and Daryls. There were Abrahams, and Carols, and Glenns and Maggies, and Carls. They came from forty-nine states and nine foreign countries. It wasn't just fans, either; some notable faces were also in the crowd. Robin Lord Taylor from *Gotham* (who also had a small role in one *Walking Dead* episode) was in the audience. Cameron and Tyler Winklevoss, the twin brothers who sued Mark Zuckerberg over Facebook, sat a few rows ahead. Elizabeth Rodriguez from the spin-off show *Fear the Walking Dead* was even closer to the stage, chatting with Nicotero, the director, producer, and makeup-effects wizard for both shows. Michael Zapcic and Ming Chen from AMC's *Comic Book Men* sat on the aisle—and those were just the stars near me, the people I could make out on the floor in the darkness. As the *Wall Street Journal*'s resident zombie expert, I was there, too.

"This is only the beginning of the most intense season of *The Walking Dead*," Kirkman said from the stage. "No one, absolutely no one, is safe." When the crowd booed at that, he gave it back to them.

"Go ahead, boo," he said, "it's still gonna happen. Who's your favorite? They're gonna get it first." Kirkman, a thirty-seven-year-old, thickset native Kentuckian with a heavy beard, does this a lot in his public appearances. Ask him about an upcoming episode, and he'll say, "Is that the one where Rick dies?" Kirkman didn't set out to make the most popular show on television, and to build a media empire around it, and to address thousands of adoring fans in New York City. He started out working in a comic book store, and figured one day that he could write his own. He seems genuinely surprised and bemused by his own success, and has a biting (no pun intended) sense of humor about it.

"There's never been a premiere in Madison Square Garden before," Gale Anne Hurd said from the stage. Hurd is a well-respected industry veteran, a producer for both the *Alien* and *Terminator* franchises.

"The fact that we got to watch it with fifteen thousand people who laughed at the right moment, who cheered at the right moment, who screamed at the right moment, it elevated the show beyond any of our expectations," Nicotero would tell me later.

I screamed along with everybody else in 1983 when Luke Skywalker toppled Darth Vader. I cheered in 2003 when Legolas single-handedly took down that oliphaunt. But those were moments that took place in theaters, with a couple hundred people. I'd never been around anything close to the spectacle staged that night at the Garden, when Rick and Daryl and Michonne wrestled with a zombie army. I don't think anybody had.

I am not an art critic. I'm not a TV critic. I'm not a sociologist, anthropologist, or any other -ologist. I am a business reporter, but for our purposes I'm mainly just a fan of *The Walking Dead,* like you are. I've been doing the *Journal*'s *Walking Dead* recaps since 2012 (season 3, episode 7, "When the Dead Come Knocking" was my first). The previous recapper had left, and nobody else in the newsroom watched the show, so I got drafted. The reality, though, is that I jumped at the chance. I'd been a loyal fan since Rick and Shane were sitting in the squad car, eating burgers and fries and shooting the breeze. While I was honing my fandom by writing my column, the show was taking a genre that was backwoods territory even for horror fans and putting it firmly in the forefront of pop culture. How'd they manage this? There isn't one single element that explains the show's success.

First, there was Kirkman's original vision of an open-ended zombie story, one that would continue well past the usual ninety-minute running time of a movie. Then there was the creative team that brought the show to the small screen.

More than those elements, though, what truly makes the show work are the characters. The people who live and often die on *The Walking Dead* aren't studies in psychology, like Tony Soprano, or powerful and duplicitous, like Cersei Lannister. They aren't the president of the United States, or Texas oil barons, or powerful FBI agents. The characters on *The Walking Dead* are so common as to almost be stereotypical: the small-town sheriff, the deadbeat redneck, the battered housewife, the army medic, the soldier, the priest, the brainy nerd, the pizza delivery boy, the farmer and his daughters. They are completely average people, and therefore completely relatable. You can be a fan of *The Sopranos, Game of Thrones,* or *The West Wing,* but most people don't see themselves as mobsters, medieval kings, or presidents (well, maybe some of you want to be president, and good luck to you). But a cop, a housewife, a soldier, a farmer, a regular working stiff? You can see yourself as that. Hell, chances are you *are* that. When these completely relatable human beings are thrust into an overwhelming reality where their every waking and sleeping moment is fraught with mortal peril, and then, through the writers' visions, are rendered as true-to-life as possible, this is more than just a television program: there's a visceral bond between the viewers and the characters that no other production can replicate.

Moreover, a key to the show's success is the time in which it appears, and I don't mean the time slot. I mean the times: our age of rolling disasters, from earthquakes to tsunamis, terrorist attacks, and financial panics. It's not surprising in times like these that a show about the end of the world might find a receptive audience. What might be surprising is that a show about the survivors of a zombie plague would have something to say about surviving our own daily challenges, big and small. Yet that is exactly what a number of people take away from it. It's like the note the teenager Enid (Katelyn Nacon) writes to herself over and over—in the dirt, on a dusty car window, even out of turtle bones: "JSS." *Just Survive Somehow.*

When *The Walking Dead* premiered, it immediately became AMC's highest-rated show. It wasn't the network's most lauded show, however. *Mad Men,* which debuted in 2007, was a critical darling, a truly inventive series about an ad agency in 1950s and 1960s New York. A year later, the network brought *Breaking Bad* to television. It was just as highly lauded. The arbiters of taste loved these shows. The Emmy Awards came in bunches. And they were good shows, both of them (I could argue that *Mad Men* should have ended the minute Don told Betty everything about Dick Whitman, but that's another story). But they never brought in viewers like *The Walking Dead* did.

The episode of *Walking Dead* that premieres at 9 P.M. on Sundays is the number-one-rated show on TV in the 18–49 age group, the most coveted demographic for advertisers. There are shows that have better overall ratings, like *The Big Bang Theory* and—at times—*Empire,* but those are network television shows. *The Walking Dead* is a cable show. Cable shows don't usually swim in these ratings waters. This zombie show is so popular, though, it goes head-to-head with the NFL's *Sunday Night Football,* with ratings that are close to or better than it (and professional football is the single most valuable television product there is these days). However—and this is the real critical point here—it's not just the ratings for *The Walking Dead.* The program that comes on after *The Walking Dead* is called *Talking Dead,* hosted by Chris Hardwick, and is literally a talk show about *The Walking Dead.* That is a top-ten-rated show on cable (and trendsetter; series as diverse as *Orphan Black, Mr. Robot,* and *Girls* have started their own after-shows). After that, at 11 P.M. most Sundays, AMC replays the 9 P.M. episode. And *that* is a top-ten-rated show on cable. Look at the ratings for October 30, 2016: Number one was the 9 P.M. airing of *The Walking Dead,* with 12.4 million total viewers. Number two was *Talking Dead,* with 4.2 million viewers. Number three was the 7:55 P.M. airing of the previous week's episode. Number five was the 11:05 P.M. repeat of that night's episode. Only an episode of *Family Guy* on Adult Swim broke up the *Dead* stranglehold on the top five. That's how the ratings usually go with this show, even with the dip in overall viewers during season 7, and to say nothing of the spin-off show, *Fear the Walking Dead,* which is the number-two-rated show on cable. You already know what number one is.

Part of this book is pure fan service: We're going to explore the show's history, how it got on the air, what goes into producing it, how the actors who are on it got on it, and what happens when they're no longer on it. A larger part of the book is going to be exploring the phenomenon of the show itself, though. How did a zombie show become so big? Is there a larger lesson? We're going to explore the history of the genre and the current cultural landscape—and its fandom as the gift that keeps on giving. Because when you see the show's ratings, and the lack of respect come Emmy time, there's a major disconnect there. Are fifteen million people just looking for a good scare every Sunday, or is there something more that brings them back?

RECAP

SEASON ONE

- **SAFE HAVEN:** Atlanta survivors' camp
- **SURVIVORS LOST:** Amy, Jim, Ed Peletier, Jacqui, Dr. Edwin Jenner
- **NOTABLE WALKERS:** "Summer" (the pajama zombie), Bicycle Girl
- **HORRIBLE HACKS:** Merle Dixon's hand

RICK GRIMES (ANDREW LINCOLN), KING COUNTY SHERIFF'S deputy, wakes up in a bed, talking, he thinks, to his friend, who isn't actually there. Nobody is. On the table next to him are dried, dead flowers. The clock on the wall isn't moving. Realizing he's in a hospital, he calls for a nurse, but nobody comes. He doesn't understand what's happened. He was shot—he knows that—stopping some armed criminals. Everything is a blank after that, and nothing seems remotely normal now.

He wanders out into the hall. The place is an abandoned, chaotic mess. The phones don't work, lights flicker. He grabs a pack of matches from the nurses' station and explores the premises using its faint light. On the floor, he sees a gutted corpse; bullet holes are sprayed across the walls. He comes to a set of padlock-barred double doors with a two-by-four through the handles. DON'T OPEN DEAD INSIDE is spray-painted on them. As he comes closer, he hears horrible groaning sounds. The doors bulge, pushed by something inside. They open as far as the chains will allow, and then gray, cold fingers slip through, reaching, probing. Rick flees in horror. Something has gone terribly, terribly wrong.

Outside the building, it is worse. Dozens of wrapped, rotting corpses are laid in rows on the ground. At the top of a hill he finds an abandoned army post outside another burned-out building. Army Ranger helicopters sit alongside Humvees and tents. There is not a soul anywhere, and Rick stumbles into town. He finds a bike and grabs it. The noise of that action stirs something on the ground nearby. It's a rotting corpse, shredded at the waist, intestines and entrails splayed out. It rolls over, groaning and growling, and reaches an outstretched arm toward Rick. He falls, his face a picture of utter horror.

It will all become clear soon enough. The world collapsed under the weight of a catastrophic plague, which killed the vast majority of people—only to reanimate them as barely alive, flesh-craving, brainless monsters. There isn't anything left to do but try and fill in the vaguest rough edges of the reason why this happened. Everything that used to make life safe and comfortable has been stripped away. Survival now is a matter of instinct, guts, and luck. For Rick and the other living, the only question is how to get through another day, another night, another hour.

Rick makes his way back to his home only to find that his wife, Lori (Sarah Wayne Callies), and son, Carl (Chandler Riggs), are gone. He notices that they took some supplies—a sure sign that the two left together, harried perhaps, but with enough time to grab the family photo albums. Outside his house, he meets two people, Morgan Jones (Lennie James) and his son, Duane (Duane actually clocks Rick with a shovel, mistakenly thinking he's a zombie). They tell him about the undead, and about a purported refugee camp in Atlanta. That's where the Joneses were headed, until Morgan's wife got infected. Now she scrapes along out in the street with the other walkers, and Morgan is too distraught to either mercy-kill his wife or just move on. Duane, meanwhile, is simply shattered by the horror of what's happened. Even the people who aren't killed by the plague physically are killed psychologically, something we'll see time and again.

Rick leaves them, grabs a squad car, and heads to Atlanta, but not before going back to the park where he saw the dismembered zombie crawling in the dirt. "I'm sorry this happened to you," he says, and mercy-kills the thing, which looks more sad and pathetic than dangerous. This is the essential Rick Grimes, a man who, at this point, will go out of his way to do a kindness for a stranger who, given the chance, would kill him. Wearing that uniform, Rick is still the law, still a representative of the old moral and ethical code.

His trip to Atlanta nearly gets him killed. He scavenges for gas a few times, but eventually ditches the car and steals a horse to get him the rest of the way. He rides into the dead city on horseback, like a sheriff out of the old westerns. When he arrives, there is no refugee camp, no survivors, no supplies or safe haven. Only the dead and more desolation. A few straggling zombies follow him. He sees a helicopter, a sign of life, and tries to track it. Coming around a corner, he gallops smack into a street choked with walkers. Hundreds of them. That's a problem. A big problem. Now he's surrounded, and forced off his horse. He loses his bag of guns. He scrambles under a tank, then through a hatch into the tank. He's safe, but trapped. A voice comes over the tank's radio. "Hey, you, the dumbass in the tank. You cozy in there?" The voice, we find out, belongs to Glenn Rhee (Steven Yeun), who is in the city scavenging with a small group of survivors, including Andrea (Laurie Holden), T-Dog (IronE Singleton), Morales (Juan Gabriel Pareja), and Merle Dixon (Michael Rooker), a drug-addled, dangerously violent man. They save Rick from the tank and then get trapped in a department store, but Merle is another problem. Coked-up and reckless, he's taking potshots at the zombies from the roof, which is just attracting more of them to the store. When the other survivors try to stop him, he gets into a vicious and racially tinged fight with the African American T-Dog. Rick finally subdues Merle and handcuffs him to an air duct, explaining the reality of the new world: there are no blacks and whites anymore; there are only the living and the dead. It's not clear whether Merle agrees.

Rick comes up with a bold plan to save the group: cover himself and Glenn in zombie guts, walk among the dead to a nearby truck, bring the truck back, and drive everybody away. It's a nick-of-time operation. The walkers bust into the department store, and in their haste to get away, Rick's group leaves Merle handcuffed and trapped on the roof.

When they get back to the survivors' camp, Rick is overjoyed to see Lori and Carl, along with his police partner Shane (Jon Bernthal). Those three, as well as a dozen or so others, have been camped outside Atlanta. Shane, the most capable one in the group, has become the de facto leader. Also, it's clear that Shane is in love with Rick's wife. Whether he was before "the Turn" isn't clear, but he sure is now, and he has some mixed feelings about his old partner showing up alive.

Merle's brother, Daryl (Norman Reedus), shows up in camp, and is infuriated about what happened to his brother. Rick, even though he just found Lori and Carl, decides to go back with a small group into Atlanta for Merle. Going back is dangerous, but Rick feels responsible, and it's the first choice he makes that involves this group. Immediately, something else is clear: Rick is somebody who isn't afraid to make hard, reasoned decisions. In this world, that is a valuable quality, and possessing it immediately gives Rick a leadership mantle. Shane had been acting as the group's informal leader, but that changes quickly. It won't be the only friction between these two best friends.

They return to the roof to find Merle gone. Only a hacksaw and his hand remain. While they're there, they try to retrieve the bag of guns Rick lost when his horse was attacked, and they have a brief but fraught run-in with some bad-looking survivors who have taken refuge in a health care facility and are caring for the old and infirm.

Back at the camp, we learn a little more about some of the

people there. Dale Horvath (Jeffrey DeMunn) is a wise, soulful sort, given to quoting William Faulkner; Carol Peletier (Melissa McBride), married to Ed (Adam Minarovich) and mother to Sophia (Madison Lintz), is a cowed, battered housewife. What goes on in the Peletier household is not spoken aloud. It involves Ed beating his wife, and apparently molesting his daughter (this is only hinted at, but it's a pretty strong hint). Andrea and Amy Harrison are somewhat sheltered sisters, distraught over the fate of their parents, who were living in Florida; Jacqui worked in the zoning department.

Before the Merle search party can get back to the camp, the worst happens: a "herd" of walkers comes through. Ed gets eaten alive in his tent; Amy gets bitten; Jim gets gouged in the stomach. Others die as well. It's a horrifying scene, even after Rick and crew get back and stave in all the walkers' heads.

The camp is clearly no longer a safe place to be. The survivors leave, with the goal of finding refuge at the Centers for Disease Control. When they reach the CDC, though, they find only one man living: Dr. Edwin Jenner, who is literally counting down the seconds until the building's generators run out of gas. The facility's computers will read that as a catastrophic failure and initiate a self-destruct sequence. Jenner, who believes the end of the world has finally arrived, aims to die, and since he let the Grimes clan in there, he also aims to take them with him. At the last second, he relents and lets them leave, whispering something in Rick's ear; what he says, we don't know. Rick's group barely escapes before the whole complex blows up, and they head out on the road, in search of survival for however long and wherever they can scratch it out.

CHAPTER 1

THE GERM

"HEY, MISTER, DO YOU EVEN KNOW WHAT'S GOING ON?"

—MORGAN JONES

(SEASON 1, EPISODE 1, "DAYS GONE BYE")

On October 31, 2010, the cable channel AMC premiered *The Walking Dead,* a new show based on a comic book series of the same name. AMC had found great success with its first two scripted dramatic series, *Mad Men* and *Breaking Bad,* but now it was taking a chance on a horror series, and, what's more, a horror series about zombies. Sure, the show had a built-in fan base from the comics, but zombies were not the stuff of prestige viewing; they were still considered B-movie material. The show had two Hollywood heavyweights behind it in Frank Darabont—who wrote and directed *The Mist, The Green Mile,* and *The Shawshank Redemption*—and Gale Anne Hurd—who produced the *Alien* and *Terminator* franchises—but it was still a big gamble for a basic cable channel that was emphatically trying to set itself apart in a crowded landscape. The series would also star Andrew Lincoln, a largely unknown British actor, which further shrouded its potential eminence. From the start, the show set a distinctive tone, though. Darabont was best known for the excellent 1994 prison film *The Shawshank Redemption,* and he brought that cinematic eye with him to the small screen. He took the zombie motif and layered a character-driven story on top of it.

AMC was born in the 1980s as a pay service, showing American movie classics (hence the acronym) aimed at film buffs. In 2002, the channel formally condensed its name to just AMC, started broadcasting newer movies like *Raiders of the Lost Ark* and *Predator,* and added more advertising. In most respects, it now looked like any other basic cable channel, and its film-buff roots were buried. Ratings were up, but so was the criticism. "The channel's focus now seems much less clear," *Newsday* columnist Diane Werts complained. She had a point. In a world of hundreds of channels, how would AMC stand out? If it was going to jettison its core audience of film buffs, who was it going to replace them with?

AMC's big gambit to attract a new audience was to turn its focus away from movies and run its own original programming. Its first scripted series, *Mad Men,* launched in 2007 to immediate, fawning acclaim. In 2008, it premiered *Breaking Bad,* which, too, was widely lauded. The critics could not say enough about these shows, which dominated the Emmy Awards. Very quickly, AMC went from being the channel that showed old movies to the channel that had the best new original series. The stunning success of those two shows meant that AMC could realistically transform itself if it could maintain that level of success. In 2010, the channel tried out two other shows. The first was called *Rubicon,* about an intelligence analyst who suddenly realizes he's in the middle of a massive conspiracy theory. Its August premiere attracted two million viewers—a record for AMC at the time. But the show quickly fizzled, and the network canceled it by November (the show's fans, true to type, had a conspiracy theory about the cancellation). That put even more pressure on the other show the network was launching that year: *The Walking Dead*.

In *The Walking Dead* AMC had both a better bet and a bigger risk. Because the show was based on a comic book series that had been around for seven years, it had a built-in audience. On the other hand, it was a horror series. *About zombies*. HBO had a respectable horror series run with *Tales from the Crypt* and *The Hitchhiker* in the late 1980s and '90s, and had a good show in *True Blood*. If you're old enough, perhaps you remember *Dark Shadows* or *Night Gallery*. Those were true cult classics, but not widely popular. The '90s gave us *Buffy the Vampire Slayer* and *The X-Files,* and while both were popular, one was horror by way of teenage angst and the other was about aliens and government cover-ups. *The Walking Dead* was completely different—far more gruesome, realistic, and graphic than anything that had come before. Clearly, it was not *Buffy the Vampire Slayer*.

I was one of the 5.3 million people who watched the premiere that Halloween night in 2010, a crowd that represented AMC's largest series premiere audience and the biggest audience for any show on television that premiered that year. I found it utterly engrossing. I remember walking in midtown Manhattan the next morning, on the way to my job at the *Wall Street Journal,* and being haunted by the sneaking suspicion that all the people on the street with me were *already dead,* as if the zombie plague had already washed over us. The show took a familiar, mostly schlocky genre and elevated it to a place it had not been before. I have not missed a second of either it or its spin-off, *Fear the Walking Dead,* since.

Zombies as we know them today, the shambling (sometimes running), flesh-craving, reanimated corpses, date back to George Romero's 1968 film *Night of the Living Dead,* wherein a group of people find themselves trapped in a house in the country trying to survive an onslaught of corpses reanimated by a radiation blast after a satellite explodes. Before Romero, zombies were mainly portrayed as people, usually dead but sometimes living, under the spell of a kind of voodoo curse (the whole idea of "zombies" originated in Haiti, something we'll explore a little later). The terror came when the witch doctor or mad scientist, or even Martians (yes, there actually was a 1950s serial involving zombies and Martians called *Zombies of the Stratosphere*), turned the zombies on the good guys. It was Romero who reinvented the zombie as a brain eater, and later refined it in *Dawn of the Dead* (1978) and *Day of the Dead* (1985). Romero's zombies truly terrorized people: a young Roger Ebert wrote a great essay about his experience seeing the movie on a Saturday morning during a matinee that literally had unsuspecting children terrified and crying. The zombies eventually got faster, like in Danny Boyle's *28 Days Later,* but they were still essentially linked to Romero's version. The ends of Romero's films usually feature one or two plucky survivors finding some kind of safe haven, or leaving whatever hell-zone they've been in to search for one. What you don't see is what happens next, because the credits start rolling. And what happens next after a Romero zombie movie ends was exactly the question that a Kentucky kid named Robert Kirkman asked himself.

Kirkman was born in Richmond, Kentucky, in 1978, and when he was still a child his family moved to Cynthiana, a small town of about six thousand people between Cincinnati and Lexington that straddles the Licking River. Cynthiana is about as American as it gets. Main Street is anchored by the whitewashed, Greek-columned courthouse and two steepled churches. Two Civil War battles were fought there. While it was originally built with the profits from tobacco and whiskey, in the postwar years the conglomerate 3M became the town's biggest employer: the Cynthiana factory was for decades the only place in the world making the famous Post-it notes. This small-town heritage bleeds through the pages of many of Kirkman's comics, especially *The Walking Dead*. While attending Harrison County High School in the 1990s, Kirkman gave no obvious indication that he was going to become a big success. He was an average student who skated by on Bs and Cs, didn't plan on going to college, and wasn't quite sure what he was going to do after high school. To all the world, he looked like a typical '90s slacker. He loved comics and worked at a local comic book store. Kirkman briefly had some aspirations to be a comic book artist but realized that, unlike his childhood friend Tony Moore, he wasn't a talented enough illustrator. However, while working in this seemingly dead-end job, he absorbed important lessons about the comic book business. One of them was this: There was essentially one distribution channel for comics. In the 1990s there had been a cutthroat war among the distributors, and one, Diamond Comic Distributors, emerged as the last company standing. Diamond had the entire North American market to itself. If you could get Diamond's attention, Kirkman realized, you could publish a comic.

Young Kirkman also learned about creator rights, and was drawn to the plight of the artist without control over their work. In the industry's early days, the people actually creating and illustrating the stories had very little control over what the publishing houses did with their work, and many lost out on countless opportunities to capitalize on their own material. In the 1970s and '80s, some of the biggest names in comics, like Jack Kirby, Alan Moore (no relation to Tony), and Frank Miller, were getting behind a movement to take control of their work. Several other prominent artists, including Todd McFarlane, Marc Silvestri, Rob Liefeld, and Erik Larsen, left Marvel in 1992 to form their own house, Image Comics, where creators would own and control their products. That was where Kirkman wanted to be, and while he knew he couldn't make it as an artist, he thought he could make it as a writer. Besides, he already had an artist in Tony Moore. First, though, the two young dreamers needed a story. Along with Moore, Kirkman created his own publishing house in his parent's basement, which he called Funk-O-Tron. His first title, in 2000, was an ambitious one: *Battle Pope.*

In *Battle Pope,* the Pontiff Maximus becomes the central figure in an apocalyptic fight between good and evil. The twist is that this pope is a foulmouthed, drinking, smoking reprobate. By temperament, he belongs on the side of evil, but Jesus picks him to do his bidding in the war on Earth (from the start, Kirkman was mining apocalyptic themes). With his self-published *Battle Pope* in his back pocket, Kirkman started angling to get himself onto Image's roster of artists. He talked his way into conducting an interview with Erik Larsen, a story he retold in an interview at 2015's South by Southwest festival, and the two hit it off. He then followed up. And followed up again. And followed up some more.

"Do whatever you can to make friends with people," Kirkman said. "Hard work is not the only thing that'll help you out." Kirkman often acts like his success is due to some galactic mistake, and like he doesn't really care about it. He cracks a lot of jokes and is very self-deprecating. He comes off like he's still that high school slacker working at the comic book store. But he is also a very driven artist who has a lot of moxie and gumption.

When he finished *Battle Pope,* Kirkman was in his early twenties, living off credit cards and using them to fund his unprofitable Funk-O-Tron. He'd moved to Lexington, Kentucky, but was still struggling to make ends meet. At one point, he recalled in an interview, "I was like $40,000 in debt and I was making about

$300 a year. And I would just lay on my floor and shake." Those years were a roller coaster ride. For a time, he was supporting himself and his wife by working at a lighting-supply store during the day and working on the comics at night. In the early aughts, Kirkman's networking and hard work finally paid off. In 2002, he began writing for Image Comics, churning out many titles and collaborating freely. Kirkman's debut at Image was a four-issue miniseries called *SuperPatriot: America's Fighting Force* (SuperPatriot was a character from an Erik Larsen title, *Savage Dragon*). After that came *Tech Jacket, Invincible, Masters of the Universe,* and *Capes*. In 2003, Image published the first issue of the title that would change Kirkman's life: *The Walking Dead.*

"When I set out to do *The Walking Dead,* I just wanted to do a really cool comic," Kirkman said in the aforementioned South by Southwest interview. At the time, he was watching George Romero's *Dead* movies, and the germ of his idea for a zombie story grew out of pondering these films' stark circumstances. "I thought, these shouldn't end. What if they just never ended?"

So he started writing the comics, with his childhood friend Tony Moore doing the artwork (Moore eventually left the series and was replaced by Charlie Adlard), which quickly built up a following. One of Kirkman's earliest fans was Frank Darabont. Darabont randomly came across a copy of *The Walking Dead* in 2005 in a comic book shop called House of Secrets in Burbank, California. "I was immediately drawn to it," he said in an interview. Darabont had seen *Night of the Living Dead* in junior high, and was a self-professed "genre nerd" (which makes sense when you realize that *Shawshank* was adapted from a short story by the master of horror writers, Stephen King). The next day, he was on the phone to his agent, talking about it.

The timing was good. TV was coming into its own as a medium. The HBO series *The Sopranos* (1999–2007) had completely rewritten the rules of what could be accomplished on television by using long-form storytelling on the small screen; there was a rush in Hollywood to meet the burgeoning demand. AMC's business-model reboot had come at the perfect time, it seemed. *But zombies?* Kirkman, for one, didn't think people would be interested. "Zombies are essentially people who eat people," Kirkman said in a *Rolling Stone* interview, recounting his thinking at the time, "so it's a cannibal show." Still, he was willing to see if television was keen on his little story. Darabont, working with Kirkman and his business partner David Alpert, shopped the show around. And it did get interest. NBC was interested, and sat down with Darabont and his agent in 2005. Kirkman and Darabont produced a pilot script to satisfy NBC's interest. NBC read the script but ultimately passed. As much as the network was keen on shaking things up and taking chances, they weren't prepared to shake it up that much. *The Walking Dead* was simply too violent for a major television network.

(A side note: This kind of story—the network that passed—isn't so unusual, and I'm pretty sure virtually every artistic creation goes through this kind of thing. In any commercial-creative medium, you're going to hear these stories. The great irony of this is that years later, when Kirkman was a big success, he experienced the other side of that coin. He and Alpert ran into a network executive at a party who asked casually what else they were working on besides *The Walking Dead*. Kirkman mentioned an idea he'd been toying around with. "Great," the executive said, according to Alpert, who told me the story when I interviewed him on my podcast, "let's make it." He hadn't written it yet, or even plotted it out, but it was sold right there. Just because he was Robert Kirkman. So he went back to his office and started working on a new comic, *Outcast;* the TV show based on it premiered on Cinemax in 2016.)

But back to the narrative: After NBC passed, Darabont showed the pilot script to a friend, the producer Gale Anne Hurd. She saw the potential in Kirkman's vision. The team now comprised Kirkman, Darabont, Hurd, and Alpert, but it was Hurd who suggested AMC as a potential home for the show. At this point, the options rights that NBC had owned to produce a television show based on the comic had expired. Now HBO and AMC had a chance to pursue those rights. HBO, somewhat surprisingly, had the same problem with violence that NBC had. They wanted it toned down, but Hurd would not budge on that issue. The violence on *The Walking Dead* may be excessive for some tastes, but all the blood, gore, and guts are there to illustrate the story. Nobody involved wanted to compromise on that. HBO couldn't come to an agreement, so Darabont's team convinced AMC to pursue the rights and order a pilot. By April 2009, AMC was negotiating with Darabont for the pilot episode. In September 2009, they signed a memorandum agreement for the script and set out terms for the potential series. AMC understood *The Walking Dead.* It took a chance, and it hit the jackpot.

At the time (and this became important down the road, after AMC fired Darabont in 2011 and he turned around and sued the company) the agreement was that Darabont would write the script and serve as lead executive producer, a role that is commonly nicknamed the "showrunner," the one in charge of everything. AMC would essentially pay an outside production company to produce the show, which is what it had done with *Mad Men* and *Breaking Bad.* As showrunner, Darabont would be entitled to up to 12.5 percent of the production company's share of the profits from the show. Darabont began by rewriting the script he'd first shown to NBC. But at the time, AMC was in a protracted fight with *Mad Men* creator Matthew Weiner over the budget for that show. It decided it would rather produce *The Walking Dead* in-house, with its own production company rather than an outside firm, a decision that almost certainly was informed by its fights with Weiner. After more negotiating, Darabont and his production team agreed to the idea of AMC taking the show in-house. Everyone got to work.

"We all kind of sensed that something special was going on, but there was no way we could have imagined or really foreseen the global phenomenon that it became," Juan Gabriel Pareja, who played the character Morales in the first season, told me. Pareja had worked with Darabont on 2007's *The Mist,* and it was Darabont who wanted him back for his new project. (Indeed, several members of *The Walking Dead* besides Pareja were in *The Mist:* Laurie Holden, Jeffrey DeMunn, and Melissa McBride. Darabont is one of those directors who likes to work with the same people.)

Pareja wasn't a horror fan himself, but the first time he read the script, he told me, his thought was "Pardon my French, but, *holy shit.*" It appeared to Pareja from reading the script that it comprised a huge vision, and he wondered how they were going to make it work. He went to the same comic book store in Burbank where Darabont had discovered the comic and started reading it himself, and he wondered again, "How in the hell are they going to do this?"

They did it because Darabont brought with him a craftsmanship honed in the movies. *The Walking Dead* wasn't filmed like a TV show. The visual cues, like the slow pacing—especially in the pilot—and the long establishing shots, came from cinema. It was even shot like a movie: Darabont ended up filming it with 16-millimeter cameras, a type of film that gives the show that somewhat grainy texture.

"Frank Darabont's vision was a particularly cinematic experience on TV," Glen Mazzara, a writer and producer on the show, who would become its second showrunner, said in a September

2015 deposition related to a lawsuit between Darabont and AMC. "It's a lot about the cinematic appeal of the show. The zombies are very visceral and grounded." The techniques, the attention to detail in the effects, the particular brand of storytelling—and we'll get into all of that later in the book—it all came together. The premiere episode was so good, the *Wall Street Journal*'s Nancy deWolf Smith wrote, "It has hooked even a zombie hater like me. . . . It plays with theatrical grandeur, on a canvas that feels real, looks cinematic, and has an orchestral score to match." For all that, she noted that the small, intimate moments were the "most breathtaking."

Tim Goodman at the *Hollywood Reporter* noted all the genre cues, as well as references to westerns—the image of the lone lawman riding his horse into town—and dystopias. He caught on to another theme as well, one that would become a recurring source of friction: "that what we're capable of doing to one another is far worse than having a zombie eat our guts." Given that it gets to tell a longer-frame narrative on television, rather than a two-hour movie, *The Walking Dead* can tell a "boldly different story" that explores "the deeper motivations in Kirkman's source work, asking what man is really capable of when pushed."

Not everybody was a fan. In its entire run, the show has garnered only two Emmy Awards, both for the show's prosthetic makeup. It has never even been nominated in a single acting, writing, directing, or drama category. As if that snub from the dilettantes at the Academy of Television Arts & Sciences weren't enough, the father of the modern zombie genre himself, George Romero, dismissed the show as "just a soap opera with a zombie occasionally."

To bemoan that the show doesn't play to the highbrow crowd or mimic the traditional conventions of the genre is to miss the fascinating things it does. Yes, it's a "zombie show," but in Kirkman's world, the undead end up representing a different kind of threat. In *The Walking Dead,* "the zombies are like part of the environment," said novelist Jay Bonansinga, who has written eight full-length novels based on the show's characters. Romero's zombies were differentiated, especially in the later films, when he'd given them their own traits and made them characters in the story. In Kirkman's zombie world, the undead shamble through in giant herds and swarms. The dead are an environmental disaster as much as anything else, he's said. In that way, they are like any other challenge we face, and what becomes important for the show's characters is how they respond to that challenge, which is really the heart of character. "I imagine that a hero is a man who does what he can," the French novelist Romain Rolland wrote in his masterpiece, *Jean-Christophe* (1904–1912). "The others do not do it." The essence of *The Walking Dead* is in characters responding to threats in the only way they can.

Another subtlety is the way gender and race concepts are handled on the show, or rather, the way they aren't handled. "There's women on the show that are really tough, and it's not commented on, 'Well, I guess she's a tough girl,'" said Kerry Cahill, who plays Dianne, one of the warriors in the Kingdom. "It's not [commented on] because it doesn't need to be." In other words, the world portrayed is a true meritocracy. In the world of the post–zombie apocalypse, if a woman, or anybody, can do a certain job, they get that job. All that matters is ability. This is made explicitly clear in the series premiere, when Rick subdues Merle after Merle's fight with T-Dog, a black man. Rick explains, in cruder terms, that black and white don't matter anymore. All that matters is the living and the dead. It's not something Merle is ready to hear, but it struck a chord with fans I talked to. This kind of social equality resonated with Cahill, who was born in a Montana town that was too small to dole out jobs based on sex. But it's also something she sees more in society today everywhere, and *The Walking Dead* reflects that new reality. It's a definite change from the world where men go to jobs and women stay at home.

"That world isn't actually how we're living as much anymore," she said. This show "doesn't bend to the gender roles, it rather owns that we have all of them."

At the first camp, outside Atlanta, the women are shown doing the laundry, and complaining about it. As the show progresses, the old gender roles quickly melt away, replaced by, well, nothing. The natural disaster of the zombie apocalypse forces these precarious communities to do away with any of the old prejudices. By season 7, Maggie Greene (Lauren Cohan) is basically running one community, Hilltop; Sasha (Sonequa Martin-Green) and Rosita (Christian Serratos) are tough enough to go take on the villain Negan (Jeffrey Dean Morgan) on their own; and Michonne (Danai Gurira) is going to be Rick's equal partner in building the new world. "The zombies and the apocalypse are what give the show the ability to take it all away," Cahill said, referring to issues of racism and sexism, "but I think the reason it resonates is because those things are going away."

The six-episode first season's ratings look pedestrian now, with the show averaging about 11.3 million viewers in season 7, but at the time they were fantastic for a basic-cable genre show (for the record, the show's highest-rated season was its fifth, which averaged 14.3 million viewers a week). After those 5.35 million watched the season 1 premiere, the audience hovered around

5 million for the next four episodes, and drew 5.97 million for the finale. The ratings would go up every year. Season 2's premiere drew 7.26 million. Season 3 attracted 10.97. Season 4, 16.11. Season 5, 17.30. The show was not only competing with broadcast television—something that was unheard of for a cable show—it was dominating broadcast.

The Walking Dead was quickly becoming a bona fide phenomenon, and not just in the United States. AMC sold the worldwide rights to the show to Fox International Channels, which rolled it out in 120 countries about a month after the U.S. premiere in 2010. In the UK, 659,000 viewers tuned in, making it the highest-rated premiere for a Fox show in five years. In Italy, 360,000 watched, the second-highest-rated showing for any Fox show ever in that country. In Spain, 105,000 viewers watched. In Southeast Asia, it was the highest-rated show on any Western channel, with 380,000 viewers across the region. In the Philippines, it outdrew every other show in its time slot by 1,700 percent. In Singapore, it was by 425 percent. Across Latin America, it was the same. In Mexico, for instance, it outdrew other shows in its time slot by 230 percent. In 2016, NBC Universo was awarded the rights to air the show in the United States dubbed in Spanish, marking the first time the show was airing in its home market in another language. It naturally became the network's highest-rated show.

Five years after *The Walking Dead* premiered, AMC had itself built out an international network, and through that it premiered the spin-off *Fear the Walking Dead* overseas in conjunction with the U.S. premiere. The show debuted across 125 territories and gave the channel its highest ratings ever. In the United States, it attracted 10 million viewers, making it the highest-rated cable premiere ever.

And, sure, there were lots and lots of average people, like most of us, watching *The Walking Dead*. But it was a big hit with stars as well. Actors Ashton Kutcher and Mila Kunis are fans (both were on *That '70s Show* with Danny Masterson, whose half sister is Alanna Masterson, who plays Tara Chambler on *The Walking Dead*). John Cusack and Ronda Rousey have both said they'd like to be on the show. Singer Chris Daughtry auditioned for the role of Dwight in season 6, though it ended up going to Austin Amelio. And while the NFL competes against the show for ratings, it presents a different challenge for fans of the show who also happen to make their living playing professional football. "I love to play in the 1 P.M. game because I love *The Walking Dead*," Carolina Panthers defensive end Mario Addison told my colleague Kevin Clark in 2015. "If we play at 1 P.M., I'll have plenty of time to relax and prepare." If the job interferes with their viewing habits, they're stuck. "When Glenn 'died,' that got spoiled for me after I went on Facebook," said Atlanta Falcons lineman Chris Chester, referring to the infamous incident in the alley in which Glenn appeared to have been attacked and torn apart by zombies (and you can bet your best katana sword we're going to talk about that incident later).

Even after ratings dipped in season 7, the show remains a global juggernaut. But the skepticism that even Kirkman had about putting a zombie show on the air doesn't completely melt away just by pointing to the ratings. Those numbers reflect the show's popularity, but they don't explain it, and there isn't actually one single thing that does. It's a combination of factors, all working in tandem to produce this crazy thing that nobody saw coming.

CHAPTER 2

THE MAGIC TRICK

"IT IS MERE LUCK WE ARE NOT ALL INSANE."

—KING EZEKIEL

(SEASON 7, EPISODE 13, "BURY ME HERE")

The Walking Dead begins after the world has ended. It doesn't show us a "patient zero." We don't get to watch the world crumble as neighbors, husbands, wives, and children turn into flesh-eating undead. It doesn't show the panic as people flee for their lives, as the army struggles to maintain order, as the world spirals out of control (*Fear the Walking Dead* would later fill in these gaps, though the plague's cause never has been revealed). *The Walking Dead* opens with sheriff's deputy Rick Grimes in a hospital room in a small Georgia town. He knows nothing except that the hospital has been abandoned and that he is utterly alone. He will leave that room, and that building, and will slowly piece it all together. In doing so, he becomes our guide through the land of the undead.

Making a believable TV show, or movie for that matter, is akin to performing a magic trick. What you are seeing is not reality. What you are seeing, literally, is nothing more than a series of images shown in fast enough succession that they appear to be moving. We all know this, of course. We are all willing participants in the magic trick. But if it's going to work, it has to be a good one, because audiences today are more sophisticated than ever. Making this trick work on this show involves not only quality writing, acting, and directing, but especially effective special effects. If the audience is going to be scared by the show's zombies, they'd better look really good. People have seen zombies on the screen for decades. Most fans have an entire visual language of them in their heads: what they look like, how they act, why they're dangerous. *The Walking Dead* has to both speak that language and create new entries within it. It's critical to make viewers believe immediately and viscerally that what they are seeing is real (or at least, real enough that they are willing to suspend their disbelief for sixty minutes).

Establishing all of that within a few minutes was the goal of the pilot episode's "cold open," the segment that rolls before the opening credits. It hits effectively on several visual and emotional levels: A police officer drives up an empty road and stops at an abandoned gas station. The visual clues show that people had once camped out there, but they've long since gone. Signs of chaos are everywhere. The cop wants to fill up a gas can, and walks cautiously through the camp to the pumps. He hears something. He gets down on the ground to look under a car. On the other side he sees a pair of dirty feet in filthy pink slippers. They stop, pick up a teddy bear, and keep shuffling along. He walks behind what looks like a young girl, in pajamas and a robe. "Little girl," he says. "I'm a policeman. Little girl, don't be afraid, okay? Little girl . . ." The little girl turns around, revealing gray skin, bloody green eyes, and a huge gash around her mouth. The shredded, rotting flesh reveals braces on her teeth. Her clothes are smeared with blood and dirt. She is a zombie—though they are never called that on this show; you can call them walkers, or biters, geeks, lamebrains, creepers, roamers, rotters, bobbers, skin eaters, infected, wasted, or *sombras* (the gangster Marco uses this Spanish word for "shades" in *Fear the Walking Dead*, and it's a word for the dead that Homer used all the way back in *The Iliad;* I thought that was a nice touch). She starts growling and rushes for the warm body in front of her. He recoils in horror but already knows what to do: he pulls his revolver, a massive Colt Python, and shoots her, once, in the forehead. She falls back and smacks down on the ground, blood draining from the hole in her skull where the bullet crashed through.

Initially, this scene was not envisioned as the open. Addy Miller, the ten-year-old who played that zombie (given the name of Summer in the credits), had auditioned for the role with the understanding that it would come at some point later in the episode. But one day Addy was in a makeup room alongside the actress Melissa Cowan when she was told by Greg Nicotero that they'd decided to make Addy's scene the opener, her mother, Jaime Miller, told me. By moving it from its chronological place in the story—which would have come after Rick had left his hometown—to the cold open, the scene had gone from what was essentially a jump scare to the table setter for the entire show. It works there, too. In one sequence, the audience is given all the visual information it needs to get what's happening in the show and what they're in store for. This scene is the reason *The Walking Dead* can dispense with a lot of exposition about the zombie apocalypse and get into the *post*–zombie apocalypse.

Addy gets just over one minute of airtime, but getting her look right was a laborious process. There were several separate sittings where head molds and teeth molds were made. The teeth were dentures that clipped over her lips, and the prosthetic on her face—the rubber mold they used to create that huge gash—covered the dentures so it looked like her flesh had rotted away.

Even the braces were fake. After that, it was a matter of pouring on the blood and dirt.

"When I got to set," Addy recalled, "Greg Nicotero added all the blood and made it all disgusting and gross—you know, zombie magic—and then I popped the contacts in, and we're ready to roll."

Miller spent seven hours on the set that day filming that one scene, which lasts just under four and a half minutes. It had to be filmed from several different angles, and the little girl performed her own stunts. For the overhead angle, she pushed herself off a ladder and onto a green-screen mattress; the head-on angle required her to drop back on the pavement (a crew member hiding behind a car slid a big pad behind her after she walked past it). "Frank Darabont [the director] blows off a gun in the far distance, and I just fling myself back," she said. "A lot of trust is used on set."

The scene works on several levels. For one thing, zombie aficionados will recognize the reference to *Night of the Living Dead*. There's a young girl in that movie, too: Karen, about the same age as Addy Miller's zombie, who hides with her parents and others in a country house (spoiler alert: she turns into a zombie). Even if you didn't catch the reference, the effect is horrifying enough in itself. That little zombie is eerie and menacing, a hair-raising apparition, because, really, there is nothing more disturbing than a child turned into a monster. The whole obviously-not-real thing is so real-looking, Addy's mother said people have actually asked her if the blood from the gunshot wound was her daughter's. That comment is, well, a bit disturbing, but it illustrates how well the production crew pulled off the effect.

"You're creating a magic trick," said Tom Savini, an effects legend in horror circles and a man who is commonly known as the "Sultan of Splatter." For Savini, who has worked with George Romero and who created *Friday the 13th* character Jason Voorhees, every special and visual effect is a sleight of hand meant to convince you of something that isn't real. "That's my modus operandi, to fool you." Savini isn't involved in *The Walking Dead,* but he does have a connection to the show. In the 1980s, while he was working on *Dawn of the Dead* with Romero, a local teenager came to the set, interested in the movie business. He was hired to be part of Savini's crew, handling the pig intestines that were used to simulate human intestines, and ended up working with Savini on several other films. That kid was Greg Nicotero, who is today one of *Walking Dead*'s key visionaries, responsible for all the visual effects, and one of its core producers and directors. On the set of *Dawn of the Dead,* Nicotero met Howard Berger, and the two, along with Robert Kurtzman, would go on to found KNB EFX Group, one of the premier special-effects shops in Hollywood today. They've worked on *Dances with Wolves, The Chronicles of Narnia, The Mist, Boogie Nights,* and hundreds of other films and TV shows. From Romero to Savini to Nicotero, there is a direct lineage of horrific zombies and grisly, bloody on-screen deaths.

"The best zombies today are the ones he's doing on *The Walking Dead,*" Savini said of his protégé Nicotero. "I'm very proud of his enormous success."

After establishing the dystopia and the horror in the cold open, the show quickly sets up its characters as the next most important element. That this story was going to be about three-dimensional humans as much as rotting zombies was evident years before it even got on the air. From the start, that focus on character was built into the comics Kirkman wrote. "I'll never forget that first issue," said author Jay Bonansinga, who co-wrote *Rise of the Governor* and several other novels based on the show. What struck him most about it wasn't the zombies necessarily, or the dystopia it portrayed. It was something smaller: In the comics, after Rick gets on that horse, he starts talking to himself, trying to cheer himself up and keep himself company. He talks about the day his son, Carl, was born, and his wife Lori's difficult caesarean surgery. It's a very quiet moment, but it is also a very human one. "Right then, I thought, 'This is completely different from any comic book I've read in my life,'" he said. While that moment didn't make it into the show, it's indicative of the kind of focus on characters that is in the show's DNA. "That's what makes *The Walking Dead* great."

The Walking Dead was going to be about people first, zombies second. "Ninety-eight percent of people are exactly the same when it comes to basic things," said the TV writer and actor Frank Renzulli, who penned the script for "When the Dead Come Knocking," the seventh episode of season 3. "If you touch something hot, you're gonna recoil. Nobody likes bad news, and so on. All the colors are there, it's all there. All you need to do is add something that isn't common to the ninety-eight percent."

This development of the characters begins in the most mundane manner imaginable: King County sheriff's deputies Rick Grimes and Shane Walsh sit in their squad car one bright, sunny day, eating a lunch of greasy burgers and fries and talking about their women troubles. Shane belittles his girlfriend's intelligence, and Rick comments obliquely about his strained relationship with his wife. They are old friends, and the conversation flows from a bond that has developed between them over many years. Shane is the tough guy who "sounds just like my damn father," as his girlfriend says. Rick is the more thoughtful one, the one who doesn't quite understand why the concept of happily ever after is so difficult. You can already see the differences between these two in this scene, and as close as they are as friends and partners, the events that will unfold will push them to the extremes of who they are as people.

While they're in the squad car, a call comes across the radio, alerting them to a high-speed pursuit. Wordlessly, Grimes and Walsh join the chase. They head out on a country highway, lay a spike strip across the road, and wait. Eventually the car comes screaming up the highway, a souped-up GTO with cops in hot pursuit. The GTO hits that spike strip and flips over. Two guys get out and start firing. Both die in the firefight. While Rick and Shane aren't looking, a third criminal crawls out. He hits Rick in the side before Shane can put him down. Rick falls to the ground, bleeding.

"You look at me, Rick," Shane says to him. "You stay with me. You hear me?"

Getting shot is not a normal thing for anybody, even a cop, but this is the last remotely normal thing that will ever happen in Rick Grimes's life. He will wake up in a bed in an abandoned hospital, though exactly how long after isn't clear. By this point, the world has been overtaken by a plague, one that turns humans into living, breathing corpses. These are the walking dead. Before long, Rick will find his hometown abandoned, his wife and son gone, most of the countryside ravaged, and the city of Atlanta overrun. Life for the survivors is boiled down to its bare, brutal essentials, no longer measured in years or decades, but in hours and days. Surviving in this hellish world requires a combination of grit, skill, and luck, and, eventually, surrounding yourself with enough people to be able to not only withstand the constant onslaught from the undead, but also protect yourself from the living as well. Surviving in this hellish world will be about fighting for every breath.

It's one thing to create frighteningly realistic zombies and to imagine a group of everyman survivors. The next step was to create a realistic apocalyptic landscape for them to live in (well, at least the ones who weren't dead already). For Kirkman, the way to do that was to dig into history. He started sketching out his vision and did a lot of research into the Holocaust and Europe after World War II. Italy, Germany, and France in those years were a pretty good parallel for the world Kirkman was creating: bombed out, society collapsed, survival dependent upon scratching out life day by day. All institutions had imploded. National borders had disappeared, and the nations themselves seemed to have disappeared, too, as government after government failed. Schools and universities shut down, and access to any news was hard to come by. Money, banks, commerce: all gone. The police, the courts: not operating. Armed men took what they wanted. There were famines and starvation. That's what Kevin Lowe described in his book about the time, *Savage Continent: Europe in the Aftermath of World War II.* "The deliberate fragmentation of communities had sown an irreversible mistrust between neighbours," Lowe wrote. "Universal famine had made personal morality an irrelevance." The only thing missing, it seemed, was the zombies.

What Kirkman came up with was a fictional universe that puts an immense amount of pressure on people every waking second. It's similar to the lawless postwar rubble of Europe, and in that devastation, with the added catastrophe and danger of the zombies, it goes even a step further. The reality of this world pounds away at the characters. Who could possibly remain rational in a world of living corpses? Who would *want* to? It is, as King Ezekiel says, a wonder they are not all insane. The tension comes from watching these survivors, these people who are, as Renzulli said, 98 percent the same, try to cope with the catastrophic, with the death that haunts them constantly. The only "right" action is the one that keeps you alive.

For example, look at Glenn Rhee. When we first meet him he is a stereotypically nerdy kid: clever but not particularly fierce, smart but not somebody who commands a room, and, in case you hadn't noticed, Asian. Glenn changes permanently, though, in "When the Dead Come Knocking" (season 3, episode 7) when Renzulli and another of the show's writers, Sang Kyu Kim, take the character in a new direction. To Renzulli, Glenn was too much of an American stereotype of an Asian, right down to the baseball cap, and was too passive. It was something, he said, that bothered Kim, too. "I said, Sang, we're gonna take Glenn up a notch. We're gonna make the Asian community proud."

In the episode, Glenn and his girlfriend, Maggie Greene, are being held captive by the Governor in Woodbury. They are being tortured for information about their community, the prison where Rick and the rest of the Grimes clan live. Glenn is bound with duct tape to a chair, and is being beaten mercilessly by Merle. Merle has not seen Glenn in a while, and doesn't remember him being as tough as he's apparently become. So he ups the ante: he throws a live walker into the room with Glenn. What follows is one of the most flat-out epic zombie fights in the whole show. Glenn gets to his feet, still bound to the chair, and holds off the zombie desperately. Eventually he slams himself against a brick wall, smashing the chair. The zombie is right on top of him. Glenn blocks the zombie's teeth with his duct-taped arm and then takes a splinter of the arm of the chair and brains the walker.

"I remember that scene very well," Renzulli said. Glenn had earned his place as a warrior of the apocalypse. "It was heroic." That event sets up a very interesting dynamic for Glenn. He does become one of the group's fighters (they all, really, become fighters). At the same time, Glenn has a strong moral compass, and despite all the suffering and violence and pain, it is something he never loses to the day he dies. It's Glenn who decides to risk his own safety to help Rick in Atlanta. It's an act of pure humanity, and it's an act that gives birth to the Grimes clan. We'll have a lot more to say about Glenn later; he's a critical piece of the show.

This story sets up an interesting challenge for the show's writers. They must take regular characters and show how they have been changed by their extraordinary events. It can turn an average teenager like Glenn into a fierce fighter, or it can turn an average middle-aged nobody into a psychotic animal, like the Governor. There's a huge range of human emotion to play with, and it's a fine line for a writer to tread. If no action is off-limits, and every character can be driven to madness by this grim reality, then there is nothing the writers *can't* put in the script. Any action can be essentially defended. Rick can go crazy over visions of his dead wife; Carol can commit cold-blooded murder; the Governor can mow down his own people; Negan can be as psychotically violent as he wants. That is a dangerous tool to give a writer, though, because it tempts them to bend the most critical element of storytelling: internal logic. Even if your characters are living in a hellscape that fractures and disintegrates their psyches, where the dead walk and eat the living, you still must try to tell the audience a coherent story. This means, for a show like *The Walking Dead,* that if certain ground rules are established, they must be maintained. If zombies are slow and loud in episode 1, they have to be that way in episodes 6, 12, and 87. Similarly, Negan can kill, but the murders must serve a purpose; indeed, Negan apparently has a rigid logic to his ironfisted rule and all his decisions.

"You have to stay in the rules," Renzulli said. "Wherever you set the bar of reality, that's got to be frozen." That bar, he said, "is the linchpin, the center of the universe that you're working from." What has set this show apart is a steadfast adherence to playing within the rules (with one big, notable exception, which I'll get into later), even when that means people must die, and in this show, people die all the time. But they must; if this show was going to work, it had to learn how to be okay with killing off major characters. And it has.

RECAP

SEASON TWO

- **SAFE HAVEN:** The Greene farm
- **SURVIVORS LOST:** Sophia Peletier, Shane Walsh, Dale Horvath, Otis, Patricia, Jimmy
- **ANTAGONISTS KILLED:** Dave, Tony, Randall
- **NOTABLE WALKERS:** Sophia Peletier, Shane Walsh
- **ZOMBIE HERDS:** Highway herd, Greene farm herd

AFTER NARROWLY ESCAPING THE IMPLODING CDC HEADquarters, the Grimes clan heads back out onto the road in search of a new safe haven. On one stretch of country highway, their path is blocked by a massive pileup of cars. Before they can navigate around it, they are scattered by a massive herd of walkers shambling down the highway. Dozens, maybe hundreds of zombies lumber by. Caught by surprise, they hide behind and under cars, and wherever else they can. This almost works, but young Sophia Peletier gives away her position, is attacked by a walker, and flees into the woods. Rick gives chase and finds her, but has to fight off two walkers. By the time he's done with them, she's disappeared again. This is the impossible-to-predict event that sends the entire group in a new direction, confronting new quandaries. How long do you keep up hope for a missing loved one? What is leadership, and who really possesses it? What moral obligations does any human still living have to any other human still living? Do any of the laws that mankind spent millennia crafting and perfecting still matter?

They search the woods, coming across a whitewashed country church, but no Sophia. Rick has a heart-to-heart with God and asks for a sign, any sign, that he's doing the right thing. He is met with silence. Back in the woods, Carl gets shot by a hunter, who was aiming at a deer. The hunter, Otis, is from a nearby farm owned by Hershel Greene (Scott Wilson) and home to a small pod of survivors, and that's how the entire Grimes clan ends up on Greene's farm. Hershel is a farmer and veterinarian, an older moral and religious man raising two daughters, Maggie (Lauren Cohan) and Beth (Emily Kinney). The veterinarian saves Carl's life, but he is wary of the newcomers. The farm is seemingly a perfect haven, protected on all sides by natural barriers and wetlands. Nobody wants to leave. They don't know the farm's secret, though: The barriers aren't perfect. Walkers do get onto the property. Hershel, however, doesn't believe the undead are really undead. He's been herding them into a huge barn on the property. His own wife and son—now among the undead—are in there.

The uneasy tension explodes when this secret is revealed. Shane has bristled at Rick's leadership and now openly rebels. He does something drastic by arming everybody and opening the barn doors. One by one, the Grimes clan mows down the walkers. For Hershel, it is overwhelming. Imagine watching your family gunned down in front of you. Then it becomes overwhelming for everybody: the last walker to emerge is Sophia Peletier. Only Rick possesses the courage to do what must be done: shoot her in the head.

The tragedy at the barn drives Hershel into a tailspin. He goes to a bar in town, one he used to frequent when he was a drinker. Rick and Glenn find him there and are confronted by a group of survivors, men who clearly don't have everybody's best interests in mind. Rick kills them, but their friends come looking for him soon after, and the situation quickly explodes into violence. One of the ruffians falls from a roof and impales his leg on a wrought iron fence. Rick's instincts as an officer of the law, and moral human being, take over and he saves the boy, named Randall, rather than leave him to the walkers. They pull him off the fence and bring him back to the barn, but this only creates another headache: the kid can't be trusted. He's a local, and knows the Greenes. If they let him go, he'd have no problem leading his gang back to the farm. Rick is unwilling to kill him after saving him. Shane, who increasingly is at odds with Rick, is not. Shane, in fact, uses the situation to his advantage. He now wants to get rid of his old friend, take control of the group, and take back Lori, who, we find out, is pregnant. Shane knows, or at least suspects, that he is the father (years later this will be confirmed by Rick). Either way, he wants Rick out.

Shane takes Randall into the woods, kills him, and then lies and says that Randall escaped. While Shane and Rick go looking for Randall, Shane tries to kill Rick. There's a struggle, and Rick stabs his friend, who falls to the ground and dies. "Damn you for making me do this!" Rick screams. Carl arrives, with a gun in his hand, and sees the whole thing. He's shocked and confused; at one point, he looked at Shane as a father figure. "Carl, it's not what it seems," Rick says, trying to keep his own son from shooting him. As Rick is talking, Shane "turns" and comes back to life—the first confirmation that every corpse does indeed turn into the undead. Carl shoots not his father, but zombie Shane. As this is all happening, a massive herd, far larger than the one from the highway, descends on the farm. It's utter chaos, and a bloodbath. The farm is lost, and everybody scatters.

The next morning, on the highway where the Grimes clan first lost Sophia, most of the crew meet up. Andrea is gone, and presumed dead (she's found in the woods by a hooded stranger leading two armless zombies on chains). They're reunited, but the recent events have made them distrustful of each other, and of Rick. While talking, he drops a bomb on them: Everyone is infected; everyone carries the disease. When you die, you turn. That's what Jenner at the CDC whispered to him. Nobody can believe it, or believe that Rick didn't tell them. They camp at night, and there is dissension and mistrust everywhere. Carol wants to leave with Daryl. Maggie wants to leave with her family. This group, after all, fell together completely at random. Is there any reason for any of them to stay together? Moreover, can they truly trust Rick anymore?

He puts this dissension down with a fiery speech. "I'm keeping this group together, alive. I've been doing that all along, no matter what. I didn't ask for this. I killed my best friend for you people, for Chrissake!" More than anything, killing Shane shows exactly how far Rick will go to protect himself and his people. This is not Officer Friendly anymore, and it's shocking to them to hear it. Carl breaks down in tears. The others just stare. Rick goes further: he challenges them to leave.

"Go on, there's the door. You can do better? Let's see how far you get." Nobody moves. "No takers? Fine. But get one thing straight, you're staying, this isn't a democracy anymore."

Welcome to the Ricktatorship.

CHAPTER 3

PATHOLOGY

"I'M SORRY, IF I HAD KNOWN THE WORLD WAS ENDING, I'D HAVE BROUGHT BETTER BOOKS."

—DALE HORVATH

(SEASON 2, EPISODE 5, "CHUPACABRA")

One Saturday afternoon in 1969, a young Roger Ebert went to the local picture show to catch the latest release, George Romero's *Night of the Living Dead.* It was the matinee showing, and the theater was packed with kids. He figured there might have been only about two dozen people there over sixteen; he wasn't so old himself, a professional film critic for all of two years out of college. The kids in the theater raced around the aisles and climbed over the seats, passing food around and even smacking their friends to shut them up. A typical raucous matinee.

Ebert had heard that the movie about to be shown was exceedingly violent. Indeed, over the previous decade, more horror movies were becoming that way. He hadn't seen a horror movie since the 1950s—flicks like *Creature from the Black Lagoon*—and Ebert felt it was time to give the genre a second chance. When the lights went down, the kids cheered. Romero's film started off promisingly enough (spoiler alert!), with a young couple being attacked in a graveyard by a zombie (though nobody called them that). The boy is killed, and the girl flees to a farmhouse, where she meets up with other people trying to fight off the ghouls (which is what Romero called them). There is a desperate attempt to escape, and two people are burned alive inside a car, which is then set upon by the zombies—who proceed to tear apart and eat the burning victims.

"At this point, the mood of the audience seemed to change," Ebert wrote. "There wasn't a lot of screaming anymore; the place was pretty quiet." It remained quiet to the end, with every character in the cast dying horribly and violently, one after the next. "The movie had stopped being delightfully scary about halfway through," Ebert wrote, "and had become unexpectedly terrifying." The children around him were stunned. Some wept. They "had no resources they could draw upon to protect themselves from the dread and fear they felt." In his article, Ebert went on a polemic about the deficiencies of the local movie codes that allowed children in the theater to even see the film, though he also figured the theater's owners wanted to show it and make a quick buck before it got completely banned. "I don't know how I could explain it to the kids who left the theater with tears in their eyes."

Night of the Living Dead changed everything about zombie stories, and about horror movies. A New Yorker and aspiring filmmaker, Romero got his start filming short segments for, ironically, the safe haven of every child's youth, *Mister Rogers' Neighborhood*. After he formed a production company with some friends in 1969, when he was only twenty-eight years old, *Night of the Living Dead* became his first feature film. Romero had started out expecting to do a riff on the Richard Matheson novel *I Am Legend,* but the project morphed into something more expansive. And morphed again. By the time it was done, Romero had essentially created a new genre; more impressively, he has continually returned to it over the decades, each time reaffirming his place as the master of the zombie story. Romero's creation put such an indelible mark on the genre that when we think of zombies today, whether they run lightning fast or shamble along slowly, we think of *his* zombies: those undead, flesh-craving mindless ghouls.

Zombie stories share some elements with other horror genres, but the nature of what makes them so terrifying is distinct from other monster mashes. How are they different? Here is a quote from Mary Shelley's *Frankenstein,* first published in 1818. The speaker is Dr. Frankenstein's monster:

> "Shall each man," cried he, "find a wife for his bosom, and each beast have his mate, and I be alone? I had feelings of affection, and they were requited by detestation and scorn. Man, you may hate; but beware! your hours will pass in dread and misery, and soon the bolt will fall which must ravish from you your happiness for ever."

Or how about this? An exchange from Bram Stoker's *Dracula,* first published in 1897:

> "Welcome to my house! Enter freely. Go safely, and leave something of the happiness you bring!" The strength of the handshake was so much akin to that which I had noticed in the driver, whose face I had not seen, that for a moment I doubted if it were not the same person to whom I was speaking. So to make sure, I said interrogatively, "Count Dracula?"
>
> He bowed in a courtly way as he replied, "I am Dracula, and I bid you welcome, Mr. Harker, to my house."

Want to think about it a bit more? Here's a paragraph from an early werewolf story, *The Damnable Life and Death of Stubbe Peeter,* by an Englishman named George Bores, published in 1590:

> The Devil, who saw [Stubbe Peeter] a fit instrument to perform mischief as a wicked fiend pleased with the desire of wrong and destruction, gave unto him a girdle which, being put around him, he was straight transformed into the likeness of a greedy, devouring wolf, strong and mighty, with eyes great and large, which in the night sparkled like unto brands of fire, a mouth great and wide, with most sharp and cruel teeth, a huge body and mighty paws. And no sooner should he put off the same girdle, but presently he should appear in his former shape, according to the proportion of a man, as if he had never been changed.

What's the difference? In a word—brains! All of those other monsters—Frankenstein's monster, Dracula, the werewolf—can be talked to, perhaps even reasoned with. Look at the lines Shelley gives Dr. Frankenstein's monster. Has there ever been a more philosophically minded nightmare? They may be darkly evil, murderous, treacherous, and unrepentant, but they resemble us in our ability to reason. It's something that connects us to all these fantastic creatures. Zombies, on the other hand, eat brains; they don't use them. At least, not the part that reasons. In the words of Dr. Edwin Jenner, the last scientist at the CDC when the Grimes clan arrives (season 1, episode 6, "TS-19"), once you become a zombie, "the human part, that doesn't come back. The you part. Just a shell driven by mindless instinct." Zombies look like us, indeed *are* us, but do not have the ability to reason. They don't talk, think, or have motivations (though there are variations on this basic theme; even Romero's later movies portray thinking zombies). They are essentially a blank slate of horror for the writer to use as a vehicle to express whatever it is that scares us, whether the goal is just a quick fright or to plumb some deeper psychological anxiety.

"Zombies are a void," Sarah Wayne Callies, the actress who played Lori, said in a 2012 speech at her alma mater, the University of Hawaii (about one month after her character died on the show, incidentally). Into that void can go virtually anything that the writer, or reader or viewer, chooses to insert, chooses to make the real bogeyman. Callies selected an interesting example of her own to illustrate this: the plays of Anton Chekhov. The university had just staged a play called *Uncle Vanya and Zombies,* part of a pop culture series that explored the zombie genre. Callies's talk was essentially a defense of the idea of putting zombies into Chekhov's plays, and in making that defense, she illustrated one explanation for why there is so much life in these stories about the undead.

Chekhov never wrote about zombies; he wrote about the problems in contemporary Russia at the turn of the twentieth century. It was a time of much social upheaval, and of course would culminate years later in the overthrow of the tsar and the establishment of the USSR. Now, Callies pointed out, to a modern audience there is a lot of subtext in his plays that simply goes over our heads. Since we don't live in turn-of-the-century Russia, we don't understand the fears of the Russian patriarchy or the plight of the Russian peasant. But that wasn't what Chekhov was writing about. What he was writing about was change, the kind of change in society that makes people uncomfortable.

"They're a placeholder, themselves nothing at all, they are a blank slate onto which we can map our fears." It could be fears about whether or not God exists, fears about your mortgage, "fears that Justin Bieber doesn't want to marry us," she said, joking. "From the mundane to the monumental, perhaps zombies allow us to fill in the blank with our own neuroses and insert them into the story as the central antagonist."

She ran through Chekhov's *Uncle Vanya* and showed how certain scenes could absolutely still work by inserting zombies into the story, how the undead effectively replace the inchoate fear of change that haunts the characters. In this very unusual and ironic way, the zombie threat ends up bolstering the real strength of Chekhov's plays, the naturalism and attention to characters and their development.

There is one way in which the zombie represents not some amorphous dramaturgical challenge, but something very, very real: the fear of death.

"We are all confronted with our own mortality at some point," said Otto Penzler, a writer and editor who published the anthology *Zombies! Zombies! Zombies!* The obsession with the afterlife underlies a lot of monster stories, like the vampire, ghost, and zombie tales. Indeed, most of the stories in Penzler's anthology don't depict the modern, brain-eating zombie, but portray a different kind of undead. Certain tales can be claimed by both the vampire camp and the zombie camp. Both share that obsession with death, dying, and what happens after. Sometimes the afterlife can be almost glamorous, like in modern vampire stories. Even ghosts can have it pretty good. Zombies, however, are the real nightmare of the afterlife.

"I'd rather come back as a ghost than a zombie," Penzler said. "I don't want to eat people's brains."

Archaeological evidence going back fifty thousand years shows that Neanderthals living in France had already developed burial rituals, preparations for the dead to enter the underworld. Some of the first epics that were written down after the development of the written word, Homer's *Iliad* and *Odyssey* as well as the Sumerian *Epic of Gilgamesh,* contained stories in which the heroes either went to the underworld or encountered the dead in the living world. In Homer's stories, the dead were called "shades." Virgil's *Aeneid* included a trip to the underworld as well. In the first few centuries after Jesus's death, a story developed called the "Harrowing of Hell," in which the savior of mankind goes into Hell and saves all the souls who've died since Adam and Eve, leaving the damned behind (the story did not get incorporated into the Bible). It was a tale that would have rung familiar to any educated person of the ancient world.

In the first centuries of the second millennium, the fictional characterization of the dead begins to change, with tales of "revenants"—Latin for "returning"—peppering the works of historians; indeed, it's interesting that the earliest stories of these revenants come from historians rather than poets. To them, these tales were not fiction. The English historian William of Newburgh collected several tales of these "prodigies," as he calls them, in his history of England, *Historia rerum Anglicarum* (1206), and explains that while "it would not be easy to believe that the corpses of the dead should sally (I know not by what agency) from their graves," the sheer number of these tales means they must be true (not the greatest application of logic, but, hey, it was still technically the Dark Ages). There are so many of these stories, he says, that writing them all down would be "beyond measure laborious and troublesome." In William's tales, the dead are buried and come back to life as monsters, terrorizing their families or towns. They are raised by some magic of Satan and usually wander around at night. Their very presence spreads disease and death. Some speak to people, others just groan and wail. He recounts the story of one man in Buckingham who died, was buried, and then rose, going every night to his wife's bed and petrifying the poor widow. After he is driven off, he starts harassing his brothers, then "he rioted among the animals." Eventually, the church is consulted. A bishop in London tells the townsfolk to dig up the corpse and burn it. They do so, and nobody ever sees the apparition again.

Another story involves a chaplain who was such a wicked priest that the citizens of the town called him *Hundeprest,* meaning "dog priest." He was "excessively secular in his pursuits," William tells us. After the chaplain dies, he rises from his grave. The holy men of the monastery prevent him from doing any damage there, so he heads to the bedside of his former mistress, one of his secular pursuits. She is so terrorized by this revenant that she appeals to a monk at the monastery for help; he is greatly sympathetic and promises a speedy remedy—after all, the woman made frequent donations to the monastery. And it is clear to see that William's stories do have a bit of moral tongue-wagging in them.

Another Englishman, and a contemporary of William's, was Walter Map, whose sole surviving work, *De nugis curialium* ("Of the trifles of courtiers," completed around 1190), is a collection of tales and anecdotes, including the history of the Knights Templar, a recounting of the 1187 capture of Jerusalem by Saladin, a comparison of royal courts with Hell, and stories of robber bands, monks, and princes. He also includes some fantastic stories about mermen, demonic pet snakes, fairy brides, centaurs, ghosts, and vampires.

William's undead, to me at least, seem more like zombies, while Map's are like vampires. However similar or different, both writers were dealt the same kind of critical condescension that zombie stories get today. Both employed satirical tones in their writing, which compromised any of their attempts to then present these stories of vampires, zombies, and ghosts as "fact." "*Ludicra*" and "*juvenilis,*" their critics sneered. You don't need to know Latin to understand what they meant.

Our societal concept of the underworld was changed forever by Dante Alighieri, whose epic poem *Divine Comedy,* completed in 1320, portrayed Hell as it had never been imagined before. Dante used his poem as a polemic to take potshots at all his political enemies, including popes, many of whom ended up in the various circles of Hell, paying for their sins for all eternity. The poem's popularity resurfaced with the Romantic poets of the nineteenth century, and it is then that we start to see the subject of the undead—both vampires and zombies—get more serious treatment. The Romantics took all this literature—the epics of the ancient world, the stories of Newburgh and Map, the vivid exposition of Hell from Dante—and started to craft a new literature out of it.

In 1845, the master of horror and Mr. Romantic Era himself, Edgar Allan Poe, published "The Facts in the Case of M. Valdemar," in which the narrator recounts his attempt to keep a dead man alive through the practice of "mesmerism," one of myriad failed scientific hypotheses that look like witchcraft to us today (or perhaps "alternative" medicine). The mesmerist believed he could somehow control magnetic fields in a body and, so, control the body. Poe's story was fiction, but apparently some took it to be a factual recounting (scientific circles in Boston and London were quite peeved when they found out it was, in Poe's own words, a "hoax"). In Poe's story, the narrator practices his arts on a dead man, claiming to revive him. The man lies on a table in a state between life and death. "There was an instant return of the hectic circles on the cheeks; the tongue quivered, or rather rolled violently, in the mouth (although the jaws and lips remained rigid as before); and at length the same hideous voice which I have already described, broke forth: 'For God's sake—quick!—quick!—put me to sleep—or, quick!—waken me!—quick!—I say to you that I am dead!'" The mesmerist tries his best, but the body—animated after death for so long—suddenly crumbles in on itself on the table, leaving only a "nearly liquid mass of loathsome—of detestable putridity."

Another writer, Reverend Samuel Whittell Key, got closer to our modern zombie. Key was an Englishman writing horror stories under the pen name Uel Key. His 1917 story, "The Broken Fang," features a hero, Professor Arnold Rhymer, a cross between Indiana Jones and Sherlock Holmes, who possesses one distinguishing characteristic: Rhymer absolutely hates the Germans. Throughout the story he refers to them by slurs used to describe Germans back then, "Hun" and "Boche." Rhymer is sent to the countryside to investigate tales of some grisly murders. The villains of the story are two German immigrants, who are actually spies and are creating the murderous zombies. When Rhymer and a policeman, Inspector Brown, first see an animated corpse, the description is close to what we're familiar with seeing today:

> As they crouched there, an accountable sense of chilliness was prevalent. Brown afterwards owned up to an uncontrollable feeling of nausea as he beheld the figure. The unearthly face conveyed features devilish in their cold and pitiless cruelty, lifeless in their immobility, vacant in their utter lack of human expression—lifeless, yet living. The eyes were lack-lustre, yet wide open and round.

Rhymer and Brown uncover and thwart the plot: The two Germans, operating out of an estate in the country, were taking the bodies of dead German soldiers, coating them in some special chemical that the Huns had concocted, and smuggling the bodies into England disguised as Egyptian mummies. They would then send them to the homes of naturalized Germans, reanimate them, and set them loose upon the countryside to kill young British men of fighting age. The villains, two men with the overtly Teutonic names of Graf Friedrich von Verheim and Otto Krupp, had been living in England for many years; it proved that "the war had been long contemplated by the Huns."

It's crazy, of course, but it shows two things: one, the idea that zombies (even though Key calls them vampires, they are much closer to our modern concept of zombies) could be reanimated corpses—and controlled by the reanimator—and, two, that the zombies could also act as a stand-in for whatever stalks the nightmares of the reader. In this case, in war-torn England in 1917, the Germans are the enemies.

As we've seen, the idea of the living dead dates far back in European culture, but it's in the stories coming out of Haiti in the twentieth century that the modern concept of the zombie first emerges. How far back these stories go isn't exactly clear, but they are a result of the mixture of a repressive society and the fascination with black magic—voodoo.

When Columbus first landed in Haiti in 1492, slavery was already a common practice across the Caribbean islands. After the Europeans arrived, it boomed and became a central part of the economy. In 1791, the enslaved Haitians revolted, eventually overthrowing the French colonial government and establishing a free nation in 1804. It was the first nation to be founded by former slaves. Though nominally free, many still lived on farms and worked under oppressive slavery-like conditions. (To this day, in fact, Haitian children from poor families, called *restaveks,* are sent to live with, and work for, more well-to-do families, where they encounter a life that is not discernably different from slavery, and the stain of a centuries-old tradition endures.)

The slavish conditions of the workers seep into the zombie tales. The stories in his collection are fiction, but some were originally presented as true life, Penzler said. People went down to Haiti to observe conditions and saw nearly catatonic workers in the field, people who looked almost drugged. Had they died and come back from the dead? No—at least, we're all kind of, sort of, sure it's no. But Penzler said he read several hundred of these tales, and the weight of them convinced him there was something going on. "I believe there is something that is zombielike about those people." The zombie tales from Haiti are just exaggerations of the conditions of the people in Haiti in the early twentieth century.

The first entry in Penzler's anthology comes from W. B. Seabrook, who penned the first true zombie story to reach U.S. readers, and who sold it as one of those purportedly "true" tales. A career journalist, Seabrook was born in Maryland in 1884, fought with the French in World War I, and had an intense interest in the occult. In 1929 he published *The Magic Island,* a travelogue of his trip to Haiti and the voodoo practices there (he claims to have been the first white man to witness these rituals). It included a story about "dead men" working in cane fields:

> One morning an old black headman, Ti Joseph of Colombier, appeared leading a band of ragged creatures who shuffled along behind him, staring dumbly, like people walking in a daze. As Joseph lined them up for registration, they still stared, vacant-eyed like cattle.

> . . . These were not living men and women but poor unhappy zombies whom Joseph and his wife Croyance had dragged from their peaceful graves to slave for him in the sun—and if by chance a brother or father of the dead should see and recognize them, Joseph knew that it would mean trouble for him.

Ti Joseph was right. The relatives of the dead working the fields did eventually recognize their brethren, restored them to their final resting place, and cut off Joseph's head in retribution. Importantly, this was the first time these undead creatures were called "zombies," and you can see from the story that they were not the flesh-craving walkers we know now, but numb, lifeless beings, dug up and used as labor. Once you know the world from which the Haitian zombie stories emerged, the social overtones could not be clearer.

Like their European counterparts, these stories were likely part of the broad folklore before Seabrook came along. That they became a staple of U.S. popular culture at this exact point was mainly due to a new kind of mass media: pulp fiction. The pulps were the descendants of the nineteenth century's dime novels and "penny dreadfuls," and in the 1920s and '30s, advances in printing technology made it easier to sell mass-market magazines at cheap rates.

"Pulp fiction was very different," said Penzler. The pulps weren't high art. They were aimed at the masses, at a mostly male readership. This was at a time when movies were a new thing, less than 50 percent of households had a radio, and television didn't exist. They were aiming for commerce, not prestige. The writers were getting paid a penny a word, and were looking to churn out as much material as possible to satisfy the voracious appetite for their stories. There was huge demand for work by talented writers, and that demand led them to not only keep pounding out the words, but also to try to top their competition and themselves as well. "More horrible, more exciting, more filled with gore and suspense," Penzler said. "They knew they were trying to entertain basically male readers with exciting stories. Well, a lot of those zombie stories are really exciting." Many of the best stories in his anthology, he said, came out of these pulp magazines.

It wasn't just the pulps where zombies found a welcome home. In 1932, a movie, *White Zombie,* was made based on Seabrook's book, starring Bela Lugosi. It strips out virtually all the social commentary and becomes a tale of a man trying to use voodoo to turn an unattainable woman he loves into his slave. It was followed by *Revolt of the Zombies* (1936) and *I Walked with a Zombie* (1943). By the 1950s, zombies were staples of B movies, the low-budget, low-quality flicks that played before feature films. These zombies were generally mute, dumb reanimated corpses, and the real threat was usually the nutbag who reanimated them, like Lugosi in *White Zombie* or the mad scientist on the mystery island in *King of the Zombies* (1941). In one 1950s serial, *Zombies of the Stratosphere,* the zombies are Martians that want to use an H-bomb to push Earth out of its orbit so Mars can move closer to the sun—really, that is the plot (and one of the zombie-Martians was played by an unknown actor named Leonard Nimoy). It's virtually unwatchable—I tried—though you have to admit, *Zombies of the Stratosphere* is a pretty good title.

That was how things stayed until Romero used this premise as a launchpad—both in terms of how zombies functioned and how they communicated messages. Romero's zombies played with several hot-button issues of the day. In *Night of the Living Dead,* the lead, Ben (Duane Jones), is a black man stuck in a house with a bunch of white people. For Romero, zombies were a way of commenting on the turbulent 1960s. "I've been able to use genre of fantasy/horror and express my opinion, talk a little about society, do a little bit of satire and that's been great, man," he said in a 2008 interview. He went on:

> All of these films, the ideas for them have come from the world. And once you know, okay, I'm going to make a movie about *this* you can glue zombies on it, easily. So it's not difficult at all. You just have to have that idea. I think a lot of people don't.

There is one other major development in the zombie genre that we haven't discussed. Sometime after *Night of the Living Dead,* zombie stories became less about individual undead and more about mass undead. Slowly, the dominant theme of zombie stories wasn't the death of a few individuals but the death of most of the human race. These stories became dominated by the theme of apocalypse. Fast zombies or slow zombies, they all belonged to this single categorical distinction.

Nobody before Kirkman had explored this apocalyptic zombie landscape in any real depth. And Kirkman didn't want to just get in, concoct a few jump scares, and get out. He wanted to stay and see what grows in a wasteland. In zombies, he found the perfect backdrop to do all that.

"It's more about that human drama," said Juan Gabriel Pareja, the actor who played Morales in season 1, about Kirkman's creation, "and more about the monsters, I guess, that us as a society can become." The show kind of forces you to imagine a "reality in which the lifestyle and the way of life that we've become accustomed to, maybe one in the future, is coming to an end, and how would we survive?"

The undead of *The Walking Dead* are plenty frightening, gory, and dangerous. But, as Jay Bonansinga noted, the way they are portrayed on this show, they are more an element of the environment than kin to the monsters of William of Newburgh, Edgar Allan Poe, Uel Key, W. B. Seabrook, or even George Romero. The hook is the zombies, but the substance is the dynamic of living in that world. What the best fantasy stories do, Bonansinga said, is ask you to accept one fantastic element and then surround that with pure realism. "To me, that's the essence of Kirkman."

CHAPTER 4

BRINGING THE DEAD TO LIFE

"THESE THINGS AIN'T SICK. THEY'RE NOT PEOPLE. THEY'RE DEAD."

—SHANE WALSH

(SEASON 2, EPISODE 7, "PRETTY MUCH DEAD ALREADY")

Little Sam Anderson, son of Alexandria, is intrigued by Carol, one of the newcomers to his community ("Forget," season 5, episode 13). One night when Carol leaves a party early, Sam follows her. He's not expecting to find her doing anything, but he inadvertently catches her stealing guns from the armory. When she realizes he's there, she tries to sweet-talk him into not telling anybody what he's seen. When he says he can't lie to his mother, this sweet-looking lady turns darkly terrifying. She says to him, "One morning you will wake up, and you won't be in your bed. You will be outside the walls, far, far away. Tied to a tree. And you'll scream and scream because you will be so afraid and no one will come to help, because no one will hear you. Well, something will hear you. The monsters will come, the ones out there, and you won't be able to run away when they come for you, and they will tear you apart and eat you up all while you are still alive. All while you can still feel it." The threat works on Sam because it preys on what he doesn't know but fears; it works on the audience, too, because it preys on what we *do* know, and fear. If the show hadn't spent years graphically depicting the horror she describes, the threat wouldn't have felt so visceral.

Each week *The Walking Dead* is tasked with creating a completely fictional world that is not only believable but the stuff of nightmares. It achieves this through a combination of effects and storytelling. The effects team goes to extremes to create monsters that groan, bite, ooze pus, explode in bursts of flesh and blood, and shred the living into little red tatters. Meanwhile, the storytelling goes to extremes to make you feel as if you are living inside a world where the only rule left is kill or be killed.

It was important to establish this deadly combination from the start. Rick Grimes heard zombies (behind those hospital doors) before he actually saw one, and the terror of his first glimpse of one is a payoff in visual terms set up by the story, by the frightening expectation: the first zombie he sees is a decomposed wraith cut off at the waist. Barely able to move, it slowly rolls over, revealing a hideous face, rotting chest, and sinewy, exposed arms. Its intestines are splayed out like bloody tendrils. Its mouth opens and an atrocious, lamentable groan escapes it. It grasps futilely at Rick, no conscious thought in its mostly dead brain. It is nothing more than a loosely connected clump of bones and muscle, yet somehow, some way, it is alive—well, *alive* might not be the right word. It is moving, a corporeal being animated but without life. Something recognizable and yet totally alien.

Making these zombies believable and terrifying has been the work of a group of very talented makeup artists who have grabbed the concept of the zombie and taken it to places never seen before on-screen. (The show's only two Emmy Awards, in 2011 and 2012 in the category Outstanding Prosthetic Makeup for a Series, Miniseries, Movie, or Special, have gone to Greg Nicotero and his special-effects team.) If viewers are going to suspend their disbelief and give in to the fantasy that is being created and rolled out on-screen, the zombies have to look as realistic as possible.

In the early days of cinema, when zombie stories were material fit for only B movies, zombies were not particularly sophisticated-looking monsters. In 1932's *White Zombie,* the undead didn't have any makeup. They were just dressed in shabby, torn clothing and walked around with bug eyes and expressionless faces. *King of the Zombies* (1941) was the same; what makes them "terrifying," if you can use that word, was that these bodies, raised from the grave, were under the control of whatever evil person did the raising. In *The Astro-Zombies,* released in May 1968, the zombies are just actors in skull-looking masks. The idea was that they were created in a mad experiment by a mad scientist—fired by the "space agency"—to create battery-powered astronauts out of dead people, because space is too dangerous for the living. It's a pretty awful movie, even if the trailer promised the most frightening film ever made: "Watch in terror! Scream in fright! Thrill to breathless excitement as these skull-faced astro-zombies strike blindly at living flesh! Tearing, ripping, and killing with blood-drenched fury! Unbearable suspense and sadistic terror grip the senses as these human transplants threaten the safety of a city." In reality, these astro-zombies are so ridiculous it's hard to believe they scared even little kids, and the movie has shown up on a number of "worst ever" lists. This was the kind of silly thing zombies got put into.

Just five months after *Astro-Zombies* came out, Romero released his take on the genre, *Night of the Living Dead.* The zombie makeup was better; these monsters had visible wounds and gaunter faces. What was most terrifying about them, though, was their insatiable hunger for human flesh—a new and unexpected innovation.

When Romero, a Pittsburgh native, set out to make his sequels, *Dawn of the Dead* and *Day of the Dead,* he called on another Pittsburgh native, Tom Savini, for help with the special effects, and it was in these movies that the zombies we know so well today started taking shape. The first challenge the team had to contend with was that *Dawn* would be filmed in color. Savini's idea was to paint all the zombies gray (although the way the production team lit the sets back then made the zombies sometimes appear green or blue instead); that way it would be easy to tell them apart from the living. For *Day of the Dead,* he got even more ambitious by trying to show the actual decomposition of the bodies. Savini studied human anatomy and death (one of his best source books is a compendium of human deaths called *Medicolegal Investigation of Death*) and consulted a famous Pittsburgh coroner, Cyril Wecht, known mostly for his criticisms of the Warren Commission's report on the John F. Kennedy assassination. For this third movie, each zombie had its own unique decomposition. "If you died in the basement as opposed to a hot attic," he said when I talked to him, "there'd be a big difference." Each subsequent film ratcheted up the realism.

Savini's main job on both films was to devise creative ways to kill zombies, and people. Sometimes it was just coming up with an idea, sometimes it involved solving a filming problem. In *Day,* they wanted a particularly gory death for the bad guy, the army captain Rhodes. One day, while sitting and brainstorming (pun sort of intended), they thought of having the zombies tear Rhodes's body in half. It was Savini's idea to pull his head off, too. "This is the main bad guy, people are going to want to see him killed in a horrible way," Savini said. "So we tore him in half."

They ran into a different problem on *Dawn* with making a head explosion happen. They'd tried blowing up the dummy head with explosives stuffed inside, but the effect wasn't working. Finally, Savini got a sawed-off shotgun and just shot the thing, splattering fake gore all over the place. It would become one of his most famous effects. He had other tricks as well: For one scene in *Dawn* where a character (played, incidentally, by Savini) brains a zombie with a machete, Savini cut a groove in the machete, put it over the actor's head, filmed himself pulling the machete away from the head, and then ran that film in reverse. In the next, conjoining shot they filmed, they put a tube on the actor's head, which spilled fake blood down his face. Spliced together, the effect looks like Savini is sinking a machete into a zombie's brain. "Part of my fame," he said, "my reputation, comes from solving these problems, and doing it in simplistic, magical ways. Like magic tricks, like stage magic."

The Walking Dead's zombies are mostly "live," which means they are actors under makeup playing out their horror in real time, though for certain shots the crew will add computer-generated effects (they did not, for instance, cut the actress Melissa Cowan in half for her role as Bicycle Girl). In terms of the undead, *Walking Dead* has two kinds of zombies: true extras, actors in makeup who are in a shot but not up close, and what the production team calls "hero" zombies, ones that are featured prominently. These monsters get an exorbitant amount of detail. For Bicycle Girl, for example, the crew made a cast of her head, her teeth, and her body. Those casts were the basis for the prosthetics that would be used. Cowan didn't just get makeup; she was completely covered from the waist up in a rubber suit. Her mouth had the same kind of prop that was used for Addy Miller: a custom denture that clipped over her lip, with another piece of foam covering the denture so it looked like her skin was torn away. It took three and a half hours to get her into that latex costume. After that, Nicotero himself added detail on the skin with paint: bite marks, wounds, and such.

Another zombie that got a ton of attention for a small amount of airtime was the one that Daryl shoots and dissects in the season 2 premiere, "What Lies Ahead." In the episode, Rick and Daryl are in the woods searching for Sophia when they spy a lone walker. Daryl shoots him, and then, to figure out whether or not this walker attacked Sophia, they rip open his insides and dissect them, looking for, well . . . Sophia. First off, like every "hero" zombie, this one (played in an uncredited role by Charlie Leach) gets his own backstory. According to costume designer Eulyn Womble, he was supposed to be a "vegan professor," and to look the role he had longish hair and a jacket and tie, but was also, of course, bloodied up. Leach had gotten the full prosthetic treatment, complete with the exposed, hideous fake teeth. After his character gets shot and lands on the ground, the dissection is made to look real by a combination of effects and camera angles: a shot from overhead has Norman Reedus holding a real knife but plunging it into a fake body. Another shot, from the side, has Reedus holding a knife without a blade, but "plunging" it into the real Leach lying on the ground, with a fake silicone chest prosthetic over his torso. This fake chest is filled with fake guts. The organs were made from sewed-up nylon sacks, stuffed with bits of material to make them look full, and splattered in fake blood. "Every single organ I lifted out of that body," Reedus said on a behind-the-scenes feature included with the season 2 DVD, "was heavy, and full, and it made, like"—and here he made a gooey raspberry sound—"noises squishing it."

One of the most memorable zombies from the entire show is the well walker, from the episode "Cherokee Rose" (season 2, episode 4). On the Greene farm, T-Dog finds a bloated, waterlogged zombie at the bottom of a well. The decision is made to pull it out and dispatch it, rather than killing it in the well, which could contaminate the water. They send Glenn down the well on a line, and he lassoes the walker. Then they pull the zombie out, but he's so saturated that at the lip of the well, he simply bursts in two, with his legs falling back down and his torso splattering all over the ground. With the walker lying there, grasping helplessly at the air, T-Dog smashes his skull in.

Pulling off this effect again included a combination of real effects, an actor, a dummy, and some CGI. Brian Hillard, who works at KNB, played the zombie, covered in a complete silicone head and bodysuit. To get the effect of a waterlogged body, they put balloons filled with water under the suit. There were four lines running into the suit: two up to his ears, and two to the fake eyes. The first two were hooked up to a fire extinguisher, which, when engaged, forced a disgusting dark liquid to pour out of his ears. The other two lines pushed air into the rubber eyes, forcing them to bulge out. The zombie that splits in two was a dummy that had bags of liquid in it, wired up to small charges that when ignited blew the bags apart. For an added touch, the effects crew filled Hillard's mouth with "gak"—his word for it—which he later spits out. The dummy was used again when T-Dog smashes its skull in. The crew filled the head with more balloons and scored the outside so that when Singleton hits it, it explodes.

While making zombies appear horrifyingly believable is paramount, the other half of the equation is the actual acting. Remember, these are still actors under all the prosthetics and makeup and shredded wardrobes. Which means they have to act like zombies. What's the best way to teach a lot of people all at once how to act like zombies?

Zombie school.

Getting all the extras to act like people who are neither dead nor alive is the very goal of zombie school, and it's just one more example of the lengths to which the production team will go to create the most realistic show they can get in front of the cameras. It's new to even the experts: "I did a lot of zombie movies," Nicotero said. "I never did a zombie school."

The idea behind the "school" makes perfect sense. While we're never told what caused the plague, we do have detailed information on how it affects the body and reanimates it. Remember Dr. Erwin Jenner, way back at the CDC, explaining how the infection enters the body and works its way up the nervous system, eventually killing its host? After either several minutes or several hours, the brain is revived, albeit with severely limited functions. Is this being dead? Alive? "You tell me," Jenner said.

The school isn't some leafy campus in Cambridge but a brick garage on set, with some folding chairs, a TV, and a DVD player. In this modest space, Nicotero and "zombie choreographer" Matt Kent give a class on zombies, show videos like *Night of the Living Dead,* teach the actors the finer points of zombies in this universe, and then take the actors through a series of exercises to help them perfect their performance. In some ways, it is an extension of what Savini did in *Day of the Dead* by making every zombie an individual. The zombie school is a chance for all these actors to spend some time picking up the nuances of being a zombie, and even incorporating something of themselves into their undead roles. "It's really important, as with any character, any actor in a film," Gale Anne Hurd said. "You want to make sure they are given a brief as to what they're doing and why. There is a backstory to everything." Even for actors whose names won't appear in the credits, who don't get a line of dialogue, it's important that they know both the rules of the show and what their own motivation is—even if that motivation is just, like, to "rip your skin off and eat it," as Frank Darabont once said.

It's also a way for the producers to see the extras, put them through a series of exercises, and get a sense of who's a better zombie. How do they turn when they hear a sound? How would they get out of a chair? How would they navigate around a chair?

The aforementioned Matt Kent is a choreographer who works with the actors, teaching these very nuances. "Each person kind of came through the doors, through zombie camp, with a slightly different take," Kent said, "Some people move a little faster, some people are stiff, some people are looser." The result is that all these zombies look like something that used to be alive, and the universe of *The Walking Dead* appears that much more real.

Zombies must be killed, of course. Which means that for every intricate effect, for every extraordinarily detailed zombie the special-effects team dreams up, the writers are going to make sure it gets killed. Still, that's *a lot* of violence, and the living aren't just using their bare hands to do all this. They use a wide assortment of weapons—from knives to bows to guns and rifles to even the occasional rocket-propelled grenade. Some of these weapons, like Rick's Colt Python, Daryl's crossbow, or Michonne's katana, act like characters in their own right, and that is not by accident: The weapons are an extension of the characters.

"I remember the first day, I went to props," said Kerry Cahill, who plays the Kingdom warrior Dianne, "and they went, 'And you get a bow.' 'Cause they already know what everybody uses. They all have it made. My bow had a job before I did." The bow, she said, has a role in the frame, it gets talked about in production meetings, and it evolves just as a character would. "There were meetings about that bow that had nothing to do with me. And it was all about what it was going to be." The only thing left to her, really, was "trying to figure out what I want to name my bow."

In Cahill's opinion, all the attention devoted to just one bow is an illustration of how much effort goes into the show. "They give everything that kind of attention," she said. To prove her worth, maybe, she picked up that bow and actually became obsessed with using it. She was never told to do that, but she said it's like an unwritten rule on the show that you put in that kind of effort. "It's kind of like showing up at Harvard. You feel the pressure to study. No one's going to tell you to, but you feel the pressure."

No weapon on *The Walking Dead,* though, says as much about its character as Lucille, the barbed-wire-covered baseball bat that Negan wields. All this killing and weaponry reached a graphic, bloody climax in the season 7 premiere, "The Day Will Come When You Won't Be," when Negan and his baseball bat quite possibly cross the line from violence done to serve the story to violence done for pure shock value.

Spoiler alert, but this is the notorious episode in which Negan shows the Grimes clan the way he runs things, which includes killing people, ruthlessly, to make a point. But you, dear reader, probably already know what happens: He has Rick and the rest of them trapped in the woods, on their knees and surrounded by hundreds of his minions. He chooses a victim, Abraham (Michael Cudlitz), and beats him to death with that barbed-wire-wrapped baseball bat. Then Daryl does something impulsive and stupid: he jumps up and lunges at Negan, landing a punch before he's restrained. "I will shut that shit down!" Negan bellows, and to show how serious he is, he metes out immediate justice. Only, he doesn't kill Daryl; he chooses another victim: Glenn. He pounds Glenn to death, shown in brutally graphic detail. Glenn's eye pops out. The middle of his skull is smashed in. Then Negan takes about half a dozen swings, shot from a wide angle. They feel like they go on and on and on. Finally, Negan steps back, and you can see pieces of Glenn's flesh hanging off the barbed wire. Negan is reveling in this brutality, vaunting his power over his captives, even to the point of using Lucille in a blatantly phallic way.

Now, for all the social resonance, all the underlying unspoken metaphorical commentary on the day and age, there is a part of this show—a big part of it—that is purely about the jump scares and the gross-out zombie stuff. The "gore factor" is a big part of the show's appeal, noted Juan Gabriel Pareja. "There's a weird combination of 'Oh, my God, that's disgusting,' but like, '*Oh my God, that's disgusting!*' Being grossed out but at the same time, almost giddy and elated by the next level of the way they gross you out, and it's a weird contradiction." Somewhere between "oh, my God" and "*Oh my God!*" is the line that the show walks.

Seeing those scraps of Glenn's flesh hanging off Negan's baseball bat, to me at least, was just too much. That was my breaking point. This is what I wrote in my recap:

> We didn't think it was possible for this show to shock us, but this did. Tonight's episode may have set a new mark for gore on television. Was it excessive? That's for individuals to decide. It certainly was done in service to the story; Negan is a brutally violent man, and this is a mad world. Still, we were fielding texts and emails right after the show, and the tenor was one of revulsion. It'll be interesting to see how people react.

Others were even more offended. "The episode went beyond depicting the gore to reveling in it, savoring the audience's discomfort with as much sadistic pleasure as Negan himself," Sam Adams wrote at *Slate*. "Glenn and Abraham's deaths were shocking, all right, but they were distasteful, too, even on a show where bodies are regularly torn apart like wet paper." This episode, which was watched by 17 million people, turned a lot of stomachs. The drop-off in ratings was steep. The next week, only 12.5 million people tuned in. For any other show, that'd still be a dream number, but it was a huge drop in viewers, and the extreme reaction to the premiere was noticed by the producers, who started to pull back on the violence where they could (given that some episodes were already complete). "We did tone it down for episodes we were still filming for later on in the season," Gale Anne Hurd said at a conference in January 2017.

The FCC received a number of complaints from viewers related to the Negan episode. "You don't show ISIS beheading people on TV, nor should you allow someone to be beaten with a barbed-wire baseball bat," one viewer wrote. Another wrote, "Watching ISIS behead someone isn't as horrible as watching this TV show," and while we could all emphatically argue that watching ISIS behead someone is categorically worse than anything on a scripted television program, the point is well taken. "I could not even sleep and I know I will not get that gruesome display of torture out of my mind ever," said another viewer. "I think this episode should be banned in its current form or banned altogether. We do not need violence porn in an already overly violent society."

The premiere was even too violent for at least one member of the cast. "The way in which it went down, it felt like it was flogging a dead horse," said Xander Berkeley, who plays Gregory, the head of the Hilltop community. The premiere's violence was the first time he'd ever seen anything on the show that bothered him. "I got disturbed for a minute or two watching it. I remember feeling that way when I watched *Taxi Driver*." What concerned Berkeley most was the possibility that showing a Negan who is cool, even sexy, and who wraps his graphic, sadistic violence in humor (and, I have to admit, Negan *is* funny), ran the risk of normalizing what should be truly terrifying. "I don't want anybody out there emulating this guy getting off on his vulgar violence." Was it over the line? Again, that is for each person to decide on their own.

How violent images on television affect the viewer has been a question since at least the early 1950s, which is to say, as soon as television started becoming a common feature in homes. "Violence is a symptom of irreconciled conflict, destruction, hurt, and waste," George Gerbner, a professor of communications at the University of Pennsylvania, wrote in a 1970 paper. "It is, in a sense, the opposite of communication. It negates the most uniquely human capacity of our species, the capacity to interact and even collide creatively through symbols and messages. Symbolic representation of violence is, therefore, a vital function of information and art in their illumination of its real-life manifestations and consequences." In other words, violence isn't just violence for its own sake. Even a violent act is communicating *something;* what matters is what that something is. "Happy are the good guys and unhappy the bad (at least in the end)," Gerbner writes. "Good guys *initiate* as much violence as bad guys, but hurt less and kill less. Good guys *suffer* more from violence, but heroes never die. Bad guys get hurt less than good guys, but, of course, they lose out in the end."

Consider two villains on this show, Negan and the Governor. The Governor was clearly psychotic and evil. His violence was never normal or even justifiable. He just killed for the sake of satisfying his own bizarre appetites, and of course, in the end he died because of those appetites. Negan is a different creature, though. Negan is "deliciously vile," Pareja said in an interview, with an "incredibly charming hatefulness." *The Walking Dead* is essentially delivering a message through Negan. That message can be that bad guys are bad and will pay for their evil, or it can even be that sometimes bad people get away with their evil; the world is certainly rife with examples of both.

All of this is good for the immediate scares, but even all these top-notch special effects on their own aren't enough. That's because the special effects aren't what make a zombie story truly terrifying, a point once made by George Romero himself. "I go to conventions and universities and talk to young filmmakers and everybody's making a zombie movie!" he said in a 2008 interview. "It's because it's easy to get the neighbors to come out, put some ketchup on them. You don't need a rubber suit or a monster effect." You need gallons of fake blood, but if you're on a budget, zombies are easier to create than, say, werewolves. This is probably one reason why zombies were such a B-movie staple for so many decades. You get Bela Lugosi and a bunch of extras, and, bang, you've got a monster movie. "But there doesn't seem to be a lot of substance behind most of it," he said. "It's just splatter, you know? I think you have to go deeper."

That deeper level is something that comes after special effects, after jump scares and exploding bodies. It's something that can be explored not through the dead, but only through the living. What makes *The Walking Dead* work is that it shows people who are broken, afraid, courageous, insane, upright, duplicitous, noble, foolhardy, and just plain hardy as all hell. In a word, it explores what's in a person's heart.

GUT-WRENCHING MOMENTS

FOR ALL THE OTHER THINGS THAT MAKE IT SUCH A COMpelling story, *The Walking Dead* would not be *The Walking Dead* if it didn't also scare you silly. Every single episode has something oozing and dripping and groaning, something repulsive and stomach-churning. It could be the sand walkers on the bridge that Tara and Heath uncover or the water zombies in the basement of the food pantry that Father Gabriel (Seth Gilliam) raids. Sometimes it is not a monster at all. Sometimes it's the fear of what waits around the bend. Here are five of the most gut-wrenching moments this show has dished up over its first seven seasons.

RICK GOES TO ATLANTA

The pilot episode, "Days Gone Bye," is a marvel of storytelling. We meet our hero, Rick, in a wounded state, we are provided with all the visual information we need to understand that the world he's living in is in ruins, and we're given all the facts to understand why that is. We see only three living people for any length of time—Rick, Morgan, and Duane—but we see viscerally what the plague's effects do to the survivors, how it figuratively and physically tears them up. Rick comes to a farmhouse looking for gas and finds the residents in their living room, dead from a suicide pact. Morgan and Duane are tortured by the fact that their dead wife and mother shambles outside among the dead. Morgan couldn't mercy-kill her before she died, once she'd been bitten, and he can't do it after. They are in fact as trapped by their guilt and indecision as they are by the undead. They can't move forward, can't do the only rational thing available to them, which is to leave.

A fair amount of running time passes between when Rick leaves his old police station and when he gets to Atlanta. We even get snippets of the camp where Lori, Carl, and Shane are, and where Rick will end up. Rick runs out of gas, ditches his cruiser, and finds a horse on a farm to take him the rest of the way. There is that iconic shot of him, alone, on the inbound lanes of the highway, like a Wild West lawman riding into town. He rolls through the empty city streets. Then he turns a corner . . . and comes upon a zombie herd. Hundreds of them, clogging the street. They turn to him, slowly. He realizes he's made an awful mistake. It's an "oh, shit" moment for the hero—and the viewer, too. With this shot, the full power of the devastation and danger is finally revealed. It quickly turns drastic. The dead surround him, throw him off his horse, and start eating the horse. Rick crawls under a tank, shooting the zombies that follow. He's got one bullet left, and is about to use it on himself; it's impossible to believe the star of the show could die in the premiere, but there is no way out. Then he sees the open hatch at the bottom of the tank. (For the record, the tank looks like a U.S. M1 Abrams, which does not have an escape hatch underneath. An M60 Patton does, but the tank isn't an M60, either; it's a British Chieftain.)

The last image, a zooming, rising shot of zombies filling the street, banging on the tank, shredding and eating the horse, shows that the survivors are massively outnumbered and overwhelmed.

THE GOVERNOR'S FIRST ATTACK ON THE PRISON

Of all the shocking moments in seven seasons of this show, nothing tops the Governor's first attack on the former West Georgia Correctional Facility, which comes at the end of "Home" (season 3, episode 10).

The Grimes clan have made themselves at home in the prison, but things look grim. They've already tussled with neighboring Woodbury and its psychotic leader, the Governor. Glenn Rhee and Maggie Greene were taken prisoner while scavenging for supplies, and the Governor molested Maggie. Daryl Dixon, an important member of the group, was part of the crew that rescued Glenn and Maggie, but when he finds his brother Merle in Woodbury, and the bad-natured brother isn't welcome at the prison, the Dixon brothers both leave. The Governor is out for blood, and Glenn Rhee wants vengeance. Meanwhile, the death of his wife has sent Rick into a tailspin. He is having hallucinations and hearing voices; he is in, as Glenn puts it, "crazytown." He wanders outside the fence, looking for whatever it is that's calling him (incidentally, Andrew Lincoln does a good crazy). Everybody else inside is trying their best to keep it together and prepare for the expected attack. Hershel goes down to the fence and tries to convince Rick to come inside. Carol watches from a distance with Axel, the last surviving prisoner, who is integrating himself into this new group. He's telling a story about his brother, and the camera is fixed on the two of them, when suddenly his head explodes. *Wham!* Then we see the end of a rifle scope and the face behind it: the Governor. Rick is pinned down in the creek. Hershel is pinned down in the field. A sniper has climbed up into a tower and has the prison yard pinned down; Carol survives only by pulling Axel's dead body over her own. The Governor holds his rifle on his hip and fires several rounds into the air, a malicious grin on his face. He's *enjoying* it.

Then he unveils his next trick. One of his goons drives a bread truck full of walkers through the outer and inner fences. The undead wander out and fill the field. The Governor and his henchmen leave, content they've gotten the prison's attention. Rick, meanwhile, is outside the fence, out of ammo. And now he's surrounded by walkers who have been drawn by the noise. He can't fight them off. Hershel is still trapped in the field; no way he can hop out on his crutches. Michonne goes off running, slicing heads off with her katana. Glenn drives up in a pickup. Rick is still on his own, fighting off walkers, which are all over him. They press him up against the fence. One is inches from his face, Rick is beset by zombies. He's barely holding them both back. It's never looked this bad. One is just inches in front of Rick's face. *OhmygodRick'sgonnadie!* Then you see a familiar bolt rip through the zombie's skull. It's a shot from Daryl's crossbow. Daryl and Merle are the grungiest cavalry ever, but they have come in classic just-in-time fashion.

This is a long fight, roughly the last quarter of the episode. It comes on suddenly, ramps up violently, and feels like it lasts forever. From the Governor's malignant glee, to the death of poor Axel, to Rick's near death and the Dixon brothers' cavalry charge, this is one fantastic, gut-wrenching sequence, and an example of the scale and magnitude the show can repeatedly pull off.

ANDREA DIES

Some fans read the comics. Some don't. This means a big chunk of the audience is expecting certain developments while others aren't. Through the years, the show's writers have deviated from the comics significantly. They have given some characters on the TV show—Denise, Hershel, and Bob Stookey—the same fate suffered by other characters in the comics—Abraham (arrow through the skull), Tyreese (beheaded by the Governor), and Dale (leg eaten by the cannibals) respectively; they've expanded upon some smaller parts from the comics for some characters, like the Governor; they've put in things that never occurred in the comics, like the trip to the CDC; and they've created characters that never existed in the comics, like the Dixon brothers. But the show totally sucker punched comics fans when it killed off Andrea in "Welcome to the Tombs," the season 3 finale.

Even though her story had already veered drastically from the comics' story line, fans were rightfully expecting her to get out of the Governor's lair. (In the comics, as of this writing—*spoiler alert*—Andrea is still alive, and a key member of the Grimes clan.) Andrea was a character who'd shown a tremendous amount of growth, from somebody who wanted to die in season 1 to a capable survivor in season 3, which is what makes her death that much more shocking.

Andrea does her best. She lands in Woodbury and falls for what the town could be. She also very, very wrongly falls for what she thinks the Governor could be. She realizes her mistake and tries to escape back to the prison. She almost makes it before the Governor tracks her down and brings her back. He lashes her to a dentist's chair deep in his private torture chambers. Then he stabs his other defector—Milton—and locks him in the room with Andrea. "Now you're gonna die," the Governor says, "and you're gonna turn, and you're gonna tear the flesh from her bones. In this life, you kill or you die. Or you die and you kill." It takes a long time for this to play out. Andrea is trying desperately to get herself loose before Milton dies and turns. She almost makes it. She's halfway out. Then Milton turns. The scene cuts to outside the corrugated walls. We hear Andrea scream, but the scene ends.

We don't know what happens to her until after the final battle with the Governor, after the Governor mows all his own people down, and after Rick, Daryl, and Michonne go to Woodbury to finish it off (all in all, it's a pretty violent climax when you think about it). They search through the torture chambers and finally find Andrea. She's alive. But she's been bitten. It's too late. She begs for a gun, to end it. "I know how the safety works," Andrea says to Rick, a reference to their first meeting in the department store back in Atlanta, when she didn't know how a safety worked. Rick hands her a semi, Michonne stays with her, and she kills herself.

HERSHEL IN THE SICK WARD

The opening episodes of season 4, when a virus rips through the prison, culminates in what to me at least is the most intensely emotional point of the entire series. As I said above, sometimes the horror and drama on *The Walking Dead* don't come from the monsters; they come from simply trying to live in a world that's lost all the safety nets that were provided by civilized society. Like medicine.

At some point after the group has made the former West Georgia Correctional Facility a functioning home for an ever-growing group of survivors, a virus spreads. Not the zombie virus, but a different kind. Whatever it is, it is severe, and without any modern medicine, it starts to take a dreadful toll. It kills one young man, who turns and attacks others. It makes a number of people severely sick, so sick that Carol takes it upon herself to kill two people and burn their bodies rather than let them infect anybody else or die and turn into zombies. Suddenly, most of the population is sick, cordoned off in a separate cellblock. Several who aren't go on a desperate run for medicine near a veterinary school Hershel knows about. Nobody who isn't sick is allowed in there. It's far too dangerous. The infected are left on their own to either live or die.

Hershel determines to not just let those people die. He goes *into* the ward with the sick, doing whatever he can to ease their pain and hopefully keep them alive long enough for the others to return. It's a suicide mission. The illness is extremely virulent, and Maggie and Rick try to stop him. He rebuts them with a great, desperate speech: "You step outside, you risk your life. You take a drink of water, you risk your life. And nowadays you breathe, and you risk your life. Every moment now, you don't have a choice. The only thing you can choose is what you're risking it for. Now I can make these people feel better and hang on a little bit longer. I can save lives. That's reason enough to risk mine. And you know that."

Hershel tends to the sick, who are getting closer and closer to dying, including his son-in-law, Glenn. He has only the most rudimentary aids—elderberry tea and a suction tube—his gumption, and wits to serve him. He saves as many as he can. Some start to die and turn. Now he's trapped in there, trying to avoid the walkers and still keep the rest alive. Maggie finally barges in and saves both her father and her husband. The scavenging team returns with the medicine that will save everybody else. If not for Hershel's heroism, those afflicted by the virus probably would have all died. It is an epic but horribly daunting scene. The danger gone, Hershel finally goes off to another cell for some rest. He sits on the bed and breaks down, sobbing uncontrollably, emotionally wasted. And I will tell you, I did the exact same thing.

GLENN IN THE ALLEY

Glenn Rhee seemingly dies in an alley (season 6, episode 3, "Thank You"), far from his friends, his wife, and his unborn child. It is the culmination of a series of entirely unpredictable events that will threaten the very existence of Alexandria. The fact that these events lead to the death of somebody as capable and resourceful as Glenn is a complete shock. Though we'll find out three episodes later that he didn't in fact die (and I'll explain in chapter 11 why I think that was a terrible decision on the part of the writers), this moment—when you don't know that he didn't die—easily stands as one of the show's most gut-wrenching.

The first three episodes of season 6 (directed by Nicotero, Jennifer Lynch, and Michael Slovis, respectively, and written by

Scott Gimple and Matthew Negrete, Seth Hoffman, and Angela Kang) are really one long, brilliantly told sequence about a massive quarry filled with the undead outside Alexandria, unfolding in near real time. There are hundreds of undead, maybe thousands, and Rick's plan is to lead them out and march them away from town. It's an audacious plan that will of course go awry, and is the trigger for everything else that happens in season 6. Glenn's plotline forms a well-contained story within that story.

With a large part of Alexandria's manpower out dealing with the zombies, the town is especially vulnerable when the maniacal group known as the Wolves attacks without warning. They ram a truck into the town's walls, which sets off its horn. That sound starts to draw the quarry walkers to the town. Suddenly everything is in chaos. As I said, the three episodes are presented basically in real time, chronicling the events of one day. The attack of the Wolves is swift and vicious and comes without a single visual or audio clue to the viewer. Most of the townspeople run, except Carol, who almost single-handedly defends the town (the story does provide Carol with several fantastic moments). Rick's group splinters, trying to regain control of the herd and running from it at the same time. Glenn, Nicholas, Michonne, and Heath end up in a town, where they have one chance to turn the herd. It doesn't work, and Glenn and Nicholas—a man who incidentally once tried to kill Glenn—wind up trapped in an alley, with dozens of walkers pinning them down.

It's the apogee of an epic plan gone horribly awry. Glenn and Nicholas climb on top of a Dumpster, without any means of escape. They are virtually out of ammo. Glenn is a hero of the Grimes clan, a fierce, resourceful survivor. This is, after all, the guy who first saved Rick back in Atlanta. But there's simply nothing to be done. They are going to die. Nicholas realizes it, whispers, "Thank you," and shoots himself in the head. The recoil sends both of them tumbling to the ground and right into that clutch of walkers.

It is a truly shocking moment that wasn't in the comics. Nobody could have seen this coming, but it makes perfect sense: The story has led Glenn to that alley. Glenn is one of Alexandria's most capable survivors. Of course he'd be part of the crew on the quarry mission. When it goes bad, of course he'd be one of the few who could possibly fix it. Only, he can't. He risks his life to try, as he has so many other times, proving himself a worthy hero. That's what makes it so shocking. In this moment, he isn't a larger-than-life savior. He's just a guy who is simply overwhelmed, and it reinforces what should be this world's only abiding lesson: anybody can die at any time. (Even though, well, he doesn't. Again, just wait until we get to chapter 11, where I have many more opinions about this moment.)

RECAP

SEASON THREE

- **SAFE HAVENS:** The West Georgia Correctional Facility, Woodbury
- **SURVIVORS LOST:** Lori Grimes, T-Dog, Andrea, Milton, Merle, Duane Jones, Donna, Ben, Axel, Oscar, Big Tiny, too many Woodburyians to count
- **ANTAGONISTS KILLED:** Tomas, Andrew, Allen, Merle
- **NOTABLE WALKERS:** Milton, Merle, Penny
- **NEW BIRTHS:** Judith

THE GREENE FARM OVERRUN, THE GRIMES CLAN IS BACK on the road and finds a safe haven in an unexpected place: a prison, the former West Georgia Correctional Facility. It's got walls, and power, and fences, and a yard for crops. Aside from the fact that they have to clear it out, because it is jammed with inmates and guards who have turned, it is ideal. The clearing is an arduous task. Hershel is bitten in the leg, and Rick impulsively amputates below the knee. But it works. They also find something else surprising: five inmates who are not dead, who've been locked in the cafeteria all this time. The prisoners have no idea what happened to the prison or the rest of the world.

This leads to a bit of a dilemma between the two groups: Who "owns" the prison—the five inmates who've been holed up in there for more than a year, or the Grimes clan, which just got there but did in fact clear it out and made it safe? Does anybody have an actual, legitimate claim on anything beyond what they can defend with guns, knives, and their lives? The question in the prison is a small-bore version of one that will play out again and again, like when the Grimes clan meets the community at Woodbury and its murderous, psychotic leader, the Governor.

They agree to a truce with the prisoners, but it doesn't last long at all, nor do the prisoners: Tomas, their de facto leader, threatens Rick, and ends up with a machete in his skull. Another one gets bitten by a walker. Rick chases away a third, Andrew, who retaliates by setting off the prison's alarms and drawing a herd of walkers. In the confusion, T-Dog dies sacrificing himself for Carol, and Lori forces Maggie to perform an emergency—an extreme emergency—caesarean section. This saves the life of her child, but mortally wounds her. Carl performs the unbelievable task of putting a bullet in his mother's head to prevent her from turning.

Meanwhile, Andrea, suffering from a flu, and Michonne are still wandering around in the wild. They come across a crashed military helicopter, where they observe other survivors. While they watch from a distance, one of the survivors sneaks up behind them. It's our reintroduction to Merle Dixon, not dead, with a metal sleeve covering his amputated hand, a long knife permanently attached to it. Merle was found at some point by a man named the Governor, and became a loyal soldier. He takes the two and brings them back to Woodbury, where they are welcomed by the Governor. On the surface, Woodbury seems almost idyllic: a picturesque town around which they've built tall, sturdy walls. Andrea is attracted to it, and apparently to its leader, but the place gives Michonne a chill. It's not entirely clear whose instincts are right. The Governor meets with the pilot of the downed helicopter and discovers there's a surviving group of National Guardsmen. He goes to their camp with news of the helicopter pilot—and then has his men, hidden in the woods, mow down all the soldiers. At that point, we know whose instinct was right: Michonne's. It's further confirmed when the Governor goes back to his apartment and settles in for the night—in a secret room where one wall is covered by fish tanks with zombie heads in them.

Glenn and Maggie go foraging for supplies and stumble into

Merle, who takes them captive and brings them to Woodbury. There, the Governor tortures them for information. The Governor sees the mere existence of another group as a threat to his rule, and in his homicidal mind is already making plans to rub them out. Michonne, out on her own, pieces everything together and shows up at the prison with the supplies Maggie and Glenn gathered up. The Grimes clan plans to rescue their comrades and invade Woodbury. They do manage to rescue the two, and Michonne goes off to find the Governor. In his apartment, she finds the horrors of the fish tanks, and the Governor's daughter, Penny, a zombified little girl. Michonne mercy-kills her in front of the Governor, and the two have an epic duel, which ends with Andrea coming in and saving the Governor, but not before Michonne gouges his eye out with a piece of glass. In the fight, though, Daryl is captured, and the group has to go back for him. Once he's rescued and reunited with Merle, the Dixons go off into the woods together, because nobody at the prison is willing to live with Merle.

Back at the prison, the psychological weight of it all has gotten to be too much for Rick, who is now hearing voices on an old phone and seeing his wife's ghost. Not only is the Ricktator not leading, he's wandering out in the woods by himself. The group is splintering and fearful, waiting for retaliation by the Governor. When it comes, it comes abruptly, and brutally. Axel takes a bullet to the brain, Hershel on his crutches gets pinned down in the field, and Rick is nearly overwhelmed by walkers outside the fence, just as the Dixon brothers return. The Governor smiles malignantly, fires some shots into the air, unloads a bread truck full of walkers on the prison, and takes off. Message sent.

Andrea arranges a sit-down between the Governor and Rick. It is the one time these two men will sit in a room together and talk. It doesn't go well. "Well, at least I don't call myself a *gover-*

nor," Rick says with condescension. Insults fly, boasts are made. The Governor agrees to back off—but only if Rick will turn over Michonne. Rick's smart enough to know it's a lie, but desperate enough to consider it. The Grimes clan needs to make a quick decision: flee or fight. Is this really their home, and if so, is it worth defending? Merle takes matters into his own hand, tricking Michonne into a trip outside and taking her captive with the intention of giving her over. But his conscience gets the best of him. Even Merle, in the end, becomes noble. On his own, he desperately tries to kill the Governor. It doesn't work. In retaliation, the Governor kills Merle and lets him turn. Daryl eventually finds him like that, and is forced to mercy-kill his own brother.

The Governor makes his plan to attack, but first deals with two traitors in his midst: Andrea and Milton. Andrea he ties to a dentist's chair in his torture chamber; Milton he stabs, then leaves in the room with Andrea. The Grimes clan decides that their home is worth defending, and they prepare for the inevitable attack. When it does come, it is far more one-sided than imagined. The Woodbury people are not seasoned fighters; the Grimes clan is. They easily repel the Governor's attack and drive his soldiers away. Lost in his own insanity and enraged at his defeat, the Governor shoots every person in his group dead, save for his two top lieutenants.

Rick, Daryl, and Michonne go to Woodbury to find Andrea, who is still alive. She has managed to get out of the chair, and has brained Milton—but not before getting bitten. She won't make it. Rick gives her a gun. With Michonne at her side, she ends it. The Grimes clan picks up the stragglers left at Woodbury, brings them to the prison, and begins the process of rebuilding, and improving, their community. This is home now.

CHAPTER 5

HEART

"YOU FIGHT AND FIGHT IT. YOU DON'T GIVE UP. AND THEN ONE DAY, YOU JUST CHANGE. WE ALL CHANGE."

—CAROL PELETIER

(SEASON 4, EPISODE 14, "THE GROVE")

"If Daryl dies, we riot" is a popular saying among fans. I don't blame them. Daryl's character is so revered and has been with these fans so long (and through so many hardships), they wouldn't know what the show would be like *without* him. That kind of attachment to the characters is one illustration of just how this show is about much more than jump scares and zombie effects.

"Character-driven stories are what *The Walking Dead*'s all about," said Jay Bonansinga, the author of the tie-in novels. Who would have believed, he wondered, back before the show premiered, or even the comics, that there would be a worldwide pop culture phenomenon about a zombie apocalypse? "It happened, in my opinion, because of character. That's what makes this so fucking interesting."

On the one hand, the people in *The Walking Dead* are literally comic book characters, sprung from the pages of Kirkman's source material. In that sense, they're, well, two-dimensional.

There's the lone sheriff. The sage old farmer. The redneck. The smart Asian. The farmer's daughter. The priest. The psychotic villain (several of these, actually). Even their names are generic: Rick. Carl. Daryl. Bob. Andrea. Hershel. Glenn. Dale. Once these cartoon cutouts are filled with breath by the cast and the writers, though, it becomes a very different proposition. Over the course of the show's seven (so far) seasons, the characters—the ones who have survived, at least—have all undergone extensive changes. They are radically different from the people they were when they were first introduced. They have evolved into fully realized, three-dimensional characters with abilities that can seem like superpowers. Ironically, one short-lived villain, a cannibal named Gareth, even goes so far as to give his enemies in the Grimes clan comic book superhero names: the Archer (Daryl), the Samurai (Michonne). Carol, who single-handedly destroys the cannibal's compound, is simply called the Queen Bitch. Despite the simplistic names, Bonansinga says, "We are not used to this kind of character depth, this almost poignant development of character. That's why people have responded to the show so much."

Character arcs are timeless. In Homer's *Odyssey,* written in the eighth century B.C., the wily hero, Odysseus, king of Ithaca, goes through hell to get back home to his wife and son after fighting in the ten-year-long Trojan War. Before he washes up on the shores of his home island, he will have lost everything: his ships, his men, even his identity. He looks no different from any other beggar. Indeed, nobody—not even his wife—recognizes him when he returns to reclaim his crown. Odysseus leaves as a king and returns as a pauper, and has to fight to reclaim what was formerly his (and bring to a bloody end all those suitors vying for his wife and kingdom). That's one hell of a character arc. Of course, what makes it so epic is that Odysseus never loses himself, never stops believing in himself as the king of Ithaca, and the story becomes a lesson in holding on to one's self no matter the circumstances.

The Odyssey is such a masterful piece of storytelling that it has basically become the template for every story that has followed it. When *Star Wars* became a massive global phenomenon in 1977, its shoot-'em-up story received intellectual support because it was seen as re-creating the so-called "hero's journey." And fans (and franchises) love heroes. *The Walking Dead* provides a different take on the hero's journey. The characters who inhabit this world are not looking for a kingdom or an adventure or a gallant fight; they are merely trying to survive and searching for some excuse to go on; invariably, they end up finding it in each other.

Every show has a protagonist who serves as the lens through which we see the world the show represents. *The Sopranos* opens with New Jersey mob boss Tony Soprano sitting in his psychiatrist Jennifer Melfi's office. Although he feigns reluctance at first, he eventually opens up to her and we experience the emotional rawness of his character through these sessions.

Sometimes these roles are split. *Mad Men* has an ostensible protagonist in Don Draper, the advertising executive with the secret past, but I'd argue the story is actually told through the eyes of Peggy Olson, who rises through the ranks of the fictitious advertising agency Sterling Cooper. In the premiere, Peggy arrives for her first day as Don's secretary and is given a tour of the office. So while Don is the star, we are really introduced to this world through Peggy.

Whose perspective we are seeing events from makes a difference. In *Cheers* (1982–1993), an engaged couple walks into a Boston bar. The man leaves his fiancée there, never to return.

She, in turn, takes a job at the bar as a waitress. So we see the world of the bar through the eyes of Diane Chambers, the outsider, which is why it seems to be full of oddballs and lunacy. If we saw it through Sam's eyes, or Cliff's or Norm's, it might appear completely different. In *Mr. Robot,* the protagonist and narrator are the same person, Elliot Alderson (technically, the protagonist, narrator, and antagonist are all the same person, but then *Mr. Robot* is a complicated show).

In *The Walking Dead,* the perspective is that of Rick Grimes, through whom we experience how the world has changed upon his awakening. Rick is somebody who sets goals: Find his family. Find a safe haven. Protect your clan. He doesn't always make the right decision—in fact, he often makes the wrong one—but he's willing to *make* the decision, and live with the consequences. There are so many examples of this I could point to, but the one that seems the most poetic to me, the most telling, involves the fate of Sophia Peletier, the young daughter of Ed and Carol Peletier, who meets her demise in the woods off the highway at the beginning of season 2 (though we won't know it for quite some time).

After the group leaves the CDC at the end of the season 1 finale ("TS-19"), they get stuck on the highway at the beginning of season 2 ("What Lies Ahead"). Sophia gets lost in the woods, and they end up on the Greene farm. Rick encourages them to keep looking for Sophia, even if he privately doubts she could still be alive. That decision doesn't sit well with Shane, who is not only Rick's best friend but increasingly his antagonist, vying for both a leadership role within the group and for the affection of Rick's wife, Lori. Shane chafes against both Rick's and Hershel's rules. When it's revealed that there are walkers in the barn, he goes ballistic. He arms the group, smashes open the barn doors, and lets the walkers loose. It's a violent challenge to Rick and to Hershel.

Then Sophia comes out of the barn. It's heartbreaking for the audience (I know some saw it coming, but I for one did not) and for the Grimes clan. Everybody stands around in shock, not knowing what to do. Carol is hysterical and overcome; everybody else is simply defeated by the reality of her death. Shane is completely neutered by it. There is, of course, only one thing to do. There is only one person to do it. Rick draws his Colt Python and shoots Sophia in the head. Because, as their leader, he's the only one who could have done that.

"Certain human beings aren't designed to heal," Andrew Lincoln said to me in an interview. "Certain people obviously keep pushing on, and he's one of those people. That's why people follow him, he's got this heart." Lincoln recalled a snippet from Ernest Hemingway's *The Old Man and the Sea,* when the old man, Santiago, is telling a story about turtles, and mentions that a turtle's heart will beat for hours after being cut out of its body. This works as a metaphor for Rick's strength, how it will go on no matter what cost or odds are placed before him. "One of the first quotes I was thinking about, when I was starting to play him, it's a really simple quote," Lincoln said. "'A hero is a man who does what he can.'"

That does explain Rick well, but Lincoln insisted that this quality is not unique to his hero character. "Look around the world; I'm constantly amazed by the tiny acts of heroism that happen in everybody's lives all the time." How do some people even get out of bed in the morning, he asked, when they know what hardships await them? Yet they do. If Lincoln is right about that, and I'm guessing he is, it's an illustration of how these characters are so like us, and why people associate so closely with them. But it's also an illustration of how ingratiated actors feel to their characters, in service of them.

Some of the characters seem to be shaped as much by the actors playing them as they are by what's in the script. This is especially evident in Andrew Lincoln's Rick, Norman Reedus's Daryl, and Melissa McBride's Carol. These three could easily be little more than cardboard heroes, flat as a page, but the actors have brilliantly transformed the black-and-white comic book characters into flesh-and-blood people whom millions of people around the world viscerally identify with. (The shame of it is that nobody ever seems to realize that come awards season.)

Every person I spoke to in relation to this book offered completely unsolicited and glowing praise of Andrew Lincoln. Lincoln is famous for being an extreme method actor on the set. He'll listen to screaming metal music, he'll scream himself, he'll punch walls, he'll do anything to ramp up his intensity to play these intense scenes. But he also takes time to work with the cast, to bring them together the way leaders always do.

"Andy, he really led by example," said Juan Gabriel Pareja. "He had a certain generosity of spirit that created a dynamic on the set that really made everybody a family. I mean, he had a lot on his plate, and even so, he was incredibly kind with his time and his energy, and it set a tone."

Xander Berkeley, who came on in season 6 as Gregory, was immediately thrown into opposition with Lincoln's Rick, and said he wasn't sure how the actor would take it. As Gregory, "I had to get up in his grill, and a lot of times actors—egos—even if it's just part of the storytelling, they flinch, they don't like anything that's going to make them look weak." Lincoln, however, was energized by that kind of dynamic. To Berkeley, it was a sign that he was working with a higher caliber of professional. Berkeley said that even people on the set for a day will find themselves getting a visit from Lincoln, who wants to make sure they're comfortable and know they're appreciated. Moreover, the level of commitment Lincoln brings to his role, both the character and his place in the cast, is something that filters through to everybody else on the set, and that Berkeley feels "somehow echoes out into the fan base. They get the vibe of the show.

"I got to say, it's pretty damn rare."

Norman Reedus is the least big-star-like big star you may ever meet. He certainly doesn't act like Daryl Dixon, the nails-tough backwoods redneck he portrays on the show, but you can see that there is a quality about the actor that translates into the character and makes Daryl a far more realistic hero.

I met Reedus when he came through New York one time on a round of interviews to promote the show. We taped a video interview, and afterward he stood around with our production crew and myself, hanging out and talking, without even a hint of pretension. Some of the guys knew him from the cult movie *Boondock Saints,* and he was telling us about the difference between *Walking Dead* fans (whom he described as loving and reverent) and *Boondock Saints* fans (loving and violent). I remember thinking, *If you didn't know this guy was one of the biggest stars on the biggest show on television, you'd never guess it just by looking at him.*

Reedus had a more circuitous route to the zombie apocalypse than Lincoln. While Rick is the clear-cut hero of the show, and Lincoln the star, Reedus's Daryl wasn't even a character when Darabont was putting the pilot together, and Norman Reedus definitely wasn't a big star. He had only fallen into acting as an adult, on the advice of a friend when he was living in L.A., and he had garnered a few credits to his name. When he read for *The Walking Dead,* it was for the role of Merle Dixon, even though the part of the evil Dixon brother had already been cast with the veteran character actor Michael Rooker. He went to the audition anyhow, because he wanted any role on the show. The producers were so impressed they brought him back, and eventually created the role of Daryl specifically for him. In the same way that Reedus could grab the mantle of Hollywood star, Daryl could grab the mantle of leader. It just doesn't seem to be in either one's natural disposition.

When we first meet Daryl, he is viewed as Merle's little brother. He hunts squirrels, is a backwoods survivalist, and constantly squabbles with Rick and Shane and everybody in the camp outside Atlanta. (In a later season, it comes out that the Dixon brothers originally planned to rob the survivors' camp and take off.) "He's kind of like a wet animal you find in an alley," Reedus told me. "If you approach him he'll snarl at you, but if you can feed him and take him in somewhere warm, he'll follow you forever." Daryl is somebody who needs "to have that glimmer of hope shown to him, he's not going to find it on his own." Over the show's ninety-nine-and-counting episodes, the wet animal has grown emotionally, allowing himself to become part of the group, and in fact finding himself through that interaction. He becomes a trusted lieutenant to Rick as well as a leader in his own right. There is a persistent vulnerability to Daryl, though, achieved via the empathy that Reedus brings to the character. (There is also ambiguity. Rumors persist that Daryl is gay, as evidenced by the fact that he's never been with a woman on the show. Reedus hasn't said one way or the other, but he did say that if it turned out that Daryl was gay, he'd "rock that story.")

The best example of Daryl's evolution comes when he's forced to choose between the prison and his brother, Merle (season 3, episode 10, "Home"). He tries to choose his blood family over his adopted one, but it doesn't take long for him to see that he simply can't live the way he used to. The Dixon brothers are back on the road, back to fending for themselves, which worked once upon a time, but not anymore. Merle plays his usual head games with his baby brother, to no avail. They find some survivors overrun by walkers on a bridge, and Daryl jumps right in to save them. He isn't Merle's little brother anymore. He's his own man now—and more than that, he's a *good* man. Out in the woods, they get into a get-it-all-out fight that reveals a few things, one being that their father beat the both of them. Daryl's had enough; he's going back to the prison. Merle knows he won't be welcome there.

"I tried to kill that black bitch. Damn near killed the Chinese kid."

"He's Korean," Daryl says.

Merle just looks at him, dumbfounded and exasperated. "Whatever," he says. The great callback there is that back in Atlanta (season 1, episode 4, "Vatos"), Daryl called Glenn Chinese, and Glenn corrected him. "Whatever," Daryl said then.

And, of course, Daryl's become such a magnet of nobility, he even manages to spark a light inside his brother. They do go back to the prison, and Merle eventually sacrifices himself in an attempt to kill the Governor. It doesn't work, but Merle goes out a hero because of the example set by his little brother. It's clear why Daryl is such a perennial fan favorite.

No single character on *The Walking Dead* has had a greater arc than Carol, played by Melissa McBride. The season 5 premiere, "No Sanctuary," portrays one of her finest moments. It was the show's highest-rated episode so far, with 17.3 million tuning in, an end-to-end action dash in which Carol returns to the Grimes clan to save them from certain slaughter inside the madhouse that is Terminus. In that moment, Carol Peletier ascended to the inner circle of the show's unkillables—unkillable because of her skills, and unkillable because of how popular she'd become among the fans.

It's worth recalling that episode's setup: Bob Stookey, Rick Grimes, Daryl Dixon, and Glenn Rhee are in a bad way, bound and being forced to kneel over a stainless-steel trough in a large warehouse. Next to them are four other men, all of whom are to be slaughtered. This is the killing floor of Terminus, where a band of cannibals (this group never really did have a settled name; I personally always preferred *Termites*) lures in strangers only to kill them, cook them, and eat them. Hey, everybody survives in their own way. The rest of the Grimes clan is in a boxcar, penned up like cattle, their fate sealed as well. In the warehouse, two of the Termites make methodical work of the first four (including, subtly enough, Sam, a hippie-ish survivor Rick and Carol met while scavenging for medical supplies). One knocks the victim out with a baseball bat, the other slits their throat. This fate awaits Rick, Daryl, Bob, and Glenn (and Glenn comes *this close* to getting whacked, twice), before Gareth, the leader of this group, comes in and has a little chat with our heroes. Rick makes a typical Rick threat to kill him, which seems just absurd, given the circumstances. Then, something happens. Gunfire erupts outside, followed by a shattering explosion.

Carol Peletier has arrived. She's like a mix of John Rambo and Josey Wales, a walking war zone with a talent for killing. She lays siege to Terminus all by herself—well, apart from the herd of walkers she guides right to the compound. She blows up a gas tank and the fences fall, the walkers trundle in—some skulking about as their rotting flesh burns—and Carol creates the distraction that allows Rick and everybody else to escape.

This is a Carol story that almost never happened, and it has as much to do with McBride's career path as it does the plan the writers had for her character.

McBride had basically given up on acting by the time she was cast as Carol. She worked steadily if not spectacularly through the 1990s, doing commercials and television, with roles on *Dawson's Creek* and *Walker, Texas Ranger* as well as a series of made-for-TV movies. In 2000, she gave up on acting and became a casting director for an Atlanta-based firm. In 2007, another casting firm brought her an opportunity. Frank Darabont was making a film version of the Stephen King story "The Mist," about a group of people trapped in a grocery store as a mist descends, carrying a variety of horrifying and deadly creatures. Did she want to audition? She eventually did, and accepted a small role as a distraught mother who leaves the store to go back to her children at home. McBride is in *The Mist* for only a few minutes, so briefly that her character doesn't even have a name; she is simply called "Woman with Kids at Home." But she gives a powerful, emotional performance as a mother more afraid for her children's safety than her own, willing to go out into the mist to get back home to them. It was on the strength of this scene that Darabont cast McBride in *The Walking Dead* as Carol Peletier.

In season 1, Carol is a battered housewife living in the survivors' camp with her husband, Ed, and young daughter, Sophia. Ed is clearly abusing Carol, and there are hints that he is doing something to their daughter, too. At this point, it is the kind of thing Carol would never even mention, much less put a stop to. Eventually she loses everything: Ed gets killed by a zombie. Sophia gets chased into the woods, and is also bitten and dies. She is a woman with nothing left and no reason to live.

Except, she does live. She picks up skills. She becomes a member of the group and pulls her own weight. She learns how to shoot. When the Grimes clan takes over the former West Georgia Correctional Facility, Carol progresses further. She joins the leadership council, where she takes on responsibilities. She (secretly) teaches the younger children how to use weapons and defend themselves. When a violent flu threatens the group, Carol adopts two young girls, Lizzie and Mika, whose father gets bitten by another resident who'd fallen to the virus and turned. Carol gives the girls a loving but stern talk about the kinds of things they need to do now to survive in this world.

Except, none of her character's change was supposed to happen. In the comics, Carol is a minor character who commits suicide early on, overcome by the brutality of this new world. Sophia, ironically, outlives her, and is later adopted by Maggie and Glenn. In the show, the writers were seriously contemplating writing Carol out during the early parts of season 3, with her character supposedly set to meet her fate in episode 4, "Killer Within." And while it is simply understood that to be cast on the show means accepting that your character *will* (eventually) die, in this instance McBride personally lobbied the producers for her character's life. She argued that Carol had more story in front of her. Sarah Wayne Callies, who played Lori, also lobbied on McBride's behalf. Maybe McBride was fighting for her job, and maybe Callies was just standing up for a friend. Either way, in the end, the story was changed, and IronE Singleton's T-Dog dies in the dark prison halls instead—along with Callies's Lori, who insists on a caesarean section that she knows will kill her.

"From day one," McBride told me in 2013, "I didn't know if I'd survive an episode. So you're grateful to live another day, and that's the message of this show and of life."

This business of who lives and dies is at the very heart of why this show is so compelling. It's not too unbelievable to say that *The Walking Dead* might be the first television show in history that could write off its leading character for no other reason than that it would serve the story, and have it actually work. Did you ever really think Captain Kirk would be killed? Or Joe Friday?

Sure, J. R. Ewing got shot, but the mystery was "Who shot J.R.?" not "Who killed J.R.?" How about Magnum, P.I.? Hawkeye? Crockett or Tubbs? Don Draper? Walter White? Tony Soprano? (I know what you're thinking, and you can stop right there. As far as I'm concerned, Tony Soprano is still alive.) But if Rick Grimes were to get bitten, or killed by Negan, or to die at the gruesome jaws of Winslow the spiked zombie, would it seem at all out of line? Shocking, yes, but completely warranted within the universe of the show. There would, of course, be a lot of upset viewers, as there are any time a main character is killed off. We in the audience form strong attachments to these characters. I found that out in a most interesting way one night while watching the show.

I will say happily that I'd become a Carol fan early on. On a show with so many strong characters, she had that diamond-in-the-rough quality. I got an idea of Carol's impact on the audience during the second episode of season 4, "Infected," about the flu. That evening, while watching, I sent out a tweet that said: "Love how Carol's become so hardcore. Who knew that bruised, battered housewife would be such a survivor?"

AMC's *Walking Dead* account saw it and retweeted it. Then it went viral. I sat there watching my laptop, the Twitter feed flying too fast for me to keep up. Hundreds of retweets. Hundreds of favorites. There was something else, too. As an answer to my question, one person wrote, "Uhhhh, only every bruised and battered woman to get away??" Another said, "As a bruised battered widowed housewife we are survivors." Yet another: "Battered women are some of the strongest women you'll ever know. We are survivors!!! No doubt." And another: "It's because she was a battered and bruised housewife that she's a survivor." Lastly, perhaps my favorite: "She survived her d*ckhead husband; zombies are nothing."

Carol best exemplifies why fans of the show so deeply identify with these survivors. She isn't a trained law enforcement officer like Rick. She isn't a backwoods survivalist like Daryl. She isn't a soldier like Abraham. She is a completely average person who finds herself an unlikely survivor, and without any of the skills of those around her. What she does have, however, is will to survive. She also can be cunning and ruthless, like when she tells Andrea to kill the Governor in his sleep to end the pointless war between Woodbury and the prison. In time, she combines all these traits and abilities to become one indefatigable fighting machine, and single-handedly saves everybody at Terminus.

"For particularly a woman coming from an abusive relationship, and to regain that power, is so strong," said Kerry Cahill, who plays one of the warriors in the Kingdom, Dianne. "We love women, and people, who go through really dark struggles and get back on their feet, get back up, and come back stronger. We love that. Because we all want to be that."

That's it exactly. Carol, more than any other character on the show, is who we are, and who we hope we'd turn into if ever pushed to the limit.

Another way we see character develop is through those who come into—or take—power within the various groups of survivors. As a sheriff's deputy, Rick Grimes had a modicum of authority; the Governor was a store clerk; Negan does not appear to have had any real power pre-Turn; Gregory, who runs Hilltop, may have been some kind of businessman; Ezekiel was a zookeeper; Gareth had a head for organization and put it to use after he learned an important lesson about the pecking order of the post–zombie apocalypse; Deanna Monroe was a congresswoman and was used to having power, and so easily, energetically, and naively assumed the mantle. Also, having a background in government already, she was eager to reestablish as much of the old world as she could, even if she alone bore the title of leader.

All these leaders came to power in different ways, and all adapted to it differently as well. Ezekiel, above all the other characters, understands how much of power is performance, and how critical the performance is to his people's morale. Gregory appears to have kind of snuck into his role, stepping into the power vacuum that is the FEMA outpost. As Paul Rovia says, he wasn't an ideal leader, but he was the one who took the role. He wears it vainly and protects it jealously. Daryl Dixon could have it, but has consistently rejected it: Daryl knows how to survive, probably better than any other person who has been portrayed on *The Walking Dead*. He also has a big heart, and while he lacks a natural inclination to leadership, it's clear people gravitate to him.

In Bonansinga's *Rise of the Governor* stories, we learn that the Governor, whose real name is Brian Blake, claimed his position as the leader of Woodbury by assuming the identity of his brother, Philip, a violent but powerful man, and it was by channeling that personality that he became a leader. Of course, that new personality was just the beginning of his descent into madness. Power quickly drove the Governor insane. One person who has spent a lot of time inside the Governor's head is Bonansinga, who wrote four books with Kirkman in which the Governor is the main character. The brother-identity swap was Kirkman's idea, but making this character feel real was Bonansinga's challenge, and that's a tall order. How do you make a murderous psychopath *relatable*?

In the comics, the Governor is a flat, purely evil villain. His daughter, Penny, is the one person who can humanize this monster. Now, Penny is a zombie, but the Governor keeps her locked up in his apartment because he cannot bear to kill her. This was Bonansinga's opening into this character's mind. "I used my experience as a father, as a parent. That's how I got inside a guy who in the comic book looks like Danny Trejo on acid," he said, referencing the character actor famous for playing menacing-looking bad guys. From there, he was able to build up the character, to give him some normal-ish motivations and desires. Ultimately the Governor goes stark, raving mad, kills a couple dozen people from Woodbury—his own people—and then wanders off into the wilderness. But even he can be brought back. In season 4, we meet the Governor again—in a story largely drawn from Bonansinga's novels. This Governor befriends a small family of survivors and becomes something of a protector and even father figure to a young girl, who reminds him of his Penny. It seems like a massive contradiction, but is it? "With evil, it's very rarely just Catholic 'evil,' demonic, pure, Donald Pleasence–talking-about-the-Shape evil," Bonansinga said (the "Shape" being the Michael Myers character from the *Halloween* films). "With great evil characters, they have their reasons." The Governor is definitely a great evil character. He also, apparently, had his reasons. Bonansinga quoted a line from Mary Wollstonecraft: "No man chooses evil because it is evil; he only mistakes it for happiness, the good he seeks."

No man embodies that sentiment quite so thoroughly as Negan, the bat-wielding, wisecracking leader of the Saviors. He loves being a cold-blooded, vicious, murdering totalitarian, and is surprisingly good at it. In the comics, we come to learn that he was a high school gym teacher married to a woman named Lucille (his backstory hasn't been explored on the show). In the world before the Turn, a high school gym teacher could never hope to become a "king," as he puts it. The Turn changed all that. Since then, Negan struts and vamps, delivers long speeches, and loves to hear himself eulogize. He plays savage, cruel games. He enjoys breaking his captives. He isn't afraid to commit the most horrendous murders.

What's perhaps most surprising is that Negan isn't actually hated by the audience. "You'll find Negan to be a strangely reasonable, strangely relatable, strangely psychotic character," Robert Kirkman told me ahead of season 7, one afternoon when he was in New York for Comic Con. I almost laughed when he said it because it sounded so outlandish. But he makes a good point. Negan *is* reasonable, in his own way. Yes, he brutally murders Abraham and Glenn in cold blood in the season 7 premiere. But that's only *after* Rick and his people murdered nearly *three dozen* of Negan's people in a sneak attack on a Saviors outpost ("Not Tomorrow Yet," season 6, episode 12) in even colder blood.

I actually pressed Kirkman about that, because it seemed to me that the smart move for Negan would have been to wipe this group out, that they were too dangerous to keep around. Kirkman was adamant that I was wrong about that, that Negan actually wanted to add pieces to his empire, and in the Grimes clan he saw a powerful piece—so long as he could break them.

And Negan is relatable, too, in a way. For one thing, he is darkly funny. He shows up in Alexandria while Rick is out scavenging ("Hearts Still Beating," season 7, episode 8) and makes himself at home in Rick's house. He has Olivia (Ann Mahoney) make a spaghetti dinner, and with Carl and Rick, they sit at the table like some typical nuclear family. It's insane, it's terrifying, but it's also so outlandish as to be darkly funny, and you get the sense that Negan himself knows all that. If the near extinction of mankind is one big joke, Negan's in on it. Of course, he is a complete monster. In that same episode, he disembowels Spencer Monroe in the middle of the street, and then orders one of his thugs to kill another resident. Olivia takes the bullet, dying on Rick's front porch. It's dangerous to make a character that violently evil also that attractive—with his black leather jacket infused with Jeffrey Dean Morgan's suave charisma—but *The Walking Dead* brilliantly walks that line.

Negan's character, and Jeffrey Dean Morgan's full-bodied portrayal of him, instantly became a big deal. At the *Walking Dead* panel during the convention, Morgan got one of the loudest ovations, even though his character had appeared in only one episode at that point. Maybe people were looking past the rank malevolence of the character and cheering the actor. Maybe the crowds will feel different now that they've seen what Negan actually does. Or maybe, like Kirkman said, there is something strangely relatable about this character. Maybe even Negan speaks to something inside of us, since, like the writer Frank Renzulli said, people are basically 98 percent the same—it's that 2 percent that can be the difference between ending up like Ezekiel and ending up like Negan.

What we've got on the show now, with all these new groups emerging over the past two seasons, is a sliding scale of leadership, with Ezekiel on one end in the role (pun intended) of philosopher-king, and Negan on the other in the form of the despot. Everybody else falls somewhere between the two, and sometimes slides from one side to the other. Rick, even though he is our protagonist, our ostensible hero, at times can be very much like Ezekiel, or a bit too much like the Governor or Negan. Even Negan at one point calls Rick an "animal," and while it's ironic coming from such a brutal despot, it's not entirely off base. You also end up with this complex network of communities with competing visions and goals, which may look somewhat familiar if you think about it. “It does remind one of the meshuggaas in our political systems,” said Xander Berkeley, who plays Gregory, “where you’ve got different people coming from different directions with different motives. I love the way the show is able to reflect aspects of real life.”

CHAPTER 6

RUPTURE

"CAN'T GO BACK, BOB."

—GARETH

(SEASON 5, EPISODE 1, "NO SANCTUARY")

On July 22, 2011, showrunner Frank Darabont was part of the team that went to San Diego to promote season 2 of *The Walking Dead* at the massively popular Comic-Con. He appeared on a panel and talked to reporters and seemed very excited about building upon the show's success from season 1. In just six episodes, the show had staked out new ground on television and within the whole zombie genre. Darabont was responsible for much of that.

Five days later, he was out of a job.

It was obvious something very bad had happened to the relationship between Darabont and AMC brass, but it wasn't exactly clear what that was. AMC issued a vague press release announcing that Glen Mazzara, who had been an executive producer, would be taking over. The network said it was grateful for Darabont's contributions. There were reports that AMC and the showrunner had gotten into a big fight over some budget cuts the network was imposing. Darabont wasn't talking. The cast was tense. Even if they wanted to speak out and come to the defense of their boss, they hesitated. After all, this was a zombie show. If they crossed whatever line Darabont had crossed, it would be easy, extremely easy, to "kill them" by simply writing them out of the show. It was a real mess.

On December 17, 2013, Darabont, his production company, and his agents served AMC a lawsuit in the New York State court.

Darabont's suit, though, was not a wrongful termination suit—at least it was not strictly a wrongful termination suit. It alleged—and still alleges, since the actual trial is scheduled to begin in 2018—that essentially AMC, which produced and aired the show, had cut itself a sweetheart deal with its broadcast arm, licensing the show for less than its production arm would have gotten it for had the show been produced independently. As the show's developer, producer, and director, Darabont was entitled to a nice slice of the profits, up to 15 percent. AMC's self-dealing, he says in his lawsuit, undercut what he would have gotten by tens of millions of dollars. In short, AMC was originally going to handle *The Walking Dead* the way it handled its other shows, by licensing them from a production company. At the time, AMC had licensed *Breaking Bad* from Sony and *Mad Men* from Lionsgate. Before *The Walking Dead* premiered, however, the network changed course. After AMC made the decision to produce the show in-house, Darabont negotiated a clause into the contract that stipulated AMC's broadcast arm would pay its production arm the same kinds of licensing fees it paid to outside studios. The entire lawsuit revolves around this one key clause. Darabont claimed that as of September 2012, rather than enjoying his share of the profits, he was getting statements from AMC showing that the series actually had a $49 million *deficit* to overcome before he could reap any profits. That should not be possible for a show as popular as this one, right? Well, that's Darabont's argument, at least. He didn't sue just because he'd been fired; he sued because, he alleged, he'd been stiffed.

The lawsuit has been acrimonious and drawn out. It has produced a mountain of paperwork, files, discovery, and one preliminary hearing after another. It has exhausted the patience of the judge presiding over it, something that comes out time and again in the transcripts of the pretrial hearings. Neither side was willing to speak to me about it, but the thousands of public documents reveal some insights into the behind-the-scenes turmoil that affected season 2 and showed up in the finished product. Reading through the court documents gives a glimpse into the business end of how Hollywood entertainment gets produced. It isn't always pretty.

Ever since Groucho Marx signed a contract in 1936 to make two movies, *A Night at the Opera* and *A Day at the Races,* that guaranteed him a slice of the films' profits—the first time an actor got such a deal—there have been fights over exactly this issue. It's actually pretty common. Go to the *Hollywood Reporter*'s home page on any given day, and there will be at least a couple of stories about lawsuits. The creative team behind the sitcom *Home Improvement* was still involved in a lawsuit with Walt Disney over that show's profits in the spring of 2017, despite the fact that *Home Improvement* went off the air in 1999. *Who Wants to Be a Millionaire, The X-Files, Nash Bridges, Judge Judy, Goodfellas,* and more have all been involved in lawsuits between the creative teams that made them and the studios that produced them.

The events leading up to Darabont's suit began much earlier. Even before the show first aired, AMC had a good feeling about its success, which factored into their decision to bring it in-house: they'd have more control over both the costs and the profits. The first season was such a surprise hit that the network of course renewed it for a full thirteen-episode second season, which premiered on October 16, 2011, in the United States. About 7.3 million people tuned in for that first episode of the second season, which showed the Grimes clan on the road, beset by a herd of walkers, and ended up with Rick, Shane, and a wounded Carl at the Greene farm. The show would average a hair under 7 million viewers that season, even better than the first. It was a real moneymaker. The $280 million question—and, yes, that is the amount Darabont is suing for—is exactly how much money did it make that season, and how much of it should be going to Darabont?

Behind the scenes, that second season was trouble from the start. According to the transcript of a deposition given by Darabont, he met with AMC executives ahead of the season, and at that time was informed that they were cutting the show's budget to $3 million per episode, back from $3.4 million. Moreover, the company planned to take a tax credit it received from the state of Georgia for filming there, and keep it, rather than putting it into the production. To Darabont's reckoning, that totaled a 25 percent budget cut, which infuriated him. "The cast and crew were earning, busting their butts, leaving it all on the field," he said in the deposition. "The fact that we couldn't then take that tax credit and put it on the screen or alleviate shooting conditions to any degree, I thought that was adding insult to injury."

In the early days, the relationship was very different. As I recounted earlier, AMC "got" the show, where other networks balked, and didn't ask Darabont and his team to water down anything. It seemed like a perfect marriage of the commercial and artistic sides of the entertainment industry. "I think AMC's such an exciting place these days," Darabont said in a "making of" mini-documentary that went out ahead of the show's premiere. Indeed, it was an exciting place. It now had prestige shows and monster hits that seemed to coexist perfectly. "It just does seem like an oddball choice for the folks who do *Mad Men,*" he said. Oddball was a good way to describe it, but it seemed genius, too.

Darabont's original contract with AMC was lucrative, and it ensured that he did actually get some money up front. He received $80,000 for the pilot script, paid in four installments. He got another $40,000 (again, in four installments) for having the sole writing credit. For directing the pilot, he was paid $125,000, with a $25,000 bonus. Because AMC picked up the series, he was hired as executive producer and paid $35,000 per episode for season 1, and $36,750 for season 2. For receiving the sole "created by" credit for the series there was a $25,000 bonus (he got credited with a "developed by" tag, but it isn't exactly clear whether this bonus was paid out), and an extra $1,000 for every episode in which he received sole "created by" credit. For sole directing credit, there was a bonus of $25,000, then a $3,000 royalty bonus for each episode for the life of the series, whether he directed it or not. The initial contract laid out the terms of AMC's plan to license out the show, since Darabont's share of the profits would come out of that arrangement. When the network changed its mind about production, the contract was amended.

For his work on the pilot alone, Darabont received nearly $300,000 altogether, and over the course of the show he was paid several million for his work. That was obviously good money, but it wasn't the real brass ring. For Darabont, what would make his work on the show truly lucrative would be his share of the profits.

In January 2011, Darabont and AMC signed another contract, for his services as showrunner for season 2. This contract included a higher level of compensation and required AMC to negotiate with him first when it came time to pick season 3's showrunner, assuming there would be a season 3 (which, of course, there was). Things seemed to be going well. The show was a huge success, a second season was a given, and considering how much material already existed in the comics (which Kirkman is still writing, as of the publication of this book, and plans to keep writing for years), there seemed to be no limit to how long the television show could run. As they prepared for season 2, though, something had clearly changed. Darabont seethed at having to accept those budget cuts from, in his words, "the people who . . . when they did rarely show up on the set . . . would drive in from the airport in their air-conditioned car, race into the air-conditioned tent we had there so the actors could have a break and not pass out from the heat, poke their heads out on occasion, and half an hour later jump back in their car and fly back to their air-conditioned office in New York. I had a tremendous lack of respect for them." If these executives expected the cast and crew to work in the Georgia heat and "pick ticks off their groin," the least the suits could do was to "put on some combat boots yourself and get out there and see what it's really like." But he kept working.

Budget issues and concerns about work ethic weren't his only problems. Darabont, based in L.A., was being sent footage daily as the crew was filming the season 2 premiere, but according to him it was not good. What he was seeing was so bad, Darabont said in the deposition, that he worried the director had had some kind of mini-stroke in the Georgia heat (the director's health, it would turn out, was not the issue). Darabont informed AMC that he was going to fly down to Georgia to personally take over shooting. "Right now we don't have a coherent enough episode to even cut it together and present it to you for you to react to," he told a network executive, Susie Fitzgerald. Time was of the essence. A large part of the premiere took place on a stretch of highway where the Grimes clan gets stuck between an immovable pileup of cars and a massive herd of walkers. In the confusion, the character Sophia Peletier runs off into the woods, which sets off everything that will follow. Converting a stretch of real highway into this postapocalyptic hellscape was a massive undertaking that could not be re-created later because of time and money. If they didn't get everything they needed while the set was up, they would never get it. That was why AMC execs okayed Darabont personally flying to Georgia. This meant he had to leave the writers' room, where the story lines for season 2 were being laid out.

His absence might have been a disaster otherwise, but Darabont had come up with a creative way of constructing the stories and using his team of writers while he was gone. One of the writers brought on for season 2 was Glen Mazzara, a veteran TV man who'd previously written and produced shows like *The Shield, Crash,* and *Life*. He'd helped hire the other writers for season 2 and helped run the writers' room; in essence, he was Darabont's number two. In his own deposition related to Darabont's suit against AMC, Mazzara explained the process they used. Rather than plotting out one episode and then dispatching a writer to actually write it, and repeating that process, the writers got together for a six-week period in 2011 and plotted out all the episodes at once, what Mazzara referred to as "breaking" them. Once that process was done, each writer was given a specific episode to write. "It was an incredibly efficient use of the writing staff," he said. By the first day of shooting, they had eight scripts written because of this process, something he called a "genius paradigm shift."

Season 2 was going to have thirteen episodes. When Darabont left for Georgia, the writers were working on the last five. He expected to be on set for a couple of weeks, working on the reshoots while still checking in with the writers back in L.A. and adding his "hands-on polish" for scripts. Another routine job of the showrunner is to have "tone" meetings with all the directors, to go over the script and lay out all the nuances, to ensure there's some continuity of vision from week to week. These meetings would loom large soon enough. In addition to all that, Darabont had also written the script for the premiere, "What Lies Ahead" (the listed credit would later go to Ardeth Bey and Robert Kirkman; Ardeth Bey, Darabont explained in his deposition, is a pseudonym for himself). In Mazzara's estimation, Darabont was working literally "around the clock" on the show.

In Georgia, AMC had a tighter budget than expected. The studio they were operating out of abutted a farm that would make for a perfect location as the Greene farm, which would be a big help logistically and financially, but the family that owned it was rather religious and didn't like the content of the show. Darabont went and personally talked them into it. (It may have helped that one of the characters, Hershel, was a sharply religious man himself, and talked about the zombie plague in terms of the end of the world, lending the entire show a somewhat religious bent.) Still, production was moving along, and expectations were high.

On July 22, 2011, while still filming season 2, Darabont was part of the cast and crew that appeared at Comic-Con. He participated in a reporters' roundtable, where he paired up with Greg Nicotero. According to myriad reports, there was no indication that anything was wrong. Darabont excitedly talked up season 2 and seemed genuinely enthused. Less than two days later, AMC's head of original programming, Joel Stillerman, contacted Darabont's agent at CAA, Bruce Vinokour. They wanted to meet with Darabont. On July 27, Darabont was called into a meeting with Stillerman and informed that he was being fired and replaced by Mazzara.

Darabont's contract was of the type known in the entertainment industry as a "pay or play" contract; if the employer fires the employee, the employee still gets paid for everything they're due under the contract. But the firing is at the employer's discretion. If AMC didn't like what it was seeing, it had the right to fire Darabont, and he would still get paid. Apparently, AMC didn't like what it was seeing. It's impossible to say at this point what Darabont presented that the network did not like. After he was let go, there were apparently major revisions done not only to the premiere but to the entire season's story arc. Moreover, season 2 is, well, problematic. The story itself isn't bad, but it gets bogged down on the farm. For example, there is a story line concerning an outsider, Randall, a kid from a group that might be dangerous who ends up a prisoner on the farm. The group has to decide what to do with him. This single decision is spread over five episodes. That's a lot of airtime for a minor character. It's impossible to tell, at least from the outside, how much of the problem was caused by production limits, how much of it was because of Darabont's abrupt firing, and how much of it was due to whatever AMC saw of Darabont's work as showrunner that it didn't like. By the summer of 2011 production on season 2 was far enough along that AMC wanted to make a change.

AMC, in documents released in July 2017, argued that Darabont's people had it all wrong. They said the two sides had never agreed to a deal in which AMC promised to give *The Walking Dead* production the same kinds of terms it gave other third-party production companies, the crux of Darabont's complaint. It also argued that in fact it had paid Darabont and CAA their share of the profit, though the paychecks only started arriving after Darabont filed his lawsuit.

Lastly, AMC claimed that Darabont was fired for cause, the cause being that he couldn't handle being in charge of a TV show. To illustrate this, they released a series of emails, composed during his time as showrunner, from a clearly stressed Darabont, in which he promised to kill writers and lambasted his crew.

AMC painted a picture of a man who simply couldn't handle the rigors of his job, and was threatening the entire endeavor.

"Fuck you all for giving me chest pains because of the staggering fucking incompetence," he wrote in one email to the production team.

Darabont, in an affidavit attached to the July batch of documents, admitted he wrote "some angry emails in extreme circumstances," but stood by what he wrote, and said he'd been "fighting like a mother lion to the protect the show."

Despite the choppy storytelling, season 2 does deliver a lot of good moments. There are some memorable walkers, like the one stuck down a well. There's the introduction of the Greene family, Hershel and his two young daughters, Maggie and Beth, the three of whom become major characters in the story (Maggie is still with us; Hershel, in season 4, and Beth, in season 5, sadly have passed on). There is a fantastic scene that takes place in a bar, with Rick squaring off against two violent survivors. There is the moment when Rick and Shane finally come to their ultimate confrontation, and Rick kills his best friend. There is the literally explosive finale when a massive herd of walkers descends on the farm. We learn what Dr. Jenner told Rick at the CDC, that everybody turns. The group dynamic turns when Rick declares that their group is not a democracy, beginning what fans call the "Ricktatorship." And, of course, there is the shock when Sophia Peletier walks out of the barn, a little zombie blinking in the sunlight. This is the emotional summit of the entire season, a gruesome revelation that forces everybody to confront the horrible reality of their circumstances.

Behind all of this was Glen Mazzara, who was eventually

promoted to showrunner, and finished up the second season and moved on to the third. By December 2013, however, Mazzara would be out, too, replaced by Scott Gimple (who is, as of this writing, still the showrunner). For a show that regularly killed off its own characters, it seemed like it was taking a drastic toll on showrunners, too.

By season 3, the show was starting to take on Scott Gimple's vision for it, and fans were happy about that. *The Walking Dead* was becoming more cohesive and its characters were far more dynamic: Rick was turning from the typical good guy into someone far darker; Daryl was evolving from an angry backwoods hick into an almost Lancelot-like hero, the indestructible sidekick; Glenn and Maggie were in love; Carl was scarred by the trauma of having to mercy-kill his own mother right after her emergency caesarean; and Carol was changing as well, after losing the last thing she cared about in this world, her daughter. The show also introduced two major new characters: the katana-wielding, dreadlocked heroine Michonne (Danai Gurira), and the Governor (David Morrissey), the psychotic leader of a neighboring community called Woodbury.

In December 2013, Darabont officially fired back, filing his lawsuit against AMC. AMC waited nearly two months to craft its initial response to the lawsuit. It denied virtually everything Darabont claimed. Of most notable interest was this paragraph from the network: "The complaint is barred, in whole or in part, under the doctrine of unclean hands." This is a pretty standard legal defense, which asserts that the plaintiffs cannot be due any aid from the court because the plaintiffs themselves did something unethical to bring about the situation in front of the court. In this case, AMC is saying that Darabont and CAA are responsible—and mainly they mean Darabont.

The suit will not get its hearing in a court until after this book has gone to print. It is currently scheduled for 2018, and given the history of similar lawsuits it may drag on far longer than that. This is not the only lawsuit related to *The Walking Dead*. The other one involves the childhood friends Robert Kirkman and Tony Moore. Unlike the AMC/Darabont suit, the Kirkman/Moore suit has been amicably resolved. At one point though, it briefly and oddly raised the prospect of *two* separate shows about the travails of Rick Grimes and his band of survivors.

Kirkman and Moore began *The Walking Dead* together, with the first issue in October 2003. But by the sixth issue, published in March 2004, Moore was out, replaced by Charlie Adlard, who continues to illustrate the comic. In 2005, Moore signed over his rights to *The Walking Dead* to Kirkman, who at the time was negotiating a deal to put the story on television. You can imagine how this went. The show gets made, becomes a massive success, and in 2012, Moore sues Kirkman, claiming the latter cheated the former out of his promised share of the profits. Kirkman countersued. Moore filed a second suit, demanding to be credited as a co-creator, with all legal copyrights to the work. That meant, theoretically, Moore would be able to legally offer TV networks *The Walking Dead*—their own version of the exact same show. Moore's attorney suggested at the time that his client might do exactly that.

This story, though, has a far happier ending. The two childhood friends settled the suit that same year, for undisclosed terms, rather than let it go to court (and, possibly, to that second *Walking Dead* show). They even repaired their relationship to the point that in 2016 their hometown of Cynthiana, Kentucky, was able to honor both men in a very public way. The Walking Dead

Day brought Kirkman and Moore back home for a celebration in honor of their work, on the first weekend of August 2016. It started when a local artist painted a mural of four characters from the show (Rick, Carl, Michonne, and Daryl) on the back wall of the old Rohs Opera House. The local chamber of commerce had come up with the idea to do a whole day honoring the show, reached out to both men, and found them both willing to come home for it.

"We're turning our downtown area into an apocalypse," Tomi Jean Clifford, the executive director of the local chamber, told the *Lexington Herald-Leader*. They brought in a wrecked airplane and turned over a couple of cars. An old jail was transformed into a zombie haunted house. Businesses on Pike and Main Streets decorated their storefronts. Moore drew a new cover for the first issue, which showed Rick staring down zombies while standing in the middle of downtown Cynthiana. It was a small celebration of everything the show is about, in the town where the two guys who imagined it grew up, where the germ of their idea first formed, far from acidic lawsuits and the hypercompetitive world of television ratings.

MINOR CHARACTERS

ONE OF THE SMALL THINGS THAT *THE WALKING DEAD* HAS always done especially well is delivering vignettes of life in the zombie apocalypse outside the main story of the Grimes clan, whether it's Morgan's encounter with Eastman, or even just showing the details inside an abandoned house. It's a way of fleshing out (no pun intended) the story of a worldwide collapse. It's a technique that you might witness in old Fellini movies, if you watch old Fellini movies, and those of Italian neorealists who were making films in the post–World War II years, the very same era that Kirkman researched to get a sense of how a collapsed world looked. In Fellini movies, the main characters pass through these other lives, interacting with people scratching out a living in the hardscrabble neighborhoods of Rome or out in the countryside. These little snippets of life outside of the lives of the main cast combine with the larger story to provide this fully rounded view of the world the director wants you to see.

On *The Walking Dead,* the Grimes clan passes through the lives of myriad people, sometimes alone, sometimes part of a larger group. But whether it's a camper who decides to hang himself or somebody who joins up with the Saviors, the appearance of these minor characters ends up painting a much wider, brighter picture of this world than you'd get from seeing just the main cast. I guess what impresses me about these characters is that they're generally "one-offs," just bodies thrown into a story so the main characters have something to play against. But rather than being cardboard cutouts, they become little character studies, and in just the briefest exposure we see a three-dimensional person. In my mind, that makes the rest of the story seem so much more credible. It's vital to the show's gritty realism.

With that in mind, here are my picks for the best one-off characters from *The Walking Dead.*

DAVE. Actor Michael Raymond-James had only one chance to bring Dave to life, but he did so brilliantly. Dave and his partner Tony find Rick, Hershel, and Glenn in a bar, after Hershel has fallen off the wagon (season 2, episode 8, "Nebraska"). Like the Governor, Negan, and Gareth, Dave is a bad man with a dangerous smile and an amity with violence. What I like about Dave is that he seems like a completely regular guy. He says he came down from Philadelphia, and it's easy to picture him as a typical Eagles/Phillies/Sixers/Flyers fan (he even has a T-shirt on for the Stafford Sharks, a youth baseball team in Manahawkin, New Jersey). Dave acts casual as can be, like he's just happy to meet fellow travelers. He's the "people person" of the two, and he shares what bits of information he's heard and what he's seen. But it becomes clear soon enough that he's sizing up these strangers, trying to find out where they're from and what they possess that he might want to take from them.

This is the first time in this show that we see a survivor who has slipped the confines of the old morality, who is ready to simply take by force whatever he can. Dave has been on the road for a while, and he has adapted.

While they're sharing what scraps of information they all have, Dave jumps over the bar, smiles, and says he's just looking for the "good stuff." Dave realizes these strangers are living comfortably—by the standards of the day—and he wants what they have. "You gotta understand, we can't stay out there," he says, sounding almost reasonable. But there is a malignant tone to him that's unmistakable. Behind the bar, he's standing right in front of Rick; Tony's behind Rick. They have him caught in a pincer. Rick has his eye on Dave—and through a large mirror on the wall behind Dave, he can see Tony, too. Dave makes the first move, goes for his gun, but Rick shoots them both dead before either can get off a shot.

Dave is only the first in a long line of smiling, malignant men who will cross Rick's path. He is also the first who will die challenging Rick, but his real significance is that he is the harbinger of this new kind of survivor.

CLARA. Here's the setup: One day Rick is in the woods outside the former West Georgia Correctional Facility (season 4, episode 1, "30 Days Without an Accident"), checking traps he's laid to catch game. While he's inspecting a dead boar, he sees what he initially thinks is a walker. It turns out to be a living woman, though given her filthy appearance, it's hard to tell the difference. This is Clara, an Irishwoman who was on her honeymoon when the world went to hell.

Played by the actress Kerry Condon, Clara emanates a sad, mad desperation (appropriately enough, the character has come to be nicknamed Creepy Clara). She lures Rick back to her campsite, and along the way she laments, without clearly saying what they were, all the horrible things she and her husband, Eddie, had to do to survive. Has she killed? How many? It's clear that whatever she's done, it has overwhelmed her psychologically. Rick is smart to be cautious.

She asks Rick for help bringing the boar back to her campsite, where Eddie waits. She wonders if he's with a group, and if she and Eddie could join. He says he'd have to meet Eddie, and ask them some questions.

They get to her camp, and the truth becomes clear: Eddie is dead—or rather, Eddie is among the undead, and Clara's been keeping him with her. In a bag. At least, parts of him. She couldn't bear to live without him, but what she's doing now is almost unimaginable. She's feeding a half a corpse, or maybe even just a head (we never clearly see) with whatever bits of dead people or animals she can find. She has lured Rick there with an eye toward feeding him to Eddie, too, and weakly rushes him with a knife. He repels her and she breaks down, the sheer mental trauma of what she's been doing crushing her. The whole episode is an illustration of the monstrosity of this world, what it does to people. While standing there, she plunges the knife into her own gut, wanting to join her husband among the undead. While she lies there, bleeding, she asks Rick to tell her what he intended to ask earlier, and for the first time we hear the Three Questions: *How many walkers have you killed? How many people have you killed? Why?*

Clara's answer to the first is that Eddie killed them all. The answer to the second is "Just me," and the answer to the third is haunting: "You don't get to come back from things."

MARTIN. Martin (Chris Coy) is the elder statesman of this group of memorable minor characters. He lasted for three whole episodes, and again as a hallucination in a fourth episode, of season 5, though his only real impact is in his first appearance, in the season premiere, "No Sanctuary." Martin is the antagonist in the B story, about Tyreese (Chad Coleman) and Judith back at the cabin in the woods. Carol and Tyreese, carrying baby Judith, sneak up on Martin, take him captive, and sequester his supplies. Carol goes off to fight, and Tyreese stays behind with the captive and Judith.

Even tied up, Martin verbally pokes and prods Tyreese. He won't shut up, in fact. "You're the kind of guy who saves babies. That's kind of like saving an anchor when you're stuck without a boat in the middle of the ocean." He wants to talk Tyreese into leaving. The actor, Coy, is somebody I'd never seen before, but he does a fantastic job in a limited space of imbuing Martin with both the weariness of this world and the pragmatism that keeps people alive. "Take her. Take the car, and go," he says, exasperated that Tyreese is even still there. "I don't want to do this today."

Martin doesn't even seem like a bad guy. He talks about the things he did before the Turn, like watching football and going to church. Now he hangs around with the cannibals of Terminus, just to survive. Martin *is* a bad guy, though. He grabs Judith and threatens to snap her neck; he makes Tyreese go outside where some walkers are lurking. When it seems like Tyreese is dead, he crashes back through the door and pummels Martin into a pulp. Tyreese kneels over him and beats him while screaming, "I won't!" Tyreese won't kill him.

He doesn't. Martin shows up later with Gareth, his face looking like a punching bag, but alive. That won't last long. Martin buys it in the St. Sarah's slaughter, and while he certainly deserved it, it's worth pondering that under different twists of fate, he could have easily been one of the good guys. He used to watch football and go to church, after all.

PAULA. We're used to seeing men adapt to the Hobbesian rules of the post–zombie apocalypse, becoming amoral, opportunistic killers. We're not used to seeing women adopt that attitude willingly, but in the character of Paula (Alicia Witt), we get that gender-bending depiction, and it adds another layer to exploring and portraying how people adapt to the end of the world.

The role of women on *The Walking Dead* has evolved significantly since the second episode, when Andrea didn't know where the safety was on her semi-automatic and the women in camp were generally relegated to "women's work," like scrubbing clothes. Obviously, in the roles of Maggie, Andrea, Beth, Deanna Monroe, and of course Carol, we see that trend that Kerry Cahill talked about, where gender doesn't matter, what matters is competence. In Paula, though, for the first time there's something else: a woman gladly embracing the new, brutal rules of the world.

The role is memorable due to a sharp performance from Witt,

who first appeared in the movie *Dune* in 1984, and is one of the more recognizable actors to play small roles on the show. But, again, in what is essentially a brief sketch of a person, we get to see the entire arc of this character. In "The Same Boat" (season 6, episode 13), Paula leads a crew of Saviors that takes Carol and Maggie hostage. They hide out at a Saviors safe house, and we start learning about Paula. She's a lot like Carol, a mirror image almost. Before the Turn, she was a wife and mother and worked as a secretary. Carol served and suffered under her husband, and Paula served and suffered under her boss. "I spent most of my days reading stupid inspirational emails, trying to feel good about myself," Paula says.

They were similar before the Turn, and they are similar when they meet: both are extremely capable of leading, planning, and killing. The big difference is how they got there. Carol took a long, reluctant road to her assassin-like persona; Paula embraced it. When the Turn hit, she got stuck not with her family, but with her boss. He didn't have a grip on what was happening, but she did: rather than let his blubbering become a problem for both of them, she simply killed him. Paula once kept a list of her kills, like Carol. "I stopped counting when I hit double digits," she says. The implication is clear: killing doesn't bother her, and it's obvious why she eventually fell in with Negan. In every important respect, she *is* Negan. "I'm still me," Paula says, "but better. I lost everything, but it made me stronger."

Throughout this episode, Carol is struggling against panic, which for the most part Paula assumes is just the fear of a weakling, a "nervous little bird," she says. When it turns out that what really frightened Carol was her own capacity for violence, Paula sees just how similar they actually are.

"You're good," Paula says. "Nervous little bird. You were her. But not now, right? Me too." There's a struggle between the two formerly nervous little birds turned entirely-too-capable predators, which Carol wins.

HUSH WOMAN. Of all the side pockets of the zombie apocalypse this show's explored and the people it's visited, the "hush woman," to me, was the most haunting (at least, I think she was a woman, but it's hard to tell). In "Twice As Far" (season 6, episode 14), Daryl, Rosita, and Denise go on an errand to find a drugstore. While Rosita and Daryl scavenge, Denise wanders around. She looks down on a display case with pictures of a happy, smiling baby boy under the glass. She looks at key chains with names on them. There's a sound from behind a door, a single walker. Denise decides to be brave and take care of it herself. What lies beyond the door is chilling. Children's books are scattered across the floor. In one corner is a crib. Then she sees what was making the noise: a mostly decomposed walker, an adult, with a cast on its leg. That isn't remotely the worst of it. On the wall this person had written: HUSH HUSH HUSH HUSH HUSH. Five times. Whoever this person is, they'd clearly chosen that room to hide out in, with what apparently was a baby, and one that was probably making too much noise. What happened? We don't know exactly, but as Denise draws an arc across the room with her flashlight, she lands on a sink—filled with murky liquid, and a baby's shoe. Whatever led to those words on the wall, and that mess in the sink, must have been truly nightmarish to live through. Trying to picture it is not something to do if you want to sleep at night, but it is the inhumanly horrific reality of the zombie apocalypse. A perfect nightmare.

RECAP

SEASON FOUR

- **SAFE HAVENS:** The West Georgia Correctional Facility, the grove, Terminus
- **SURVIVORS LOST:** Patrick, Hershel, Lizzie, Mika, Karen, Lilly, Meghan, Martinez
- **ANTAGONISTS KILLED:** The Governor
- **HORRIBLE HACKS:** Hershel's head

THE FORMER WEST GEORGIA CORRECTIONAL FACILITY HAS become a thriving community of survivors, with more arriving by the minute. The Ricktatorship was surrendered peacefully, and a leadership council now runs the community. Rick tends to pigs and his fields and tries to be a father to Carl and Judith. Things have settled down so much that there's even time for normal human interaction: Tyreese has a girlfriend, and Beth a boyfriend. The prison is the sole thriving, surviving outpost of humanity amid a sea of the undead.

Carol Peletier has been emotionally transformed. She is a light of the community, a hardened survivor who understands that anything and everything is acceptable when the goal is to live another day. She secretly teaches the young children in the camp how to use weapons and defend themselves, and takes two sisters, Lizzie and Mika, under her wing.

Tranquility, such as it is in the post–zombie apocalypse, doesn't last. The problem comes in the form of a deadly flu that sweeps through the prison, possibly spread from Rick's pigs. The signs are there, though not noticed. Outside the fence are walkers with blood streaming from their eyes. One of the newer members, a kid named Patrick, is infected. He dies inside the prison complex and returns as a walker. Before anybody even knows what's happening, there are two viruses racing through the community: the swine flu–like one, and the zombie virus. The prison doesn't have any of the medical resources available before the Turn to deal with the flu, and it's quickly becoming a big problem. Tyreese's girlfriend, Karen, also catches the bug. He goes to visit her but finds her dead body. She and another person who was sick, David, have been burned alive by an unknown attacker. Before that mystery can be solved, a team—Daryl, Michonne, Tyreese, and Bob—is tasked with going to a veterinary school Hershel knows about where there might be medical supplies. Meanwhile, more and more people are getting the flu, including Glenn and Sasha. There aren't many healthy people left, but Rick and Carol are among them. During a quiet moment, Rick asks Carol if she killed Karen and David. "Yes," she says flatly. Rick and Carol go to a nearby town to scavenge for any supplies they can find. They come across two survivors, kids really, who don't seem very well equipped for the new world. All this time, Rick is digesting what he now knows about Carol, and he decides she cannot come back with him. Sure, Rick has killed before to protect the group, but he sees his actions in a different light than hers. He simply will not let her back. She is shocked, but sees how it's going to go. She loads up a car and vanishes.

Daryl's group does eventually come up with supplies that will help, and they also find one odd, random clue: a radio broadcast they hear in the car. "Sanctuary . . . those who arrive, survive." Meanwhile, Hershel is back at the prison, almost single-handedly keeping the sick alive with a broth of herbs and the few medical supplies they had handy. He is risking his life, and knows it, but defends his actions vehemently. "You step outside, you risk your life. You take a drink of water, you risk your life." It's a powerful statement that cuts to the heart of why people like Hershel, Rick, and the others do the things they do.

Elsewhere, we are reunited with the Governor, who, after

committing a horrifying atrocity, has lost most of his mind. His two henchmen, Martinez and Shumpert, abandon him, and he wanders aimlessly through the desolation. He comes across a tiny band of survivors: two sisters, Lilly and Tara Chambler; their infirm father, David; and Lilly's daughter, Meghan. They are living in a mostly abandoned apartment building. They take the Governor in, warily, though they'd be much warier if they knew his past. He tells them his name is Brian, and he starts to become friendly with them, and useful. When David dies, the Governor is the only one who knows what must be done. They leave that town, eventually falling in with a new camp of survivors, led by the Governor's old henchman, Martinez. Quickly, the Governor kills Martinez and takes over the group, and then prepares them for another assault on the prison. He does this under the guise of safety: Where they are isn't safe, he says, but he knows of a place. The people in it, though, are bad and must be driven away. He convinces his new group that an overwhelming show of force will be enough to drive the occupants out. One of the survivors, Mitch, is an army vet and has a tank. That's something the Governor didn't have before. He also has hostages, whom he stealthily went out and captured: Michonne and Hershel.

The Governor goes to the prison with his new army, his tank, and his prisoners. Rick nearly talks them out of the attack. But the Governor isn't interested in a truce. He also isn't interested in just driving off Rick. He cuts off Hershel's head with Michonne's katana, and attacks. It's a brutal attack, and destroys the prison—his mad, obsessive goal all along. The Governor himself is killed in the assault, and most of his people die, too. The Grimes clan is forced to scatter, everybody fleeing in different, random combinations. Their small groups are utterly separated, the odds of ever finding each other miniscule.

Glenn, still getting over his flu, is left behind. He grabs as much gear as he can carry and leaves, finding Tara Chambler sitting in the prison yard, horrified at what she's been part of. The two take off down the road, Glenn determined to find Maggie. They are picked up quickly by three strangers: Sergeant Abraham Ford, Rosita Espinosa, and Eugene Porter, an odd, mullet-topped man who apparently is carrying with him a great secret: the zombie cure. They are trying to return him to Washington, D.C.

Rick and Carl escape together—without Judith. Rick was so badly injured in the fight, he seems very much like he might die. Michonne is completely alone, and takes up her old habit of walking with zombie decoys. Sasha, Bob, and Maggie are together, as are Daryl and Beth. These two take shelter in a graveyard mortuary. Walkers descend on the house, the two are forced to flee, and Beth is mysteriously taken away by somebody in a car. Eventually, Daryl's found by a gang, the Claimers, that crosses paths with Rick, Carl, and Michonne. There's a fight. The Claimers aren't the victors.

Tyreese has left with Lizzie, Mika, and baby Judith. They are soon found by Carol, who didn't go very far, saw the rubble of the prison, and came looking for survivors. These four eventually find a home to occupy, which seems safe enough. The problem, though, isn't walkers, or other outsiders: it's Lizzie. She's just a little girl, really, and the horrors of this world are too much for her fragile psyche. She's convinced that the walkers aren't dangerous, that they're just people, and that she could be like them. To prove her point, she kills her sister. Carol and Tyreese realize the girl is dangerously insane and cannot be trusted around people, ever. They have no choice. Carol walks the young girl out into the yard, the very young girl she took under her wing. "Look at the flowers," Carol says to the crying girl, who is upset enough that it's clear she understands that *something* is about to happen, if not quite exactly what. A moment later, a shot rings out.

Despite being separated, eventually all the wandering members of the Grimes clan converge on one place: Terminus. The radio broadcast was real. It's an old rail terminal and depot, and it seems like a safe place, with a large group of survivors. Rick is wary, though, and very soon his wariness is proven to be well-founded: this place brings in newcomers, but it takes them captive. It seems like they do this with everyone. The place isn't a sanctuary. It's a death trap. Rick, Carl, Michonne, and Daryl are herded into a railcar, where they meet up with most of the others, except Tyreese and Carol. "They're gonna feel pretty stupid when they find out," Rick says.

"Find out what?" Abraham asks.

"They're screwing with the wrong people."

CHAPTER 7

EXPANSION

"YOUR WORLD'S ABOUT TO GET A WHOLE LOT BIGGER."

—PAUL "JESUS" ROVIA

(SEASON 6, EPISODE 11, "KNOTS UNTIE")

Even before the show debuted in 2010, it was clear that the world Robert Kirkman envisioned and brought to life was big, and went way beyond what Rick Grimes could see with his own eyes. For one thing, the entire planet had fallen to the zombie plague, which meant there were plenty of abandoned towns for survivors to come through and dangerous brigands for them to fight. Thus, more places to explore! But there's a larger reason why this setup has proven such fertile ground for writers beyond Kirkman, who have spurred tie-in books and spin-off shows. That reason was summed up by something Cliff Curtis, who plays Travis Manawa in *Fear the Walking Dead*, said to me in an interview in the spring of 2016, before the show's second season aired. He was talking about Travis and his struggle to come to grips with what has happened to the world, to come up with a new code of survival, and to not lose the person he used to be: "The struggles he's going through are human and grounded in reality." It's that kind of strife and trial that marks the show and opens up a rich territory for exploring extraneous characters and stories. How would *you* react if the world ended? Where would you go? What would you bring? Would you kill somebody?

(Personally, I know exactly where I'd go: my hometown's library. It's a sturdy brick building. Board up the windows and it's very defensible, and it's got a fireplace, a heat source. It's next to the police station, which I could raid for supplies and weapons. And, while it's got all the books I could ever want to read, it's not just a *Twilight Zone* nerd's fantasy: it's got all the *practical* information I could ever need. Anything I didn't know how to do, I could just research. If the world ever does end, you'll find me holed up there.)

Jay Bonansinga had been writing horror stories for years when his agent came to him one day in 2010 with a proposal: to cowrite a novel with Kirkman based on *The Walking Dead*. At this point, the show hadn't even premiered yet, but Bonansinga was interested. "Originally when I heard about the gig, I figured it was a standard novelist job, a tie-in," he said. "I had no idea what I'd walked into."

In the book world, a tie-in book is a pretty standard product, something that is produced mainly to put some extra merchandise on store shelves. Usually it's a novelization of the show or movie. Bonansinga even had a direct tie to zombie royalty: he had worked with George Romero on a movie version of his first novel, *The Black Mariah*. Though the film never made it to the screen, the experience helped him years later: "I played the Romero card" with Kirkman, he said. Of the several writers considered, Bonansinga got the contract.

Bonansinga assumed he'd be sent a script of the pilot or the first few episodes as a template to work from. Instead, in his first conversation with Kirkman he learned what the vision really was: a "full-bore literary work," a separate story that would tell the entire background of the notorious Governor. It would eventually turn into a series that currently comprises eight books, and has expanded from the Governor's story to that of the people of Woodbury, as well as introducing characters that Bonansinga has come up with on his own, one of whom, Tara Chalmers, would end up as a character in the show (they changed her last name to Chambler).

"He is the most self-possessed man I've ever known," Bonansinga said of Kirkman. "Zero pretention, droll sense of humor, doesn't suffer fools." Perhaps this is because Kirkman presents an "aw shucks" persona, which you can gather from his interviews as well. But you don't just go from working in a comic book shop in Kentucky to presiding over a small media empire without some drive, and that drive is what Bonansinga saw firsthand. "Kirkman has this innate sense of what he wants," Bonansinga said. "He has this gauge inside that knows what a fan really wants, deep down, the fan might not even know."

The Walking Dead: Rise of the Governor, their first novel together, made it onto the *New York Times* bestseller list, as did the next one, which was a continuation of the first story. The Governor has a small but pivotal role in the comics, and despite that role expanding in the TV show, we still know almost nothing about him from that medium. These books fully explore the character's small bits of good, and his very large doses of really, really bad. *Rise of the Governor* opens after the Turn with the story of Brian Blake and his brother, Philip. Philip is the strong one, the leader of the small group they end up with; Brian, though older than Philip, is a weaker man. The brothers make their way across the ravaged countryside along with Philip's daughter, Penny, and arrive in Atlanta, where they briefly stay with the Chalmers family: sisters April and Tara, and their father, David (a version of this story is shown in season 4, with the Tara character turning into a series regular).

The brothers take their gang back on the road, where, at one point, Penny is attacked by a zombie and turns. Philip refuses to either stave in her head or leave her, so they keep the zombified Penny with the group, which as you can imagine is not easy (it's like trying to keep a rabid cat, an insane thing to do, but it certainly does illustrate how the end times can make you nuts). Eventually they arrive in Woodbury, though it is a different Woodbury than the one we see on TV: there is no Mayberry-like main street, no sunshine, no hope. It is an outpost of madness, with people barely surviving day to day and living in abject fear of the group of National Guardsmen running the town, led by Major Gene Gavin. Soon enough, Philip goes stark, raving mad, and there's a battle between him and another man from the original group, Nick: Nick shoots Philip, Brian shoots Nick, and then Brian shoots Gavin, effectively taking over the town. One of the people there, Caesar Martinez, asks his name, and he says "Philip Blake." Brian Blake becomes Philip Blake, and then becomes the Governor (this twist, Brian taking on his brother's persona, was Kirkman's idea, Bonansinga said). That is where the book ends, but it's clearly just setting up for the myriad terrible things "Philip" Blake will do in Woodbury as the Governor, and for the band of people who will outlast his maniacal administration.

The novels were the first major expansion of the vision, but there would be much more. While the Kirkman-Bonansinga team was writing their books, the show's production crew were experimenting with other ways to tell stories about life in the post–zombie apocalypse. They began with a series of webisodes, short videos that ran on AMC's website and take place in the

Walking Dead universe. The three original webisodes are each tangentially attached to the main show. (If you haven't seen these, go watch them. They aren't very long, and are definitely worth your time.) "Torn Apart" tells the story of one family's fate at the outset of the zombie plague. The mother sacrifices herself to the undead to save her children and becomes a zombie. Not just any zombie, either, but "Bicycle Girl," the cut-at-the-waist, pathetic wraith Rick finds in the park after he wakes from his coma. "Cold Storage" focuses on a survivor, Chase, who hides out in a storage facility only to find another survivor already there, who has made himself at home, to the point of keeping a girl locked up in one of the units. The connection to the show becomes clear when Chase rifles through a storage unit, checking out the possessions of somebody who's probably long dead. He comes across a picture of a familiar family: Rick, Lori, and Carl Grimes. "The Oath" sees a couple, Paul and Karina, seeking medical help at a hospital, only to run into a cracked doctor, who's taken it upon herself to offer assisted suicide. Karina takes her up on it. Paul defangs her and bring his zombified companion with him out of the hospital. Before he leaves, Paul bars a set of doors in the hospital and spray-paints a warning to others: DON'T OPEN DEAD INSIDE.

The most audacious expansion of the universe, though, was of course the AMC spin-off series *Fear the Walking Dead,* which premiered on August 23, 2015. *Fear* moved the clock back a bit. In the premiere, the zombie plague is just starting to hit the edges of society, and most people simply don't believe what is happening around them. The show focuses on a small group of people: Madison ("Maddie") Clark, a high school guidance counselor; her boyfriend, Travis Manawa, who is the school's English teacher; and their families (Travis is divorced, Maddie's a widow). Travis has a teenage son, Chris, and an ex-wife, Liza. Maddie has two children, Nick and Alicia. Their father died some time earlier in an auto accident.

Even with *Dead*'s monster ratings, there was a question about whether there was enough demand for a second show about zombies. To distinguish itself from its sibling, *Fear* focuses on average people. To an extent, *The Walking Dead* focuses on "regular" people, but *Fear* takes that even further. The Clarks and Manawas aren't cops or outdoorsmen, or anything special, really. They are also a somewhat dysfunctional group: Chris resents his father. Nick is a heroin addict. Alicia just wants out of town. Maddie struggles with the guilt of how her husband's death affected her children. Their daily lives are concerned with matters as mundane as trying to save money by fixing the kitchen sink without calling a plumber (as somebody who had to learn his own fair share of plumbing skills in order to save money, the scene where Travis fixes the sink immediately put me on this show's side).

The premiere of *Fear* came in between the fourth and fifth seasons of *The Walking Dead,* when the original show was surging toward its highest ratings. That tailwind helped: the opening episode of *Fear* attracted 10 million viewers, making it the highest-rated premiere for a scripted cable show ever, and while the ratings have trended down since then, it has remained the second-highest-rated show on cable, second only to *Dead.*

Judged on the ratings alone, *Fear* is a success, of course. But it still has to live in the shadow of its sibling, and that makes for persistent and inevitable comparisons. "I think season two will establish our show as its own show," Cliff Curtis said back in that 2016 interview. Yet, much like its predecessor, *Fear* suffered from an uneven second season. There were things about it that worked very well, like the whole idea of taking the cast onto a boat and exploring the world offshore, which was a creative way to show a part of the zombie apocalypse that isn't seen very often but is often mentioned as an escape by fans of the genre. There were also aspects that didn't work quite as well, like a midseason finale that ended in a literal fire that felt forced.

Curtis's character, Travis, occupies an interesting space on the show. Despite serving as the male lead, Travis is no Rick Grimes. For one thing, he's an English teacher instead of a cop. More important, he's got enough survival instinct that he isn't among the first ones killed when the Turn occurs, but he has a hard time giving up his morals and ethics. He still envisions a society put back together, where he can raise his son and be with Maddie, and maybe go back to teaching Jack London and other classic literature. And as tiresome as it can get watching Travis try to make good in a world gone horribly wrong, it's also necessary. From a story standpoint, you need a Travis to be one end of the morality continuum, the good side of the trust-humanity/screw-humanity dynamic. Travis's impulse to still do good while everything else is turning very, very bad become the friction within the group that creates drama among the survivors. The biggest pain for him is that his own son, Chris, eventually moves to the opposite end of the spectrum. Here, though, the morality tale becomes a reaffirmation of the value of goodness, because Chris's moral journey ends up costing him his life.

The dynamic turns as new survivors become part of the group. First there are the Salazars: Ofelia (Mercedes Mason) and her parents, Griselda (Patricia Reyes Spindola) and Daniel (Rubén Blades), a simple barber with a horrifying past. Victor Strand (Colman Domingo), another character, doesn't show up until late in the first season, in "Cobalt" (episode 5), but as soon as he does, the whole tenor of the show changes. Most of the other characters are busy trying to figure out what's going on around them; Strand doesn't care. He's a smiling hustler, and Domingo gives him a voice that almost purrs as he's pulling his little strings.

Strand is stuck in a holding cell in a military facility (with Nick Clark, it will turn out). He turns on another man in the cell, Doug, and slowly drives him mad. Strand taunts Doug about his wife, about how Doug wasn't strong enough to take care of her but how in this new world she is attractive enough that she'll be able to find a new man who will. It's almost like Strand is exercising a skill, like a quarterback throwing balls in a drill. Strand's true intentions are kept hidden long enough that you really don't know what his game is. But he's critical to the group's survival. He's the one with the boat, the *Abigail,* on which the survivors hitch a ride and barely escape a burning Los Angeles. Eventually we learn that Strand's motivation is simple: to get back to his partner, Thomas Abigail, a rich Mexican businessman. Strand's mission to get back to Thomas becomes the focal point around which the entire second season revolves, and lands the "Abinauts" in Mexico. The show even inadvertently hit on a piece of the cultural zeitgeist in the season 2 finale, which aired on October 2, 2016, in the middle of the real U.S. presidential election, where the Mexican border and Donald Trump's plan to build a massive wall across it were a major flash point. Toward the end of the finale, several of the characters—after sailing down to Mexico—find themselves back at the U.S.-Mexican border, Ofelia alone and Nick leading a large group from a town of survivors. Ofelia is seemingly taken captive by a lone armed gunman. Nick's group comes under fire from some paramilitary-looking dudes as soon as they cross the old gates that let cars into America. Zombies or no zombies, the border is something people care about.

Whether it's *The Walking Dead* or *Fear the Walking Dead,* the novels, the webisodes, or the ongoing graphic novel, people have a virtually inexhaustible appetite for zombie material. The expansion of the world Kirkman and Moore first sketched out in the panels of a comic book page has tapped into something inside people, and they have responded viscerally. They want more.

The Walking Dead returned for its second season on October 16, 2011, but it didn't come back alone. AMC knew it had a hit on its hands, and a ratings smash. The question was how to capitalize on that. Traditionally, a network will try to line up one or more shows to run the same night, creating a block of programming to keep viewers glued to the station. AMC had a different idea. Over on the Bravo channel, producer Andy Cohen had taken his *Real Housewives* franchise and done something unusual with it: built a talk show on top of it. Called *Watch What Happens: Live,* it featured Cohen and various stars from Bravo's shows, as well as seemingly anybody else who happened to be in New York that night. Oprah. Cher. Whoever. The show was, and is, consciously goofy—and always involves actual drinking (there is nothing quite like watching actor and *Housewives* superfan Michael Rapaport with a couple in him talking about Bethenny's latest fight with the Countess). It appears that AMC's brain trust saw that model and found it exciting, and thought, *Hey, we can do that, too . . . without the drinking.* Cohen's show was pulling in about a million and a half viewers, and *Housewives* wasn't doing near the business that *The Walking Dead* was doing. And producing a talk show was far more affordable than another scripted drama.

In the summer of 2011, AMC ordered a pilot, hiring the same production team behind *Watch What Happens.* They brought in stand-up comedian Chris Hardwick as the host for this unaired test. Hardwick was a good choice with great nerd cred. He'd moderated *Walking Dead* panels at San Diego Comic-Con, hosted

Doctor Who specials for BBC America, and had a podcast called, appropriately enough, the *Nerdist Podcast.* The pilot worked, and the network made plans to bring it along as a live show. Thus *Talking Dead* was born.

The first episode aired with two guests on the set, comedian Patton Oswalt and writer-director James Gunn, along with Hardwick. Kirkman appeared via satellite. The whole idea was less about capturing Cohen's booze-fueled goofiness and more about tapping into exactly what was already happening online surrounding the show, which was (and still is) people talking about it, passionately, seriously, in minute detail. On air, the host and guests took calls, read questions from online viewers, and gabbed about all the tiniest points. *Did that zombie that Daryl and Rick dissected really swallow a woodchuck whole? Is that even possible?* Gunn, Oswalt, and Hardwick got into a discussion about how they would want to be killed before they became zombies, and the finer points of fast versus slow zombies. (Incidentally, Gunn wrote the screenplay for the 2004 remake of *Dawn of the Dead.*) They argued about the perfect weapon for a zombie apocalypse: Hardwick favored the katana, but Oswalt agreed with the writer Max Brooks, who expressed in his bestselling book *World War Z* that a .22 is best. Gunn wanted a Gatling gun. Later on, Hardwick made Oswalt admit, groaningly, that the two had played Dungeons & Dragons together, and then launched into a discussion of players' moral, ethical "alignment," and how Kirkman changes the moral alignment of his characters under these harsh conditions.

"You're losing every viewer you have right now," Oswalt said, "but you're getting one *really* devoted viewer."

The show drew about 1.2 million people for that first episode, after the season 2 premiere of *The Walking Dead,* "What Lies Ahead," drew 7.26 million viewers, a record for *The Walking*

Dead at the time and a sign of what was coming. The plan actually worked better than AMC could've hoped; *Talking Dead*'s ratings climbed from that premiere, and kept climbing. In its second season—the third for *The Walking Dead*—*Talking Dead*'s audience went from about 2 million to 5 million. In its third season, it went from 5 million to 7 million. The show was a top-ten-rated program for Sunday nights. Not only that, but the 11 P.M. repeat of that night's episode itself was a top-ten-rated show. *Talking Dead,* it seemed, was a good lead-in for a repeat of the episode people had just watched. People were watching the show, watching a discussion about the show, and then some were watching the original show *again*. What's more, *Talking Dead* was so nerdy that it even went online after it went off the air. In other words, even the after-show had an after-show. Suddenly, AMC had three hours of the most-watched programming on Sunday nights in addition to the Internet sensation that commented on all this content. Look at the week of December 5 through 11, 2016, for example. That week, the top-rated show on cable was *The Walking Dead,* which drew 6.5 million viewers in the key 18–49 age bracket. *Monday Night Football* was second (the Colts-Jets game), with 3.3 million viewers. *Talking Dead* was third, with 2.5 million.

Talking Dead was conceptually easy, but in its popularity it was suddenly a hot ticket. Besides actors from *The Walking Dead* and members of the production team like Kirkman, Gimple, Hurd, and Nicotero, the show attracted a wide range of guests. People who had nothing to do with *The Walking Dead,* beyond being fans, stopped by to sit on the couch and fanboy it up with Hardwick. The director Kevin Smith (who also has a show on AMC, *Comic Book Men*) is a frequent guest, as are Wil Wheaton, Dave Navarro, Aisha Tyler, Keegan-Michael Key, and Marilyn Manson. The guests have been as varied as CNBC morning anchor Joe Kernen and former Pittsburgh Steelers running back

DeAngelo Williams. The actress Yvette Nicole Brown is a frequent guest, and she is such a massive fan that she arrives on set with a notebook filled with her thoughts on the show.

It was impossible to miss what a gold mine AMC had found. Suddenly, a lot of shows with obsessive fan bases started getting their own after-shows. BBC America's *Orphan Black,* which is an excellent show that finished its fifth and final season in 2017, got its own after-show, *After the Black. Game of Thrones* got one. *Mr. Robot,* another show I love, received one, too. *Sons of Anarchy . . . This Is Us . . .* They even did one for Destination America's *Mountain Monsters,* about a group of West Virginian hunters searching for evidence of Bigfoot and other fanciful monsters with colorful names like Hogzilla, the Cherokee Death Cat, the Snallygaster, and the Grassman (don't ask).

Not everybody was a fan of this new format. "The real problem with these after-shows," *GQ*'s Scott Meslow wrote in a critical piece, "is that they originate from the same brain trust that produces the shows being analyzed." *Is Hardwick ever going to trash an episode? Is one of the stars ever going to complain about a plot point?* "In practice, these post-shows are basically just a PR-friendly brand extension—a pep rally for TV shows that already have an obsessive following." It should be noted, Meslow is not a fan of *The Walking Dead,* either.

So what do you do when you're the most popular, bloodiest show on cable? You strive for enrapturing the world of academia. Since starting research for this book, I've come across quite a few academic essays on the show, and it seems PhD types are as interested as the rest of us. The zombie apocalypse can be gruesome, it can be gory and violent and terrifying, but that doesn't mean it is just mindless escapism. Think about the show beyond zombies: the collapse of society, a grim fight for survival, and a struggle to rebuild some semblance of that shattered world. Most zombie stories never explore those themes very deeply, if at all, because they don't last long enough to do so. *Night of the Living Dead* is literally about one night. *28 Days Later* shows society after a complete collapse but doesn't get past the mad scramble to get out of London and a fight with some very dark soldiers. *Dead Set* gives its reality-star brats some time to stew and bicker, and gets points for satirizing reality TV, before the zombies take over the set—and the world. *The Walking Dead,* on the other hand, was from the outset aimed at consciously exploring the aftermath of the zombie apocalypse. It's a show about the *post*–zombie apocalypse. That means there are a lot of themes to explore—everything from politics, to sociology, to medicine and the study of pandemics. And that's what a small group of professors at the University of California, Irvine, realized.

Society, Science, Survival: Lessons from AMC's *The Walking Dead* was an eight-week noncredit online class that the UCI professors taught in 2013. Designed in conjunction with AMC, it was what's called a MOOC, a massive open online course. The series explored the basics of individual survival and featured thought experiments like *Can you really eat squirrels?* (Daryl Dixon would growl if you asked that in his presence.) Or *What is Maslow's Hierarchy of Needs, and is just surviving reason enough to live?* The course moved into larger questions of social structure, explored through various settings on the show—from the Greene farm to the community at the prison to the dictatorship of Woodbury. It looked at "social identity," the kinds of roles and stereotypes the characters fit into. It looked at health issues, too. How are infectious diseases spread? What is the role of the medical profession, from local doctors to the Centers for Disease Control? It even explored the psychological damage done to people who do survive similar ordeals. What's the effect on somebody's psyche of always sleeping with one eye open?

For UCI, it was important that the course be taught on a college level, if the school was going to participate at all. Four professors were selected to run the MOOC, and they split up the various courses: Joanne Christopherson, a lecturer in the School of Social Sciences; Michael Dennin, a professor of physics and astronomy, Sarah Eichhorn, associate dean of the school's Distance Learning Center, and Zuzana Bic, a lecturer on public health. They each proposed different topics, and AMC ended up selecting eight of them for the course, with an eye toward themes that would be emerging in season 4, since the online course went live ahead of that season's premiere (though the network would not share so much as a line of dialogue from the new episodes with the professors, for fear of giving away spoilers). Two of Christopherson's got selected, one on the hierarchy of needs and another on leadership styles.

Christopherson had taught online classes before, one of the reasons she was chosen for this, but she herself had never even seen the show. "I'm kind of a *Downton Abbey* person," she said. She binged the first three seasons of *The Walking Dead* and found herself intrigued. Then she'd go online and look up the old recaps. It all got her mind racing. "It was very rich to write about," she said. She would think of an idea, watch an episode and take notes, go read a recap, and other ideas would pop into her head. "I had to limit myself to three topics" for the MOOC, she said. Her interest in how characters deal with living through a disaster was the underlying source of her module on the hierarchy of needs.

The course ended up getting sixty thousand participants, from ninety countries, which was enlightening to Christopherson, because it illustrated that the show wasn't attracting just violence-soaked American kids. Four fifths of the participants said they spent more than an hour a week on the coursework—meaning they spent more time on that than they did watching the actual show—and 60 percent of them said the course made them bigger fans of the show. And, while it may be a benefit none of them ever need to draw upon, 80 percent said they felt the course improved their odds of surviving a zombie plague.

The positive feedback turned out to be good for Christopherson's reputation on campus. The course got a lot of attention and was written up in the media. On campus, she is still invited to come to dorms and talk to the students about the show, and is asked to sit with them to watch new episodes. "I've kind of become the professor who knows about *The Walking Dead,*" she said. "It's been a whole phenomenon to me."

CHAPTER 8

MARCUS AURELIUS AND ZOMBIES

"DON'T YOU WANT ONE MORE DAY WITH A CHANCE?"

—MICHONNE

(SEASON 5, EPISODE 9, "WHAT HAPPENED AND WHAT'S GOING ON")

The financial panic of 2008 ushered in the worst economic downturn most of us had ever seen, and destroyed lives across the globe. In 2008 and 2009, in the United States, hundreds of thousands of people were losing their jobs every month. While this wasn't quite the same thing as a zombie apocalypse, it dawned on me that there might be some connection between the fictional world of the show and the real world of the viewers. My main job at the *Wall Street Journal* back then was, and still is today, to cover the markets. During the day, I wrote about the movements of the Dow Jones Industrial Average, earnings reports, oil prices, the dollar, the economy, GDP reports, unemployment, consumer spending, industrial production—the whole gamut. I had a front-row seat for Wall Street's epic meltdown. The economic catastrophe was well inside my circle of friends and family. I knew people who'd lost their jobs, people who were struggling to pay the bills and put food on the table. Nearly a decade later, we are still trying to get past it.

The twenty-first century has already seen its share of disaster, including, in the United States alone, the September 11 attacks and 2005's Hurricane Katrina. There have been myriad calamities around the world, too. There was the Indian Ocean tsunami of 2004, which killed nearly 300,000 people across India, Sri Lanka, Kenya, and South Africa; there was Japan's 2011 earthquake, the fourth-most-powerful earthquake in the world since 1900, where 15,894 people died and the Fukushima Daiichi power plant came within hours of a nuclear catastrophe. London, 2005. Paris, 2015. Aleppo, 2016. You might say that the real world, in which so many regular people were thrust up against the worst humanity and nature had to offer, had sadly prepared viewers well for the fictional world of *The Walking Dead*.

"At its heart, *The Walking Dead* is a show about a group of ordinary people trying to survive in a world that has suddenly and violently changed on them," I wrote in a recap ahead of the season 4 premiere. "That resonates in a nation where millions of people have had their lives suddenly and violently changed over the past five years."

The success of a show like *The Walking Dead* "always has something to do with the age in which it first appears," author Jay Bonansinga said. He pointed to Bram Stoker's novel *Dracula,* with its subtexts of sexuality standing in opposition to society and religion, as something that struck a nerve in the Victorian era. Today, he said, "the age that we live in is messed up, on many levels." It's terrorism, unemployment, the economy, the market, not having health insurance, *having* health insurance . . . the list goes on. "You can shoot it in the head this month," he said, "but it just keeps coming up. If it swarms up on you, you're dead." It's dreading going to the mailbox and seeing the new bills you can't pay, it's dreading hearing the phone ring and knowing it's a collector, it's waiting for the next unexpected disaster to crash into your life.

"It's a lot like real life," Norman Reedus said when I interviewed him in the *Journal* offices in 2014, referring to the show's propensity for killing off characters, another aspect that makes it seem more real. "You always feel like you have more time with people. When that person's ripped from you it's a shock."

The Walking Dead uses zombies as a metaphor for real-life terrors, yes, but it also does something more: in portraying a group of constantly threatened, morally challenged survivors, it gives us the guts of a template for attacking all those real-world terrors, a sort of modern Stoicism that sees every day as a chance. "Don't you want one more day with a chance?" Michonne asks. The show is practically a how-to manual on developing the kind of gumption you need to survive tough times. Kirkman wasn't looking to make a grand statement about the world when he first envisioned his comic; he just wanted to do a story about zombies. But the world changed to meet him, and that is what makes the series so visionary and prescient.

How this message gets delivered is unique in itself. A man named Stuart Hall, a professor at the University of Birmingham in the UK, explained all this back in 1973, in a paper that sought to explain how television has its own "televisual language," and how that language is used to disseminate cultural messages. In essence, it's one giant circuit, from the production team, through the cable network or over the Internet, into the home, through the television (or these days, laptop, desktop, tablet, or smartphone), and into, well, your brain. That last step, though, is not merely the result. You are not just the dumb receptacle at the end of the circuit. What is being delivered to you, Hall says, is a coded message. How you decode that message is what gives the medium its power. "Television is a discourse," he writes, "a communicative, not simply behavioral, event." Tying all this together, what we have in *The Walking Dead* is a show that makes use of a handy metaphor in the zombie for whatever anxiety the audience has, appearing at a time when the audience has a lot of anxieties. In this environment, that discourse Hall talked about took on a life of its own.

It was amplified by social media. Live performers—theater actors, musicians, even street performers—are very familiar with the connection between themselves and their audience, and how that produces a dynamic that is unique to each individual and performance. Television actors don't get that same feedback, but if they happen to be on Twitter when their show is on, and many are these days, they can get a facsimile of that "live" reaction to their performance. In that sense, social media gives television an entirely new channel for its televisual language. Today, with people watching television and at the same time talking about the shows on social media, you end up with an even more complicated circuit than the one Hall pondered in 1973. "Watching television is a link in the chain of sacred storytelling," Diane Winston wrote in *Small Screen, Big Picture,* "a latter-day version of Western traditions, such as hearing scriptures, 'reading' stained glass windows, or absorbing a Passion Play." In an age of social media, when the interaction between viewer and program is far more kinetic than in the past, the unspoken messages contained within a show like *The Walking Dead* are shaped more than ever by the viewer as well as the production itself.

It's interesting that Winston makes those religious comparisons. Indeed, in a world in which going to religious services has lost any meaning or coherence for many, television—for better or worse—has emerged as a real conduit through which cultural values are explored. "Television converts social concerns, cultural conundrums, and metaphysical questions into stories that explore and even shape notions of identity and destiny—the building blocks of religious speculation," Winston said. In *The Walking Dead,* we get plenty of religious overtones, and while the show does not exactly provide a religious answer to the big questions of our age, it does, I believe, provide the kinds of answers that people usually turn to religion or literature for in the first place. In the modern age, television shows are our parables, says Sonya Iryna, a freelance writer who covers the show for the fan website Undead Walking. "I always relate it to a quote from Neil Gaiman, from *Coraline,* where he said, 'Fairy tales are more than true, not because they tell us that dragons exist, but because they tell us that dragons can be beaten.' And I think that's really the appeal of the show."

"A show like [*The Walking Dead*] tells us that no matter what happens, if you are loyal to the people you love," she said, "you can conquer anything."

About 23 percent of Americans now consider themselves unaffiliated with any religion, according to a 2015 survey by the Pew Research Center. This unaffiliated group, moreover, is composed of younger people over time, and their overall numbers are growing, while Catholics and Protestants, for instance, are getting older and their overall numbers falling. It's a phenomenon Pew calls the growth of the "nones." I believe the show takes certain religious reference points, reinterprets them, and uses them in a way that appeals to both the religious and the nones.

If you've watched enough of *The Walking Dead,* you've certainly caught the religious overtones of the show. Some characters are very religious, like Hershel Greene, while others aren't at all. Churches have been used as sets, and the whole show has a very Book of Revelation feel to it. "And the seventh angel poured out his vial into the air; and there came a great voice out of the temple of heaven, from the throne, saying, It is done." That's a verse from Revelation (16:17). After the seventh angel poured out the last of the bowls of wrath, this happens: "There were flashes of lightning, and rumblings, and rolls of thunder, and a great earthquake, the likes of which had not occurred since men were upon the earth—so mighty was the great quake."

That verse, rendered in the familiar notation of REVELATION 16:17, is listed on the marquee outside the Southern Baptist Church of Holy Light—the church where the Grimes clan goes looking for Sophia in "What Lies Ahead." It's a subtle but unmistakable reference. And that isn't the only time the show will insert Bible verses. Inside Father Gabriel's parish church, St. Sarah's, there are five Bible verses indicated on the message board for that week's sermon, what must have been Father Gabriel's last. For the record, here they are:

> **ROMANS 6:4** "Therefore we are buried with him by baptism into death: that like as Christ was raised up from the dead by the glory of the Father, even so we also should walk in newness of life."
>
> **EZEKIEL 37:7** "So I prophesied as I was commanded: and as I prophesied, there was a noise, and behold a shaking, and the bones came together, bone to his bone.
>
> **MATTHEW 27:52** "And the graves were opened; and many bodies of the saints which slept arose."
>
> **REVELATION 9:6** "And in those days shall men seek death, and shall not find it; and shall desire to die, and death shall flee from them."
>
> **LUKE 24:5** "And as they were afraid, and bowed down their faces to the earth, they said unto them, Why seek ye the living among the dead?"

Lastly, on the arch above the pulpit is another verse, John 6:54: "He who eats my flesh and drinks my blood has eternal life, and I will raise him up at the last day."

There is an exchange at the end of season 2 that crystallizes the show's subtle indication that it is portraying the end times as prophesied in the Bible: The farm has been overrun by a herd of walkers, and the Grimes clan has scattered. Rick, Carl, and Hershel are back on the highway, at the original spot where the group first stopped. "I can't profess to understand God's plan," Hershel says, "but Christ promised the resurrection of the dead. I just thought he had something a little different in mind." You could read all of *The Walking Dead* as one extended meditation on the end of the world.

Our institutions have not collapsed like in *The Walking Dead*, but if we're being honest, they've collapsed at least a little. In medieval times, society was broken up into "estates." The first estate was the clergy, the second the nobles, the third the commoners. In the eighteenth century, people added the fourth estate: the press. Well, today, none of those estates is in particularly high standing: the churches are losing parishioners; the nobles are losing popular support; the commoners—what today we'd call the 99 percent—are being squeezed from every angle; the press is being gutted by the Internet. How the show addresses what people think of institutions can be summarized by looking at how the Grimes clan approaches the church.

There are two churches that make an extended appearance on *The Walking Dead*, the first of which appears in "What Lies Ahead," the season 2 premiere. "At this point in the story of *TWD* as a whole, God exists, people believe, and they feel as though they have a relationship with God—albeit a strained one," wrote two professors, Erika Engstrom of the University of Nevada, Las

Vegas, and Joseph Valenzano III of the University of Dayton, Ohio, in a 2015 paper about the show and its depiction of religion. The Holy Light church is depicted with reverence. It's a beautiful, pastoral, white country chapel. Both inside and outside it looks like it did on any other day during its existence. Indeed, the speaker system that plays a recording of church bells still works—it's what the Grimes clan first hear that attracts them. When they enter, there are three walkers sitting in pews, looking like parishioners waiting patiently for the Lord. Even after the searchers realize that Sophia isn't there, they linger. Daryl snidely asks the statue of Jesus for a sign. Carol prays. Rick, although not a religious man, prays as well. He stands underneath the statue of Christ, bargaining for some signal that he's doing the right thing for the group. Previously, at the CDC, he admitted that he had no hope for their survival. Yet he still fights for it. He isn't going to get the answer today, however. In every shot, the camera shows Rick from the vantage of Jesus looking down from the cross at him, Engstrom and Valenzano point out. Rick is "lowered" in relation to Jesus. "As a composite, these angles and placement of religious images create the impression that Rick, the human, is just a human," they write. God still has a commanding place in the lives of these survivors.

That will change. The next time they come across a church, it is St. Sarah's, another country congregation, led by Father Gabriel Stokes. This happens just after the near-death encounter at Terminus with the cannibals, at the beginning of season 5. Carol had come along and single-handedly saved the Grimes clan—destroying Terminus at the same time—and now the cannibals invade the church seeking vengeance. Thinking they're attacking while Rick and a core group have left, the Termites instead find themselves trapped when Rick comes back—the whole thing a giant ruse.

All the visual signs of "the church" from one episode to the other have been transformed. Whereas the scenes at Holy Light were shot in bright daylight, and the church itself appeared pristine, St. Sarah's is different. The walls have been marked and scarred. Somebody, not shown, has scrawled YOU'LL BURN FOR THIS onto the outside wall, a message for Father Gabriel, or possibly for God himself. At Holy Light, zombified parishioners sit quietly, as if the dead are reverent there. At St. Sarah's, the only one there is Father Gabriel, a scared, impotent, murderous coward, a poor representative of God on earth. Even Rick has been transformed. At Holy Light, he was still Officer Grimes, still the good-guy hero who risked his life for others, quick to forgive and see the good in people, even those who threatened his life. At St. Sarah's, we see a very different version of him. The uniform is gone. With his thick beard and long hair, Rick resembles an Old Testament fire-and-brimstone prophet. The first Rick was about forgiveness, but this one is about revenge. He forces Gareth to kneel in front of him, replacing the Jesus of Nazareth who was exalted with his own version. He toys with Gareth the way a cat plays with a mouse, and then, recalling his promise, pulls out his red-handled machete and hacks Gareth to pieces—Rick literally smites his enemy in that formerly holy place. Now, as Maggie says in the wake of the slaughter, "it's just four walls and a roof." Engstrom and Valenzano go further: "This is not merely Old Testament vengeance because even that is accompanied by a belief and value for the Almighty. No, these actions are bereft of faith and elicit the idea the characters have given up on religion—and God."

Either the depiction of religion on the show is a commentary on religion itself, or religion is a stand-in for the idea of institutions overall. The scene at St. Sarah's could be *The Walking Dead*'s "God is dead" moment, a sort of Nietzschean epiphany.

Or it could be seen as an *affirmation* of religion. Remember, Hershel didn't disavow God, he just thought God had something different in mind. The trials and travails that the Grimes clan, and all the other survivors, endure are symbolic of a Job-like test from the Almighty. In that sense, the entire show illustrates a testimony for faith, not a rejection of it, which is how Ann Mahoney, who played Olivia, views it. She noted that in the epic battle with the dead inside Alexandria's walls, Father Gabriel says that God has given the Alexandrians the answer to their prayers, which is "to go take care of it, go out and deal with it."

"I don't think God, in my opinion, deals with an actionless human," she said when I talked to her. In this same way, she feels she has to let her own children "earn the things that they know, because that's how they grow." You need to look horizontally, not vertically, Mahoney said; vertical thinking is worrying about the next moment while horizontal thinking is looking toward a higher power for spiritual growth. There is a frequently quoted line from the book of James that sums this up: "Even so faith, if it hath not works, is dead, being alone" (James 2:17). I've heard it paraphrased as "faith without works is dead."

Action, not actionless, was built into the very fiber of mankind, according to the Bible. Look no further than the book of Genesis. "Then the Lord God took the man and put him into the Garden of Eden to cultivate it and keep it" (2:15). God didn't just put man into the garden without any responsibility. Far from it; man was put there specifically to work the land, to maintain it. Action and work were part of the bargain from the very beginning. Of course, another part of the bargain was that man would not eat the forbidden fruit, but that's another story.

Even if you're not particularly religious, the Bible is a rich source of symbolism, and one Bible story seems a tragically apt parable in season 7. Abraham, the father of the Hebrews (and by extension the Christians and Muslims), was an obedient servant of his Lord. He left his home and settled in a new land at God's command. God had told him to do these things, and promised that his offspring would rule the world. When he was one hundred, an age that even Abraham thought was old, he and his wife, Sarah, were blessed with a son, Isaac. Isaac would become the focal point of God's sternest test: the Lord commanded Abraham to kill his son as a sacrifice of obedience. Abraham took his son to a mountaintop, built an altar, tied Isaac to it, and pulled out a knife. He was going to go through with it, much as it pained him. An angel stopped him, though. The Lord had seen enough.

For all its controversial violence, the season 7 premiere, "The Day Will Come When You Won't Be," is a sort of demented take on the Abraham and Isaac story. Rick and his family have traveled long and hard and have seemingly come to their own promised land. Of course, they run into the Saviors, an ironic name if there ever was one, and Rick is eventually, after much horror, put to the same test as Abraham: told to sacrifice his son. Abraham may not have understood why he was asked to make this sacrifice, but Rick sure does—Negan is going to kill them all if he doesn't go through with it. Did you think Rick was going to do it? I sure did. And, the thing is, Rick *was* going to do it. At the last minute, Negan decides in his own sick, maniacal way that he's made his point, and stays Rick's hand. In that moment, Negan has symbolically taken on the power of God, at least over this group.

In a way, Rick is a little bit of both Jesus and Abraham. He isn't just the hero, valiantly fighting and beating his enemies; he is also the shepherd to a flock. Through him lies the path to, if not salvation, at least survival.

Now, we've discussed this show from a Christian viewpoint, because the references to Christianity are many, but I'm not just trying to set it up as a Christian parable. Indeed, I think there is another way of looking at the world, a philosophy that explains the show and its characters' motivations to an even greater degree. In fact, I think that what I'm about to show you is the biggest single reason for *The Walking Dead*'s unusually strong following.

Just Survive Somehow.

In "Them" (season 5, episode 10), Rick delivers a speech that dives a little deeper into this mantra and worldview, which shows that the only way to survive in this world is to basically forget about yourself, to not concern yourself with any of the things with which we in this real world of ours do concern ourselves. You have to stop caring about things like right or wrong, love or hate, even living and dying. *Especially* living and dying. The speech, maybe the most important in the whole show, is worth printing here in its entirety:

> When I was a kid, I asked my grandpa once if he ever killed any Germans in the war. He wouldn't answer. Said that was grown-up stuff. So, so I asked if the Germans ever tried to kill him. But he got real quiet. He said he was dead the minute he stepped into enemy territory. Every day he woke up and told himself, "Rest in peace, now get up and go to war." And then after a few years of pretending he was dead, he made it out alive. That's the trick of it, I think. We do what we need to do, and then, we get to live. But no matter what we find in D.C., I know we'll be okay. Because this is how we survive. We tell ourselves that we are the walking dead.

The last bit, "we are the walking dead," is an iconic line from the comics; there Rick says it in the prison, trying to explain the difference between civilization and barbarity, and how the line between the living and the zombies is a thin one indeed. In the show, the line is still delivered by Rick, but in a completely different setting, in a completely different speech. It comes after the fight with the cannibals of Terminus, toward the end of the slog to Washington, when the group is exhausted and near starvation, on the brink of complete collapse. While they rest in a cabin in the woods, too tired to do anything else, Rick gives them that grim pep talk.

The concept—*we are the walking dead*—is made far more contemplative, nuanced, and meaningful by Rick's captivating speech. Rick is talking about a way of life, one grounded in the extreme mental gymnastics a soldier had to perform in order to survive the horrors of war. The only way to do it is to tell yourself it's all over already, the worst has happened. "We do what we need to do, and then, we get to live." A perfectly Stoic Rick Grimes line.

Stoicism as a character trait still has some cultural currency, but as an approach to life it is not very well understood anymore. In ancient Greece and Rome, it was a major school of thought. Stoicism, first developed by a Greek named Zeno of Citium around 300 B.C., teaches self-control and acceptance as a means to overcome emotion, to practice a kind of measured denial of material concerns in order to achieve peace and calm, and to live a virtuous life. The ultimate goal of Stoicism is to relieve suffering. I've always thought of it as a determination to remain focused on the single most important thing, life itself, and not be sidetracked by all the external troubles and problems we can't control anyhow. The goal isn't to withdraw from the world, but to find a way to live with all the craziness that invariably comes with being part of it, accepting it for what it is, and not letting it drive you crazy, too. Rick's speech, seen in this light, is nearly the essence of Stoicism. Contrast it with these quotes from Marcus Aurelius, a second-century Roman emperor whose *Meditations* is one of the great works of Stoicism:

> Just that you do the right thing. The rest doesn't matter. Cold or warm. Tired or well-rested. Despised or honored. Dying or busy with other assignments. Because dying, too, is one of our assignments in life. There as well: "to do what needs doing." Look inward.
>
> Think of yourself as dead. You have lived your life. Now, take what's left and live it properly. What doesn't transmit light creates its own darkness.

In Stoicism, Aurelius found his refuge and guidepost through the world. Rome was in a rough way in his years. The empire was beset from the east by the Parthians and from the north by Germanic tribes, and most of his rule was spent fighting wars. Soldiers returning from the Parthian campaign brought a plague with them, which ran across the empire for years. "As for pain, a pain that is intolerable carries us off, but that which lasts a long time is bearable," Aurelius wrote in *Meditations*. In other words, if it doesn't kill you, it can't be all that bad.

The most Stoic character on the show, if you ask me, is Glenn Rhee. Nobody else has quite the same commitment to virtue and badassery no matter the circumstances. Glenn gets to Alexandria and gains a mortal enemy in Nicholas, who actually tries to kill him. Even so, Glenn turns that situation into one of personal virtue, and he works with Nicholas to make a him a better man. Why would he do that? Because doing so makes himself a better man. Remember when they were escaping Terminus, in the season 5 premiere? Glenn hears somebody in one of the railcars and demands they rescue him. Now, Glenn had just been about one second away from having his throat slit, yet he is still concerned about a stranger. Hell, go all the way back to the pilot, when Glenn goes out of his way to save Rick, a decision that, as Maggie points out in her speech in the season 7 finale, really gave birth to everything that's been built by this group since then. Glenn's mix of grit, guts, and hope is the perfect Stoic message for our times.

This approach to life shows up outside of Stoicism, too, of course. There is a concept in Japanese culture called *gaman*—the University of Nevada's Erika Engstrom introduced me to it when I ran this theory by her—which is sometimes translated as perseverance, but means something more like "psychological endurance," a beefier and more cerebral concept. And doesn't that sound like a good description of Rick's speech?

I came across a CNN clip from 2011, in the aftermath of Japan's awful earthquake, tsunami, and nuclear crisis, when the network brought on *Star Trek*'s George Takei to specifically talk about how *gaman* affected the Japanese people's response to the disaster. It is this *gaman,* Takei said, that helped the Japanese endure the nightmare. It was *gaman* that kept individuals from rioting or looting, from surrendering all norms of society, and it was *gaman* that gave rescue workers the courage to go into the Fukushima nuclear plant to help stabilize it, even though they were exposing themselves to the deadly radiation leaking all over the plant. "They are members of a community," he said, "so they know that they're taking a high risk, but they bear it, they endure it, [with] fortitude, and for the sake of the others, they go in."

Now, that is doing what needs to be done.

If you're still not sure that *The Walking Dead* is basically one extended rumination on Stoicism, take this test. Guess who said the following statements: Marcus Aurelius, second-century emperor of Rome and noted Stoic, or Sergeant Abraham Ford, foul-mouthed survivor of the zombie plague?

> "A cucumber is bitter, throw it away. There are briars in the path, turn aside from them. This is enough. Do not add 'and why were such things put into the world?'"

"Why are dingleberries brown? Just the way shit is."

"How ridiculous and unrealistic is the man who is astonished at anything that happens in life."

"You'd have better luck picking up a turd by its clean end."

"Pass then through this little space of time comfortably to nature, and end thy journey in content, just as an olive falls off when it is ripe."

"Suck my nuts."

Okay, so that wasn't a hard quiz. But it illustrates that there is a lot of Stoicism in *The Walking Dead*. Stoics strive to endure any suffering and pain, seeing them, rightly, as things beyond their control. When Abraham tells Negan "suck my nuts," even as Negan is about to murder him, he's employing a form of Stoicism. Extreme, yes, but nonetheless.

I've taken you some ways away from where we started, but there is a reason for it. There are interesting things happening here on several levels that translate directly into the show's success. The writers are picking up cues from religion and philosophy to bolster their stories. Those cues, and the values that underlie them, are being retransmitted through a new vehicle, namely a television show. They are being absorbed, energetically, by a large and global audience. And even though they're being transmitted through a story about a global apocalypse, they're being received as a positive, hopeful message for millions of people, certainly some of whom are struggling in their own lives. This is happening, moreover, at a time when people are becoming *less,* not more, religious.

That last bit is curious. Recall the Pew study, which found the change in attitudes toward religion so stark there's an entire group now it called the "nones." That's a clever title, but I think it misses a crucial piece of the story. People may indeed be turning away from organized religions. But that doesn't mean they have stopped asking the questions that give rise to religion in the first place. *Why are we here? What's it all about? Why am I made to suffer?* Man's search for meaning, a phrase the great Viktor Frankl used, is eternal, as are the answers. It's up to each of us to find them on our own. If people don't connect with the answers given by religion, they will just go look someplace else. It is not nuts to suggest they are finding them in a TV show, even one about zombies. After all, in Ann Mahoney's view the show and her faith are basically using different stories to teach the same lessons.

TOP TEN EPISODES

IN OCTOBER 2017, *THE WALKING DEAD* WILL BEGIN ITS eighth season with its one-hundredth episode, a notable milestone and a sign of its longevity. It's a hard mark for any television show to hit, and it's even harder the way shows are built and aired in the era of Peak TV. In the old days, you might film twenty-five episodes or so a season, but that number has been cut for many shows. The competition is stiffer as well. There are hundreds of channels, on broadcast, cable, and the web, and hundreds of shows, to say nothing of all the homemade stuff, available on YouTube. *The Walking Dead* started with six episodes, then expanded to thirteen in season 2, and has been filming sixteen a year since.

With that in mind, let's look at the best of the best, the top ten out of the first ninety-nine episodes of *The Walking Dead*. To help me with this list, I've recruited two of the writers of the popular *Walking Dead* fan site Undead Walking—Adam Carlson, the site's founder, and Sonya Iryna, one of its staff writers.

10. "ARROW ON THE DOORPOST" (SEASON 3, EPISODE 13)

Tensions are high between the prison and Woodbury. Rick Grimes and the Governor meet at an ostensible peace parlay, but both come away from the fractious meeting more prepared for war than ever.

Paul says: This is the only time that Andrew Lincoln's Rick Grimes and David Morrissey's Governor really are in an episode together, and it's a rare treat to watch these two actors play off each other. The setup is a peace conference between Woodbury and the prison, held in an old feed mill, but neither leader is in the mood for peace, and as they parry and joust, it becomes more and more apparent. Rick snarls, the Governor smiles, but they've both got mayhem on their minds. When Rick mocks him, "At least I don't call myself a *governor,*" and says, "You're the town drunk," you can see the condescension. The Governor meanwhile toys with Rick's emotions, pokes him about his daughter and the fact that she isn't his (at the time, we didn't know for sure that this was true, but Rick later confessed it to Michonne, so Rick knew at this time that it was indeed true). Neither one backs off, and both are ready to go to war, Rick with trepidation, the Governor with glee. There's also the B story: the aides-de-camp outside the Esco feed mill. Watching Daryl and Martinez engage in a zombie-killing skills competition is fantastic.

9. "JUDGE, JURY, EXECUTIONER" (SEASON 2, EPISODE 11)

On the Greene farm, the group debates the fate of a prisoner. In the balance is not only the prisoner's life but the moral soul of the group.

Sonya says: "Judge, Jury, Executioner" is one of my favorite episodes because it showed the group struggling to hang on to humanity. While I felt the Randall story line dragged on, I appreciated that the writers used that story line to address the characters' rules about morality in the new world. Dale tells the group, "The world we know is gone, but keeping our humanity, that's a choice." And he's right. Those questions about morality come up again and again throughout the series. Now that the communities are heading toward rebuilding some semblance of civilization it's an issue that they will have to define and figure out again in the context of building a society.

This episode also had one of my favorite moments of the entire season, a moment that is even more poignant now that both Glenn and Hershel are gone. The scene where Hershel gives Glenn his heirloom pocket watch and tells him, "No man is good enough for your little girl, until one is." The watch has become a symbol of humanity throughout the show. Glenn carried Hershel's legacy of humanity in the face of horror, and now Maggie is carrying it for Glenn and for Hershel.

8. "HERE'S NOT HERE" (SEASON 6, EPISODE 4) *In a flashback we see the evolution of Morgan Jones through his encounter with a man named Eastman, and how this encounter sets him on a path of peace at all costs.*

Adam says: Morgan is such a unique character. You'd already seen him earlier on when he brought Rick in ("Days Gone Bye") and then you learned about his son's death (season 3, episode 12, "Clear") and how that made him just absolutely crazy. In "Here's Not Here," you get to see this character development that's been happening over multiple years. And Eastman is a complicated character on his own, who mirrored a lot of characters in a lot of ways, especially Rick, when he was talking about how he had to kill Shane, and how Eastman had to kill the guy who took out his family. So I felt a lot of the parallels there were great . . . and Lennie James, he's a fantastic actor.

7. "INTERNMENT" (SEASON 4, EPISODE 5) *A virus tears through the prison, infecting most of the residents. The sick are cordoned off in a separate cellblock, but the situation is getting worse. Hershel goes in to try to keep them alive with an herbal remedy and what scraps of medicine he has. It's an epic race against time, and Hershel pushes the very limits of his endurance.*

Sonya says: I thought "Internment" was an important episode for the development of the story because it addressed something that hadn't been addressed before: the issue of pandemic. So much of the survivors' story has been about dealing with walkers or dangerous people, and the issue of illness was really not addressed before season 4. But in that world, with having large numbers of people living in grim and unsanitary conditions, it would be easy for disease and sickness to spread fast. I thought "Internment" showed a new facet of the fight for survival when they had to fight something inanimate that they might not be able to beat. Walkers and people can be killed, but illness is an enemy with no face. I also thought Scott Wilson's performance was simply amazing. Hershel had some great moments throughout the series, but "Internment" was his shining moment for sure. He embodied that deep faith in the power of humanity. It was sad and beautiful.

6. "THE DAY WILL COME WHEN YOU WON'T BE" (SEASON 7, EPISODE 1) *The Grimes clan finally comes face-to-face with Negan. As they kneel before him, captured by his goons, he exacts his revenge for their earlier attack, killing Abraham. Then he kills Glenn, and he breaks Rick's will before finally releasing them, subjects now in his expanding empire.*

Sonya says: This episode was by far the roughest one. But it made my favorites list because it was probably the most iconic moment of the series and the comic. They had to get the arrival of Negan exactly right or it would damage the show. And I think they did get it right. It was the most devastating piece of TV I've ever watched, and I've been watching horror movies and shows since I was seven years old. Watching Glenn's death made me physically sick. To make people that emotionally invested in a fictional character is a pretty difficult thing to do, but *The Walking Dead* does it so well.

Even though the episode was raw and incredibly painful, I have to count it as one of the most extraordinary episodes that the show has done. And even after the deaths of Glenn and Abe and the humiliation of Rick, Maggie and Sasha were ready to fight. That spirit of survival, along with the bond between the survivors, is the heart of the show. Even though the episode was terribly painful it was filled with that unshakable belief in the power of love, loyalty, and family.

5. "FOUR WALLS AND A ROOF" (SEASON 5, EPISODE 3) *After escaping, and destroying, Terminus, the group finds shelter in a church, where they are attacked by Gareth and his few remaining comrades. Rick draws his enemies into the church, traps them, and viciously slaughters them.*

Paul says: For whatever reason, the third episode of most seasons tends to be epic, and "Four Walls" is certainly that. It caps off the Terminus story, but more importantly, it reveals the complete evolution of Rick Grimes, from well-meaning officer of the law to ruthless leader of a group of *really* tough survivors. The tension is fantastic. It does seem like Gareth and the Termites have invaded St. Sarah's Church and are going to kill and cannibalize. Then Rick comes through the shadows, turns the tables, and takes his place in the pulpit, towering above Gareth. With that beard, he looks like some mad prophet from the Old Testament, and he smites his enemy without any remorse. This is the new covenant of the blood.

Adam says: Everything came together in a great way, a powerful episode. I liked Gareth and I wanted him to stick around a bit longer. It's one of those episodes where things flew by.

4. "DAYS GONE BYE" (SEASON 1, EPISODE 1) *The pilot episode. Rick Grimes wakes up in a hospital bed, recovering from a gunshot wound and coma. The world he knew is gone, replaced by an apocalyptic nightmare where society has collapsed and the undead own the world, while the living struggle for survival.*

Adam says: The one that got everybody hooked. One thing I love about the pilot is how it's not perfect. There are scenes that make absolutely no sense—like Summer, the little girl, who picks up the teddy bear, or the walkers outside that grab a rock to smash the door. You can kind of tell *The Walking Dead* was trying to feel things out, trying to figure out how the show was going to work and everything. At that point they didn't have a real identity. When I watched the episode the first time, I thought, *Wow, this is amazing.* Going back to it and watching some of the changes that they made over the years and how [the changes have] kind of been relatively forgotten has been a lot of fun, and I think that's what makes that re-watchable.

3. "NO SANCTUARY" (SEASON 5, EPISODE 1) *The Grimes clan is trapped in Terminus, in line to become food for cannibals. Carol Peletier leads a herd of walkers to the compound and single-handedly rescues everybody while destroying the Termites.*

Paul says: In terms of an "action" episode, it is so hard to beat this one. From the opening on the killing floor to the reunion of Rick and Carl with baby Judith, it never lets up. There are explosions and hails of gunfire and jump scares galore. There are also tons of zombies lurching around—the ones who keep going after walking into fire are especially gnarly. Above all, it is the episode where Carol becomes a full-fledged action hero, tapping her brains and courage to rescue the group (even after Rick had banished her earlier).

2. "THE GROVE" (SEASON 4, EPISODE 14) *Carol and Tyreese find a haven in an old farmhouse. But little Lizzie is dangerously insane, and Carol is forced to make one of the hardest decisions of her life.*

Sonya says: "The Grove" was such a beautifully heartbreaking episode. Melissa McBride's performance was so nuanced and emotional; it was just stunning. There were a lot of layers in that episode that were so well done. One of the things that stood out to me was the juxtaposition of the domesticity they craved so badly and the horror of the world they live in. The opening scene where Carol is making tea and where Lizzie appears, playing tag with a walker that is trying to kill her, is brilliant.

Paul says: One of only two episodes all of us agreed belonged in the top ten, and I can't imagine it would be left off anybody else's list, either. If "No Sanctuary" is the episode where Carol becomes a full-fledged action hero, "The Grove" is the one where she becomes a full-fledged tragic hero. Carol has already proven she is somebody who isn't afraid to decide, to act, but now she must make a decision to kill a little girl whom she essentially adopted. When Carol says, "Look at the flowers," your heart just breaks for both of them. It's an awful yet beautifully rendered story.

Adam says: "The Grove" is a classic. You can't talk about *The Walking Dead*'s best episodes without mentioning it.

1. "NO WAY OUT" (SEASON 6, EPISODE 9) *After the attack from the Wolves, walkers break down Alexandria's walls and threaten to destroy everything. Rick Grimes leads an epic fight against the undead to save the town.*

Paul says: The other of the two episodes that all of us agreed on, which made putting it in the top slot an easy choice. I think it is the show's high point.

Adam says: There's no way to sum that up, other than saying that the last couple of minutes are some of the most intense moments in television. When the Alexandrians were trying to make their way through that crowd [of walkers], you've got Carl, you've got the hand getting chopped off, you've got [Jessie] trying to protect her son, you've got the son that is just overwhelmed by everything around him. Just a powerful ending to that episode. Fantastic.

Sonya says: What I really liked about this episode was that it hit on one of the enduring themes of the show—that ordinary people can do extraordinary things. This episode had Eugene's one moment of bravery, when the people of Alexandria, who had been relying on Rick and the others, stepped up and fought for their community and their lives. And they did it. They stepped up.

RECAP

SEASON FIVE

- **SAFE HAVENS:** St. Sarah's Church, Grady Memorial Hospital, Alexandria Safe Zone
- **SURVIVORS LOST:** Bob, Tyreese, Noah, Aiden, Reg, Pete
- **ANTAGONISTS KILLED:** Gareth, Mary, Martin, everybody at Terminus, Dawn Lerner
- **HORRIBLE HACKS:** Bob's leg
- **ZOMBIE HERD:** Terminus herd

THE GRIMES CLAN IS TRAPPED IN A RAILCAR IN THE CANnibal haven of Terminus. They are not going to just sit there and become dinner, though. They are ready to fight, with anything they can get their hands on: pieces of wood, belt buckles, strips of leather. The Termites are canny, though. They hit the car with tear gas and take the group, four at a time, to a killing room. Their first captives: Rick, Bob, Daryl, and Glenn. They are herded over a stainless steel pig trough with four others. They will get clocked over the head with a baseball bat and have their throats slit. The Termites are extremely efficient cannibals. They have a system. Gareth, the leader, comes in to check on the progress and to ask Rick about a bag he buried in the woods. Rick tells him what's in it, including a red-handled machete, "which I'm going to use, to kill you." It's a crazy boast, given his current situation, and Gareth laughs at it. Then there is a noise outside. Then something rocks the entire building.

As we will soon find out, it's Carol. She and Tyreese, baby Judith in tow, have snuck up on one of the Termites out in the woods, a young man named Martin. They tie him up and push him into a cabin, where Tyreese and Judith remain with him. Carol takes some fireworks (Martin was using them to distract walkers away from Terminus), a poncho, and some heavy firepower, and heads over to Terminus on her own. There she begins an epic one-woman assault. She shoots holes in a large gas tank in the yard and then fires a bottle rocket at it. The rocket hits the gas escaping through the bullet holes, setting off a huge explosion that knocks down the gates and opens the yard up to an approaching herd of walkers.

Rick and the others use the distraction to kill their captors—although not Gareth, who's left the room—and begin their own escape. There are walkers everywhere, and the Termites are trying to fight them off. Carol, searching for her people, finds a treasure room, where victims' belongings are piled up. She finds Daryl's crossbow and Rick's wristwatch. She also comes across Mary, Gareth's mother. They fight, and Carol shoots her in the leg. There's a brief conversation, and we hear the hard-learned philosophy of the Termites: "You're the butcher, or you're the cattle." Carol opens a door, lets in some walkers, and leaves Mary to die. Everybody is finally freed, and they escape into the woods. Rick wants to go back and finish the Termites off, but nobody else is up to that; they're just happy to be alive. Then Carol shows up. Only Rick knows why she was gone in the first place, but now all is forgiven. She leads them all to the cabin where Tyreese is waiting with Judith, and Rick and Carl see that she's alive.

Now the whole Grimes clan is reunited, but they're not going anywhere. Eugene hasn't yet told them about his "mission" to get to Washington with his cure for the zombie virus, but he sees in this group a force that could help him. They come across a priest, Father Gabriel, fighting for his life alone in the woods. They save him, and he takes them back to his parish, St. Sarah's Church. It's clear to Rick, at least, that there is something off about this man and his church. And there is. Something terrible happened here: as they will discover later, Gabriel locked himself inside the church and let his parishioners die outside.

Gabriel leads them to a food pantry in town where there are supplies in a water-logged basement filled with walkers. They figure out a way to get down there and get the supplies, though it seems at one point that Bob may have been bitten by a walker. He tells his friends that he's fine. They go back to the church and have a great feast. Abraham makes a grand pitch for heading to Washington, and Rick agrees. Bob slips away, though, and goes outside. He's crying—we don't know why—and gets knocked on the head by somebody. Elsewhere, Carol also quietly leaves, and is tracked by Daryl. This will be a recurring theme with Carol, who has turned into a fearsome survivor in the post–zombie apocalypse but has a hard time psychologically squaring away the things she must do. While they stand by an old car, another car zooms by, with a familiar cross marking that Daryl's seen before—the car that took Beth. Off they race after it.

Bob wakes up to find himself captured by the Termites, at least the ones that survived. They'd been hunters before Terminus, and are now hunting down Rick and his crew, with vengeance on their minds. They cut off Bob's leg and begin eating it, which he for some reason finds hysterical. "Tainted meat!" he screams, pulling the collar on his shirt to show the bite mark that he got in that water-logged basement.

The Termites dump Bob back at the church, and he tells the group what's happened. Rick devises a cunning plan. Aware that they are being watched, he takes a group with him, at night, into the woods. Soon after, Gareth and his survivors invade the church. Thinking that they are hunting, they find themselves instead caught in a trap. Rick comes back in, holds them at gunpoint, and makes Gareth kneel in front of him. Gareth begs for a deal, but Rick has no intention of letting these people go. "I made you a promise," he says. He pulls out his red-handled machete and hacks Gareth to death as Sasha, Abraham, and Michonne take care of the others. It's a bloodbath. The next morning, there's a vigil for Bob, who soon dies. Abraham, Rosita, Eugene, Glenn, Maggie, and Tara set off for Washington in the St. Sarah's Church bus. The rest are waiting for Daryl and Carol to return.

Daryl and Carol follow Beth's trail to Atlanta, and a hospital called Grady Memorial. It is an outpost of humanity among a sea of the undead, kept running by a squad of local police, led by the harsh Dawn Lerner. It quickly becomes apparent that there is a violent hierarchy here. The cops get whatever they want, by either consent or force, and the rest "work off" the debts they incur—one way or another—for the privilege of living in safety. It is not something Beth is going to put up with, and with another captive, Noah, she plots an escape. Noah makes it out while Beth doesn't, and he runs into Carol and Daryl in the city. As they go looking for Beth, Carol is hit by accident by the cops, who then scoop her up and take her back.

Farther along the road, the crew taking Eugene to Washington runs into several obstacles, but Abraham will not be deterred. The former sergeant is all business, and he intends to complete his mission. Their bus flips over, but they walk on until they find a fire truck, which they use. Their way is blocked by a herd of walkers a thousand strong. Still, Abraham wants to plow through them. A fierce debate erupts about what to do, and Eugene can't stand it anymore. He tells them, finally, the truth: He isn't a scientist. He doesn't have the plague cure. He's just a scared, smart nerd with a mullet and a talent for lying.

The remaining Grimes clan has a tough nut to crack in rescuing Beth. Rick's plan is to quietly break into the hospital and kill all the cops, but Tyreese comes up with a less drastic plot: capture two of theirs and elicit a hostage exchange. That's exactly what they do, bringing their prisoners to the hospital, and it nearly works, until . . . Beth turns to Dawn, her captor, says cryptically,

"I get it now," and stabs Dawn in the chest. Dawn instinctively grabs her gun and shoots Beth in the head. Abraham's group, which had turned back south looking for everybody else, arrives just in time for Maggie to see her dead sister.

Now the group continues north, in the hope that Eugene was at least right about Washington having survived. It's a grueling trek. They eventually run out of everything and are near death. They find a barn and hunker down amid a fierce storm. The next morning, Maggie and Sasha meet Aaron, who's from a nearby community and offers to shelter them. The community is called Alexandria, and it's run by an unshakable optimist named Deanna Monroe. Aaron is unlike anybody else they've met. He's a capable survivor, but he hasn't been driven mad by the world. It's almost like he's from a pre-Turn world. He seems . . . normal. His offer is too tempting to reject. The group doesn't really have a choice, but they've been on the road for so long, it's not at all clear they can even live among others anymore.

They arrive at Alexandria, and the Grimes clan does its best to fit in. Carol bakes cookies. Rick takes a job as the constable. Daryl joins Aaron in the recruiting forays. It's an uneasy union. The Alexandrians have been behind the town's tall, corrugated steel walls almost since the beginning. They don't really understand how the world works now. They *need* the Grimes clan. But Rick isn't interested in babysitting a bunch of lilies. He is prepared to either make it work, or simply take over the town—whichever shakes out better for him and his people.

CHAPTER 9

THE WALKING DEAD'S GREATEST MOMENT

"WE'VE BEEN PRAYING, TOGETHER. PRAYING THAT GOD WILL SAVE OUR TOWN. WELL, OUR PRAYERS HAVE BEEN ANSWERED. GOD WILL SAVE ALEXANDRIA, BECAUSE GOD HAS GIVEN US THE COURAGE TO SAVE IT OURSELVES."

—FATHER GABRIEL

(SEASON 6, EPISODE 9, "NO WAY OUT")

Season 6 of *The Walking Dead* is essentially two separate stories combined into one. The first tells of the quarry walkers and the plan to get rid of them that goes horribly wrong, bringing Alexandria to the very brink of complete destruction; the second is about the expansion of the world we've been seeing up until now—the introduction of Hilltop, and of Negan and the Saviors. While the second half is a setup for the bloody hell to come down the road, the first half is its own self-contained story, a marvel of storytelling that ends with what I think is the show's greatest moment: the final stand the Alexandrians make against the horde (episode 9, "No Way Out"), when these scared, wounded, scattered people forge a new bond and finally become one unified group. Like Eugene says before going out to the fight, "this is a story people are gonna tell."

Throughout the course of the show, the Grimes clan has grown from a small band to a thriving community living inside an old prison to a small band again, and then, when combined with the survivors in Alexandria, into a large, thriving group. There are two factors driving this transformation: One is the Grimeses' realization that nobody survives on their own very long. "People are the best protection against walkers, or people," Rick tells one prospective survivor he finds in the woods (she doesn't quite make the cut). So there's the drive to bring in numbers as self-preservation. That is a cold rationale, though, and no group would likely survive the inevitable infighting if it were *only* a numbers game. The second driving force is the more lasting one: the bonds of brotherhood. There's a word in ancient Greek, *storge,* which translates loosely to familial love. (It shows up in the Bible in the book of Romans 12:10, when Paul writes, "Be kindly affectioned one to another with brotherly love.") It's the love of family and tight friends. That term isn't ever referenced on the show, but it runs throughout the story of these survivors. This is the new social glue of the post–zombie apocalypse, and it's this *storge* that spurs Rick to go running into the woods to find Sophia (season 2, episode 1, "What Lies Ahead"). Or inspires Merle, Merle of all people, to go and try to kill the Governor on his own (season 3, episode 15, "This Sorrowful Life"). This concept of familial love is at the very center of Maggie's speech in the season 7 finale, "The First Day of the Rest of Your Life," when she talks about how the group has grown "not as strangers, but as family." That's the essence of *storge.* This episode is really the realization of everything we've just been talking about, a melding of *storge, gaman,* faith plus works, and extreme Stoicism. That is what makes this moment the show's greatest.

Before this epic fight, the integration of the Grimes clan into Alexandria had not been smooth, to say the least. They gave up their guns, but Carol stole some back. Rick was attracted to Jessie, and fought with her husband, the hard-drinking, abusive Pete—whom he later kills. Glenn is fighting with the guys who lead scavenging runs, Aiden Monroe and Nicholas. One Alexandrian, Carter, wants to kill Rick before he does any more damage. While some of Rick's people are entranced by Deanna Monroe's plan for Alexandria to become a new flowering of the old world, Rick is just as prepared to take the town by force.

This friction comes to a head when two antagonists descend upon the town. One is that group of walkers. The other is the Wolves, a group of seriously deranged survivors—marked by a bloody *W* cut into their foreheads—who hack and pillage everywhere they go. Their handiwork has been hinted at earlier, when the group came across a completely ransacked town in the ninth episode of season 5, "What Happened and What's Going On."

Rick's plan was to lead the walkers out of the quarry and down a highway, away from town. As he directs a group in this task, the Wolves attack Alexandria, and the noise pulls at least half of the quarry walkers off the road and toward town. No sooner is the attack of the Wolves repulsed than the zombies start arriving, pushing up against Alexandria's corrugated walls. The walls cannot hold, and the town's perfectly laid out and manicured streets are overrun by the undead.

The situation is desperate. People are trapped in their homes.

Nobody can communicate with each other. Rick is in his house with Carl and Judith, Michonne, and Jessie and her two boys, Sam and Ron. Gabriel is there, too. Rick's idea is to cover themselves in guts-drenched tarps—just like he and Glenn did back in Atlanta—make their way out to some cars, and lead the herd away. So off they go. Rick gives Judith to Gabriel, who brings her to the garage that is his makeshift chapel. Back on the street, little Sam can't control himself, and when you think about it, you can't blame him. He's just a kid who has seen the apocalypse, watched his dad get killed, and had to endure Carol's harrowing threat speech. It's too much for him. So Sam cracks, which attracts the walkers. He goes down, and Jessie goes with him. Then *Ron* cracks. He pulls a gun on Rick, whom he blames for pretty much everything (not without reason, really). Michonne guts Ron before he can get off a clean shot, but he does get off a shot, which catches Carl in his right eye.

At this point, everything is falling apart. Rick grabs Carl and runs for the infirmary. Denise is there with Heath and Spencer. Although Denise has been rattled by the very idea of performing medical duties, she steels herself and prepares to take the patient. There is a lot of nervous activity in that room. Rick is understandably overwrought. He stands there, aghast and helpless. He doesn't know what to do, except . . . the light Denise needs in order to operate is attracting walkers outside. They could easily break into the house. If Carl has any chance, any chance at all, that can't happen. So Rick grabs his hatchet, steps outside, and starts braining walkers, by himself. It seems like a suicide mission, as capable as Rick is; there are simply too many. Michonne, though, isn't going to leave him alone. She loves both these men, Carl and Rick, even if this is before she and Rick become a couple. She can't do much for Carl except hold a suture in place, but she can do a lot to help Rick. She kisses Carl's forehead and runs outside to join Rick. Heath and Spencer are moved enough by this to join the fray as well. This is the turning point for the Alexandrians, and for the Grimes clan as well. Not only is this the moment when they come together as one, but after this night, these people will never be afraid of the monsters again. It's a hugely critical moment in the show.

Filming this episode was almost as dramatic as the episode itself, and the marathon shooting session that produced it adds a distinct touch of realism upon second viewing. Ann Mahoney, who played Olivia, walked me through the filming of that sequence.

"Most of us were called at five or five thirty," she said. "We knew what we had ahead of us." Indeed, the plan was aggressive: they were going to film the entire thing on the Alexandria set in one night. It was a huge production. For one thing, virtually every member of the cast was involved. They shot multiple scenes in multiple locations, both inside the homes and out on the streets. There was the special-effects issue of lighting the town's manmade lake on fire. To top it all off, the shoot required about 250 extras to comprise the zombie horde that invades the town.

Everything was done in stages. The scenes inside the houses, when most of the characters are indoors hiding, were shot first. After that, the crew moved outside and shot in increments. "We'd shoot in one part of the street, move ten feet further, then shoot that." At each new spot, the crew would add more blood to the fighters and muddy up their clothes a bit more, so that as the sequence wound on, they looked increasingly caked in the battle.

"If you follow it," she said, "it's beautiful continuity. We literally did twelve hours of jumping, running, and fighting."

Back in the story, it's not clear at first what Rick is doing when he goes outside. Either he sees fighting these walkers as the only thing he can do to help his son, or he is just enraged beyond control and is taking it out on the undead. His emotions seems to suggest both. But his reasons don't really matter. What matters is that the others see what he's doing. For somebody like Michonne or Carol, the choice to fight is easy: if Rick's doing it, they're doing it. For the others, and the Alexandrians especially, the decision is not so simple. But even the meekest are inspired by what they see Rick doing. He almost certainly wasn't trying to inspire his compatriots to fight, yet that is exactly what he does.

Everybody is scattered. Father Gabriel is with Judith and a group of parishioners. Denise was actually outside, with Owen, the one living member of the Wolves whom Morgan captured but didn't kill, and who escaped from the town jail. Rosita, Eugene, Carol, and Morgan are in the row house where the jail is. Olivia and Eric are in a house. Aaron, Heath, and Spencer are in the infirmary. Maggie is trapped, alone, on a lookout tower by the wall. Glenn and Enid are actually just coming back to town. And Daryl, Sasha, and Abraham are somewhere out on the road. They are all scattered and separate, there's no way to even talk about what they might do, if they could. That doesn't matter. Rick's action is signal enough.

"This is it," Heath says. Michonne, Aaron, Heath, and Spencer rush out to join Rick. The five of them stand among the hundreds of zombies, hacking away. There is no turning back, no running. They are in it now. Others see this, peering through their drawn shades. "Knock them away, drive 'em down," Rick says. He sees Olivia and Eric come running out of a home. Eric, incidentally, still has a cast on his foot, but he runs out anyway with nothing more than a small knife. Rick suddenly is not alone. He has a group with him. He has comrades. He has his family. "We can beat 'em!" he yells. They continue hacking their way through the throng. In the small converted chapel, Father Gabriel is holding Judith. He can hear Rick shouting directions outside. Gabriel hands off Judith and picks up a bloody machete.

"Gabriel," Tobin says, "what are you doing?"

"We've been praying, together," Gabriel says. "Praying that God will save our town. Well, our prayers have been answered. God will save Alexandria"—he's almost smiling—"because God has given us the strength to save it ourselves."

Throughout, Mahoney said, the person who kept the group going was Andrew Lincoln. "Andy Lincoln is a real leader," she said, "not only is he a leader as the character, but he leads by example in the cast as well." Lincoln does seemingly crazy things to get himself into character, and when your character is Rick Grimes, you have to do crazy things. I've seen outtakes of him screaming and punching walls, one in which he punched right through the Sheetrock.

Mahoney was filming inside one of the houses, since her character, Olivia, was still hiding, and she watched Lincoln, as Rick, "out in the street, hacking away."

"There wasn't a lot of acting involved," she said. "It was just so inspiring to watch him." At this point, Rick has lost a woman he cared for—he actually cut off her arm—plus her two sons, and his own son was grievously wounded. Yet he's out there, fighting against overwhelming odds with every last ounce of his strength. "He's still fighting, so how can we sit back and let him do that? We have to do this," she said, recounting essentially what was going through her character's mind. That's what prompts the Alexandrians to leave the safety of their homes and join the fray.

Outside, the cast and crew continued to shoot the fight in segments, moving down the street and through town, but essentially in sequence as it ended up in the episode. They shot in the streets, then the actors turned their backs to each other, forming a circle against those hundreds of extras, "and then they were coming in from all sides, and we shot that, and then we shot when we finally started beating them back over the field toward the wall. And then finally," she said, unable to contain a chuckle at the thought of it, "at the very end, we shot the moment where Daryl blows up the lake."

It was, she recalled, a tremendous amount of work to try to fit into one night, and they were constantly pushing to move on and beat their one unmovable deadline: sunrise. Throughout the night, their biggest motivator was Lincoln, she recalled. "There'd be times when Andy would just look at us and say, 'Are we doing this? We're doing this!'"

Elsewhere, Glenn and Enid are back in town and trying to save Maggie, who's trapped atop that guard tower. There's no time for anything more than the most desperate plan. Enid climbs up to Maggie, while Glenn makes as much noise as possible to try to draw off the walkers. It works, though it seems—again—as if Glenn is about to be consumed by the undead. He is saved by a hail of gunfire—Abraham and Sasha stand on top of the wall with high-powered rifles. At this point, you don't even ask how they managed to kill dozens of walkers with a spray of bullets and not hit Glenn even once. You don't ask that, because, one, Glenn is seemingly unkillable (so far), and, two, the tension has been ratcheted up so high at this point, the drama is so intense, you're not even thinking about continuity flaws. "Can you open the gate?" Abraham says, smiling. "Appreciate it, pal."

This is the tide beginning to turn. The entire Grimes clan is back in one place, and the Alexandrians are out in the streets with them as well. There is still the issue of several hundred zombies, though. Daryl comes up with a novel plan. Since they arrived in a gas truck, and since Abraham found a rocket-propelled grenade launcher out on the road, they pour gas into the town's man-made lake and launch a grenade into it. (Now, it probably would've been smarter to save the grenade for another day, and just light the lake with a Bic or something, but that's a quibble. Also, it's less dramatic.) The lake bursts into flames, which attracts the attention of the lamebrains. They slowly, stupidly, start walking into the lake, into the fire. But not all of them. Now everybody is hacking away at the undead, slashing and stabbing and braining, one after another after another. "Don't let up!" Rick screams. As Bear McCreary's soundtrack builds to a crescendo, we see a series of increasingly fast cuts of all of them: Glenn braining a walker; Morgan swinging that long staff of his; Daryl slashing with a knife; Maggie, Sasha, and even Eugene are there; Father Gabriel is hacking with his machete, and now it's getting faster. There is a cacophony of yelling and grunting, stabbing and slashing.

It was a lot of work, and the cast and crew were tired, Mahoney said, but despite that, nobody's enthusiasm flagged. "We'd stop, we would joke around, we would pump each other up," she said, "everybody just kept in really good spirits.

"Just like in the scene," Mahoney said, "between all of us actors we felt like a team, we had to bring the drama and momentum to this. It was a great night." They filmed until the sun came up, and that scene of all of them on the front porch looking filthy and exhausted was the last thing they shot that long night. The dirt and the blood were fake, but the exhaustion was real. "It was just a beautiful bonding moment," Mahoney said. "As we wrapped that morning, you could feel the euphoria in the group. We knew we had accomplished something."

Mahoney herself didn't get to see the final cut of the episode until the night it aired. Filming it piece by piece gives you a different perspective than seeing it put together. On the set, she said, you carry the momentum with you as you play the role, but you don't see the momentum building the way it does in the finished product. When she sat down to watch it that Sunday night, she said, "I was cheering."

Mahoney acknowledged ruefully her one disappointment about this night: apart from one shot where Olivia comes running out of the house, you don't really see her in the fight. Her shots ended up on the cutting room floor, as they say in the business. "I slashed a lot of zombies," she said, "and you didn't get to see a lot of it." She also defended the Alexandrians, who before this episode had not shown a lot of fighting spirit, against complaints from viewers. "Well, this would be you guys in the apocalypse; none of you are Daryl, none of you are Rick." The Alexandrians were also, she noted, the first group the Grimes clan meets that isn't either duplicitous or outright murderous. They're a good group that wants to do good, and when they are finally pushed, in this one epic night, they don't shrink from the challenge.

"The Alexandrian people are nothing to sneeze at."

The point comes together in the final frames, which is cut so fast it's impossible to tell who's who (unless, like an obsessive, you sit there and start and stop the video enough times to pick out everybody, which I did one night). It's just so many slashing, waving arms, coming so rapidly. It's not like a lot of different people, but one singular body. That's what they are now, all of them. One. They are one great, powerful, fighting wonder of the zombie world. They have taken back control. It has been a long time coming, for both the Grimes clan and the Alexandrians. And whether you think God is dead or alive, this moment of triumph works. They have found the strength within themselves to rise up, to fight for themselves, and together they have found a new, collective strength they didn't have before.

It doesn't mean all their problems are over. Far, far, *far* from it. Even as this challenge is met, there is a larger one, more deadly, on the horizon: the Saviors and Negan.

CHAPTER 10

FOUR WALLS AND A ROOF IN CHARLOTTE, NC

"ANYTHING IS POSSIBLE UNTIL YOUR HEART STOPS BEATING."

—FATHER GABRIEL

(SEASON 7, EPISODE 12, "SAY YES")

"Let's go see Jesus!" the young girl said to her father. They were two people amid hundreds congregated on a Sunday in a cavernous building in Charlotte, North Carolina. On almost any other Sunday, in any other large building down in the Bible Belt, amid a congregation of the faithful, the Jesus in question would be the Lord and Savior of the Christian people. On this day, the girl was not talking about Jesus of Nazareth, however, but Jesus of Hilltop. More precisely, she was talking about Tom Payne, the actor who plays the character Paul Rovia, who, with his long, dark hair and thick beard, is nicknamed Jesus.

To understand the popularity of *The Walking Dead* it's not

enough to just watch the show on Sunday nights, even with a Twitter feed open. If you want to understand why people are so passionate about this zombie show, how it's more than just some well-done jump scares and slick special effects, you need to actually meet the fans face-to-face. You need to go to a Walker Stalker Con.

In Charlotte, the Park Expo and Conference Center sits just a few miles outside the built-up, busy uptown, but it feels much farther. The city's center is full of cranes and new construction; new hotels; office towers; the modern, and fast-looking, NASCAR Hall of Fame; and a mall-like pavilion called the Epicentre, full of restaurants, a movie theater, a bowling alley, and the like. "The Park," as the expo center is called, sits in a quiet part of Charlotte, off the highway and between a Montessori school and a small coliseum. It doesn't boast any fancy architecture or bright lights. The week before, there'd been a gun and knife show. In January, there was an RV show. The Charlotte Fire Department administered its entrance exam there. The inside is essentially just exposed girders and cement walls. Maggie Rhee would probably call it just four walls and a roof.

The Walker Stalker conventions started in 2013, when two fans of the show, Nashville music executive Eric Nordhoff and his neighbor James Frazier, organized a fan convention in Atlanta. It was a surprising and immediate success, and they quickly capitalized on it. Now there are half a dozen each year, held all over the country, overseas (London), and even *on* the seas (really, there's a Walker Stalker cruise). They have grown in size and scope, but many, including the one I went to in Charlotte in December 2016, have a coziness to them. Some of the other conventions are larger and get more of the top names—virtually everybody from the show was at Walker Stalker Atlanta, for instance, which author Jay Bonansinga described as being like the "Super Bowl."

But these aren't like other conventions: they are not designed so much to sell you stuff (though there is that going on, too) or to be a marketing vehicle for some new show. The Walker Stalker conventions are more narrowly focused: they are held in order to bring together the people who make the show and the people who watch it.

It is an almost stunningly successful formula.

Saturday was gray and damp in Charlotte, cold enough that the clouds unloaded a steady stream of alternating snow and rain. The convention center is utilitarian-looking to begin with, and the lousy weather didn't make it any more attractive. The only clue outside the building about what was happening inside was a big inflatable archway with WALKER STALKER written in huge white letters against a red background surrounded by Kirkman-comic zombies. Despite the weather and the nominally ominous zombies, the crowd was in exceptionally good spirits. And why wouldn't they be? They were all about to meet their heroes. Or, to be more precise, their heroes had come to meet *them*.

Unlike Atlanta, Walker Stalker Charlotte didn't bill the top names like Lincoln, Reedus, Gurira, and McBride. But it did have a lot of actors from the show—both current and recently departed—and the convention had already gotten big enough to attract actors from other shows: R. J. Mitte and Giancarlo Esposito from *Breaking Bad*; several of the actors from SyFy's *Z Nation,* like Keith Allan and Russell Hodgkinson; Kane Hodder, who played Jason in several of the *Friday the 13th* movies; and, randomly enough, Zach Galligan from *Gremlins*.

The convention floor was broken up into three long aisles: one for actor booths and two for merchandise. The actors' aisle began with Michael Cudlitz on one end and ended with Chandler Riggs on the other, which were consistently the two most crowded booths. Other actors there whose characters are currently alive were Josh McDermitt (Eugene), Christian Serratos (Rosita), Alanna Masterson (Tara), Seth Gilliam (Father Gabriel), Khary Payton (Ezekiel), Tom Payne (Paul "Jesus" Rovia), Ross Marquand (Aaron), Xander Berkeley (Gregory), and Austin Amelio (Dwight).

Apart from that basic layout, the floor was randomly arranged. There were a few large exhibits, scenes set up for fans to step into and take pictures. The most elaborate one, without a doubt, belonged to "Cecil Grimes," an Andrew Lincoln look-alike. Cecil's booth certainly wins the prize for tallest exhibit: a mini-recreation of the West Georgia Correctional Facility, with a guard tower probably fifteen feet high—that had a Glenn Rhee mannequin in it. Below that was a chain-link fence and a small prison yard, where Cecil, dressed as a King County sheriff's deputy, posed for pictures. He had a scruffy-looking guy in dark glasses with him, who pulled off a good-enough Daryl Dixon. Cecil had a line outside his set of people waiting to pay $25 for a picture with him, $30 for a "bro-mance package" that included Cecil and Daryl, or $45 for the convention special, which included an autographed photo and some other merchandise.

Elsewhere, Robert Bean, a tall, thin man with a mustache and Vandyke goatee, had set up his "Tactical Field Response Team"—an SUV loaded for the apocalypse. Inside were gas masks, shotguns, automatic rifles, clips, shells, hatchets, blankets. And more clips. Lots of clips. He had an arsenal outside, too, an entire shelf of various handguns, rifles, machetes, and swords. The guns are all modified air rifles, and for a price, you can pose in front of the SUV with some really deadly looking weaponry and a couple of zombie mannequins. Yet another vendor was selling *real* katanas. He had a variety of them, including AMC-branded ones for $250. For another $100, he'd sharpen it for you, too.

As Saturday morning climbed toward noon, the crowd and lines started growing. In front of each actor's booth was a queue with aluminum rails for the long lines, but many lines were out past these rails and onto the main causeway. There were a lot of families here, parents with their kids: One little girl was dressed as Addy Miller's pajama zombie from the premiere's open, with full-on zombie makeup and a teddy bear. She positively went running for Miller's booth, leaving her mother behind, the excitement visible.

The vendors there were mainly doing something related to the show, or at least the horror genre. One booth was giving people zombie makeovers, for instance. The actor Eugene Clark, who played the zombie "Big Daddy" in Romero's *Land of the Dead,* had his own booth set up, selling merchandise. There were lots of T-shirt vendors and clothing and jewelry sellers. There were several artists, too. One of them, Rob Prior, had a double booth, and was putting on a show. He was painting a picture of Jesus—*The Walking Dead*'s Jesus—with a paintbrush in each hand, moving fast while listening to some hard-rock song. It was a very good painting. The Charlotte Area Paranormal Society (CAPS) had a booth. Skybound, Robert Kirkman's media company, had a booth, selling Lucille bats, key chains, and baseball caps with a wavy *D* on them, a reproduction of the hat worn by the character Clementine in the video game. And comics, of course. Lots of comics.

One of the more unusual aspects of Walker Stalker Con is that it is not just about actors on the show *now;* actors whose characters have died have a complete second life here. Michael Cudlitz, who played Abraham Ford, obviously has a big following. The line in front of his booth snaked through the aluminum tubes used to form aisles, out onto the floor, and over to an overflow area, where it folded back on itself half a dozen times. But he wasn't the only popular actor there. Scott Wilson, Chad Coleman, Michael Rooker, IronE Singleton, and Lawrence Gilliard Jr. (Bob Stookey) all had crowded booths for both days of the convention. Even actors who had only small roles on the show—those who appeared only in zombie makeup, and are completely unrecognizable in the flesh—have dedicated fans at these conventions.

The actors aren't just phoning it in, either. Depending on how busy or slow it is, they may spend anywhere from thirty seconds to several minutes talking to fans, but they greet every single one enthusiastically. They give everybody a hug or a fist bump. They exchange chitchat. They answer questions. They share backstage stories. I know that these are actors, of course, but none of it seemed forced.

One teenager I talked to was Abby Johnson, a sixteen-year-old from Statesville, North Carolina. She walked away from Chandler Riggs's booth, her elation obvious. She had never met a celebrity before. She was shaking, and buried her head in her father's shoulder. "He followed his dreams," she said. "It inspired me to follow mine." I thought at first she was talking about Carl, the character, which didn't make much sense to me because Carl is not really right in the head most of the time, but I learned she meant Riggs, the actor.

By midday Saturday, the crowds had slowed a bit. People were off getting lunch, actors and fans included. But there was Kyla Kenedy, who played Mika, still at her booth, talking to a father and son, who were the only ones there. The son was severely physically handicapped and in a wheelchair, but he was alert and engaged, and was enjoying the chance to speak with one of the show's stars. Kyla for her part seemed completely happy to talk, and in no rush at all. Without anybody else around, the three just sat there for some time, talking. I tried to imagine how much harder it must have been for that father to bring his son here than for all the other parents whose children weren't handicapped, and wondered what they hoped to get out of it. Just some entertainment, or something deeper?

On Sunday, the crowds were about the same size as on Saturday. One young woman, Brittney Taylor, a twenty-three-year-old from Raleigh, was dressed as Michonne, with extensions on her own real dreadlocks to perfect the look. She was with three friends, and they had seen a few of the actors, like Tom Payne, Chad Coleman, and Michael Cudlitz. What she likes about the show, she said, are the "real life lessons" it teaches, and I wasn't sure at first what she meant. Real, life lessons, or real-life lessons? It can't really be the latter, as we do not (yet) live in a world where we must combat zombies daily to stay alive, but it did sound that way. Of course, she meant the former. Sure, these characters are fighting fictitious ghouls, but in their travails, they show personal growth and endurance, she said. Michonne, for instance, lost everything in her life (indeed, we didn't know until season 4, when Michonne is hastily forced to hold baby Judith—and reacts painfully to that—that she had a child), and must find a way to cope and rebuild herself as a person. That's what attracts Brittney to the show.

Her friend Debra Ulmer liked a different aspect of *The Walking Dead*. "These people are forced to work with people they wouldn't normally be around," she said, pointing especially to the initial conflict on the roof between Merle and T-Dog. Merle is a violent racist and hates T-Dog because of his skin color. They fight, the Dixon brother gleefully pounding T-Dog. It's Rick

Grimes who intervenes and lays down the new rules of the world. It takes Merle a few seasons to get that message, but he does. Eventually. But it's something Debra picked up on and that keeps her invested in the show. Because who doesn't want to see that same thing in the real world?

Another thing about this convention is that you have a very good chance of bumping into one of the actors. I was interviewing another fan, Ron Rosaly; his daughter, Lex; and his granddaughter, Harley. We were standing by the live stage, and the actor R. J. Mitte walked by, on his way to his panel session. He was running a few minutes late, but still took the time to stop and talk to us.

Being here, Lex said, puts the average fan on the same level as the actors. "They're not on a pedestal. They're humanized."

A few minutes later, I was standing in line for a root beer, next to a woman whose boyfriend was at the counter ordering. Tom Payne walked by us. The woman next to me stood frozen, a big smile creeping across her face. "I'm trying to control my face," she said. She was failing. You see this a lot. The actors end up walking through the hall and simply have no choice but to be among the fans—not that it seems like any of them would do otherwise anyhow. There is a real and genuine appreciation of the fans at this convention. At other conventions, where the whole goal is to publicize whatever it is you're promoting, media are a big deal. Not here. The media are allowed, but not elevated. The fans, however, *are* elevated. The great Joe DiMaggio was once asked about why, in a meaningless game in 1951, he hustled on a meaningless play. "There is always some kid who may be seeing me for the first time," DiMaggio said. "I owe him my best." I was reminded of that quote watching these actors meet and greet these fans.

There were two things I did to try to get a feeling for the fan experience. The first was to wait in a line to meet an actor (with my press credentials, I could have gone into a VIP line, but I didn't want to do that). Some of the actors would do a meet-and-greet, where you could just say hi and talk to them for a minute or so without buying an autograph or picture. Josh McDermitt, whom I'd met once before and interviewed, was doing the meet-and-greets, so I stood in his line. The people in the line were friendly, happy, excited to be there, talkative with each other. There was absolutely no pushing or shoving or jockeying or anything. People who'd never met talked and shared details of their lives. While I waited, I noticed McDermitt talking to a family with two teenage boys. In just that brief moment he got all the broad brushstrokes of the family; one of the boys was sixteen, and apparently struggling a bit with it. "The longest year," McDermitt said knowingly. "Good luck."

I ventured some more. For about an hour, I was a fly on the wall at IronE Singleton's booth. I'd asked if I could stand off to the side and just watch one of the actors and the fans. I didn't take notes, didn't take pictures, didn't interview any of the fans afterward. I wanted to get a true sense of the dynamic between fan and actor.

Singleton is one of the more interesting cast members. He was raised in Perry Homes, one of the most notorious housing projects in Atlanta. He never knew his father. Together with his brother and alcoholic, abusive mother, he lived with his grandparents and extended family in one home. Grinding poverty and violence were his daily reality. By the time he was eighteen, his mother was dead. He could have easily become a statistic, but through sheer determination, he got out of the projects and found success in the entertainment industry. It's a story he tells often and openly, using his life itself as an object lesson. The story resonates; people gravitate to him.

"People tell me the most intimate things," Singleton told me while I stood there. He thinks it has to do with the fact that he's so open about his own life. That's almost certainly true. A stream of very different people came to see him: some black, some white, girls, boys, locals, a couple from England. He treated all of them warmly. Two young white girls who were in school told him they wanted to go into theater; he talked to them about it, about the importance of putting in the time it takes to master the craft, and keeping up their grades. The couple from England apparently had met him before, and there was the warmth of old friends running into each other again. They expected to see him in England when Walker Stalker goes to London. Every single person told him that they wish T-Dog were still on the show.

Sunday afternoon. The last major interview on the main stage was with Michael Rooker, who had a large crowd. His character, Merle, was one of the most, well, unique on the show, and Rooker, a veteran character actor, was alone among the cast in being generally recognizable (at least in the States) when the series began. Rooker took a few questions from the moderator, a few from the fans, and then grabbed the microphone, hopped off the stage, and started working the crowd on his own. He flirted with the girls. He played friendly with the guys. From the audience came questions about Merle, questions about his marital status, questions about his next projects. He approached one boy, whom I couldn't quite see, and angled the microphone down to him.

"What is the meaning of life?" The question was unusual enough that I looked to see who had asked it. It was the boy in the wheelchair I'd seen the day before talking to Kyla Kenedy. *What is the meaning of life?* That question, coming from anybody else would have been just rhetorical. Coming from that boy, it wasn't. He had come all this way, endured whatever discomforts traveling brought, had this one chance to ask a meaningful question, and it was this one. A perfectly suitable question to ask. Now, the greatest minds in human history have grappled with that question. Hell, we all have. It's an eternal, unanswerable question, and it wasn't exactly fair to expect Rooker to be able to answer it off the top of his head. He took it seriously, though, and gave it a shot. "The meaning of life is to live," he said, "and to enjoy every single second." Not a bad answer, really. It may seem odd to think that a show literally about the death of mankind ends up answering questions about the meaning of life, but it does. Or at least it tries to. "We do what we need to do, and then we get to live," Rick Grimes says in the show, and while it was under far different circumstances, that's about as good an answer as you're likely to ever get. It's not comforting, but it's not some lying fable, either.

It was getting late and the convention was winding down. A lot of the talent was still there, though. Scott Wilson, IronE Singleton, Josh McDermitt, Michael Cudlitz, Lawrence Gilliard Jr., John C. Lynch (Eastman), Michael Traynor (Nicholas), Jason Douglas (Tobin), the *Z Nation* cast, Chad Coleman, Addy Miller, and others were still meeting fans. McDermitt hugged a group of girls, who all walked away smiling. Wilson high-fived a little girl. R. J. Mitte stood at his booth chatting with fans in the style of people meeting at a bar. A Charlotte cop stood chatting with Kane Hodder.

Romero was 100 percent wrong about this show when he said it was just a soap opera with zombies. I watched all these fans, and the actors talking to them, sharing things with them, engaging them and laughing with them and offering them encouragement in their own lives, and I realized that the key to understanding the show's success is this: In watching the weekly struggles, people draw hope that they can cope with whatever problems they have in their own lives. That there is a future. For one weekend, the four walls and a roof of the Park Expo and Conference Center were transformed into a kind of church of *The Walking Dead*.

By four thirty, the Con's volunteer staff were getting their chance to meet the actors. There were still a few fans around, but the lines were almost completely full of the volunteers in their maroon shirts. They had worked all weekend for this moment. The actors knew it, too, and a lot of them hung around. McDermitt, Berkeley, Singleton, Gilliard, Lynch, Payton, Mitte. Cudlitz had a huge line waiting for him. Other volunteers were breaking down the piping, taking down banners and drapes, carting off boxes of unsold merchandise. But these actors were acting (no pun intended) like they had all night. The volunteers were eating it up. There was almost nobody left here to see this, which is really too bad. These Hollywood-star types were absolutely off the clock now. They were doing this solely because they appreciated the effort that these volunteers, who after all are also fans of the show, put in.

Five P.M. The show was officially over, yet the actors were still there. Five oh five. Five fifteen. I saw Cudlitz's handlers trying to get him to wrap things up, but he ignored them. A forklift passed by, and the sounds of hollow aluminum pipes banging around echoed through the hall. It was now down to Cudlitz, McDermitt, and Berkeley for last actor standing. At 5:20 Cudlitz was finally dragged away. A few minutes later, McDermitt, too, left, and I caught up to him as he walked across the empty floor.

"Me and Cudlitz are usually the first ones here and the last to leave," he told me. He understands the fans, he said, because before he got the role of Eugene Porter, he was one of them, and he appreciates all the work that the volunteers put in over the weekend. "I was a fan of the show, too. I get it. We're blessed to be here."

I looked back and noticed that Berkeley was still talking to volunteers, meaning that McDermitt wasn't actually the last to leave. "I don't know why Xander is still there," he admitted, deadpan. "That pisses me off." It's a badge of honor to him to be last.

It's a badge he doesn't win this time. Xander Berkeley is the last cast member to leave the floor.

WEAPONS

"WEAPON CHOICE IS ALSO CHARACTER CHOICE," KERRY Cahill has said, and it's true. The characters on *The Walking Dead* and *Fear the Walking Dead* will use absolutely anything they can get their hands on—a piece of driftwood, a cane, a screwdriver, a shovel. Sometimes the weapon *is* their hands, like when Nick Clark gouges a walker's eyes out with his thumbs, jamming them all the way into his brain (which looks as nasty as it sounds). Ideally, though, these characters have actual weapons.

What these characters use to defend themselves are in many ways extensions of themselves. Can you really imagine anybody else using Rick's Colt, for instance? Sometimes characters lose their weapons, and it's as if they have been defanged; when the weapons are returned, it's like Samson getting his hair back. Michonne finds her katana among the gear that Gareth was carrying with him. Carol finds Daryl's crossbow. Daryl swipes Rick's Colt from the Sanctuary and returns it to him, and that's like Rick being restored to, well, Rick. He's ready to fight again. Weapon choice is indeed character choice.

Let's look at some of the most iconic weapons on *The Walking Dead*. For background on these weapons, I'm indebted to both the Internet Movie Firearms Database website and the Walking Dead Wiki site.

COLT PYTHON .357 MAGNUM. Rick Grimes is the A-1 alpha male of the post–zombie apocalypse, and his revolver screams it. The .357 Colt Python is not the most powerful handgun ever made—that title belongs to the Smith & Wesson .500 Magnum—but it is powerful enough, and more than that, it is a visually distinctive handgun made by the same company that made the iconic Peacemaker, "the gun that won the west." The one Rick uses has a six-inch barrel and a nickel finish, and that size and the glint of the nickel make it stand out. This is a loud, powerful handgun, and the person who wields it needs to be powerful as well. It's also a classic-looking, beautiful gun, and a revolver, too. This is an old-time gun, for an old-time lawman. The Python is the perfect weapon to illustrate that.

It makes some sense, too, that a cop would use this gun as his service revolver—some police departments did issue it—as opposed to the Smith & Wesson, which is really just too big for a day job. More than that bit of realism, though, Rick's Colt Python is big and bad and just looks plain intimidating. It isn't as outrageous a phallic symbol as the gigantic sword Toshiro Mifune's Kikuchiyo carried in the Akira Kurosawa classic *Seven Samurai,* but it is at least as intimidating as Harry Callahan's .44 Magnum in the *Dirty Harry* movies, and the point is made whenever Rick whips it out. This is not a man to be messed with.

If you still have any doubt, just try to imagine Rick's weapon of choice being some random Glock, or anything else. It just wouldn't be the same, would it?

HORTON SCOUT HD 125 AND STRYKER STRYKEZONE 380. The Horton Scout used by Daryl Dixon in seasons 1 and 2, replaced by the Stryker in season 3, says everything you need to know about him. "See, a man with a rifle, he could've been some kind of photographer, soccer coach back in the day," says Joe, the leader of the Claimers (season 4, episode 13, "Alone"), a gang that finds Daryl on the road. "But a bowman's a bowman, through and through." Daryl Dixon isn't just any survivor. The bow is an ancient weapon, and his skill with it exemplifies all of Daryl's primeval survival skills. Those skills may have been near useless in the old world, where survival was guaranteed by myriad modern conveniences, but when it all went to shit, as they say, everything about Daryl Dixon became paramount, a point that is emphasized every time he launches a bolt. (Don't call them arrows, they're bolts!) Anybody can learn to fire a rifle. But a bowman is a different breed.

Now, one of the downsides of both handguns and crossbows, especially in the wake of a societal collapse, is ammunition. The show does an admirable job of clearly showing how Daryl will fire off several bolts and then recover them later. But even the best-stocked group of survivalists can find themselves low on ammo. That's when the following weapons show their superiority.

HAMMER. There's nothing special about a hammer. It's an extremely blunt instrument. But in the hands of Tyreese, it becomes a symbol of sheer physical power. Think about the scene in "Isolation" (season 4, episode 3) when Tyreese takes on a herd of walkers armed with nothing but that hammer. It's a big hammer—it looks like a twenty-eight-inch framing one—but still. A man who can physically brain zombies armed with nothing but a hammer? That is a blunt force for the ages. Tyreese, as is made clear in other episodes, isn't very good with a gun, but he's deadly with this. The irony is that despite all his power, using it is traumatic to him and goes against who he is as a person. The friction eventually becomes unbearable for him. The hammer even reflects the two sides of Tyreese. After all, a hammer can be a weapon of destruction, or it can be a tool used to build.

BASEBALL BAT WRAPPED IN BARBED WIRE. Lucille is thirsty. Lucille is hungry. Lucille is a stickler for the rules. Of all the weapons on *The Walking Dead,* none gets anthropomorphized as much as Lucille, the barbed-wire-wrapped baseball bat carried by Negan. No other weapon acts as such an obvious totem of its user's power, either. Negan talks about the bat as if it is the one making the decisions.

Of all these characters, none gets so much pleasure out of using their weapon of choice as Negan does his bat, and there is something nearly pornographic in his gleeful violence. Of course, that's half the point. Negan is putting on a show, and the bat is part of that. Much like Rick's Colt, Negan's bat is physically intimidating, especially with that barbed wire wrapped around it. It's a big, visual weapon, which is perfect for a showman like Negan. B.B. King's guitar was famously named Lucille, and of course the baseball bat is a critical piece of equipment in America's national pastime. It makes sense that Negan's weapon would be something from a game, since he seems to treat everything like a game. Even the barbed wire is for theatrical effect—after all, the blows from the bat alone should be enough to kill you. The wire just shreds skin and creates a bigger mess, a further intimidation to anybody forced to watch these ritual murders.

When Negan hands the bat to Rick to hold for him (season 7, episode 4, "Service"), and later to Carl, too, you can almost feel the transfer of power. Negan understands what the bat represents. He puts it in his enemies' hands not for convenience's sake but as a direct challenge to their own power. *You can have my power,* he's saying, *if you've got the stones to use it.*

BO STAFF. Morgan Jones's bo staff is just, like, a big stick. But the staff says everything about what Morgan has become in this world. It's one of the few weapons in the show's entire run, in fact, that essentially gets its own backstory. After leaving Rick's hometown in Kentucky—and after leaving most of his senses even earlier—Morgan wanders the countryside in a quite insane state of mind (season 6, episode 4, "Here's Not Here"). He eventually comes across a man named Eastman, played by the great character actor John Carroll Lynch, who takes him in, tames his insanity, and gives him a new guiding philosophy: aikido, which teaches him new ways to fight and live in this world. This not only is important for Morgan—it does, after all, restore him to some measure of sanity—but his newly acquired pacifism becomes an important plot point in several episodes down the road. Morgan's ability to use his bo staff with such precision shows that he has the power to kill, even though he refuses to use it.

The bo staff that Morgan carries with him is not widely used by aikido practitioners these days. They use a shorter staff called a jo. Still, in the post–zombie apocalypse, it helps to carry a big stick, even if you don't want to hurt anybody.

KATANA. Michonne's katana sword is, in my estimation, the single best weapon on *The Walking Dead.* It's lethal, it will never run out of ammo, it's long enough to use before a zombie gets too close, and in the right hands, it can cleave a head in two or cut it clean off in a single swing. The katana, too, is the perfect weapon for Michonne. It represents everything that she is: fast and lethal, sharp and deadly. The sword itself represents both grace, in its long, curved blade, and power, in its extra-long grip, which allows the user to hold it with both hands. Indeed, Michonne is not unlike the samurai warriors who first used these weapons, a virtually unkillable fighter who also adheres to a complicated moral and personal code. Like the bow, the sword is a weapon whose roots go deep into human history, five thousand years or more. So there is something mythic about Michonne's use of hers, and indeed, when we meet her, covered in a robe and hood, leading two defanged walkers on chains, she appears entirely mythic. If I had to place a bet on one single character to outlive everybody else on this show, I'd bet on Michonne and her katana.

RECAP

SEASON SIX

- **SAFE HAVEN:** Alexandria Safe Zone
- **SURVIVORS LOST:** Carter, Nicholas, Jessie, Ron, Sam, Deanna Monroe, Denise, Eastman
- **ANTAGONISTS KILLED:** The Wolves; many, many "Negans." But not Negan.
- **NOTABLE WALKERS:** Deanna Monroe
- **ZOMBIE HERD:** Quarry herd

RICK AND MORGAN DISCOVER A LARGE QUARRY A FEW miles away from town, filled with hundreds of walkers. The more that stumble in there, the louder it gets, which attracts even more. It's like a magnet for the undead, which is why Alexandria has been relatively zombie free. But it won't last. The roads out of the quarry are blocked by eighteen-wheelers, but the roads are crumbling. Eventually the walkers will get out, and probably find Alexandria. Rick's plan is to lead them out and march them far off, twenty miles away from town. In the beginning, it works. Daryl on his bike, and Abraham and Sasha in a car, lead the herd down a road. The others act as wranglers, keeping the undead from straying. Then, something unexpected happens. Far off, from the direction of Alexandria, an air horn goes off. The walkers are drawn to the sound of it, far too many for the small band of wranglers to handle, and they start shambling toward Alexandria. The plan is unraveling.

Shortly before, back at Alexandria, all is quiet. Carol bakes a casserole while watching Mrs. Neudermeyer outside smoking a cigarette. Suddenly, a man comes running up and slashes Mrs. Neudermeyer with a machete. Without any warning at all, Alexandria is under attack by the Wolves, the homicidal band with a very disturbed philosophy about the new world. They run through town armed with knives and machetes, hacking to pieces anybody they can find. Most of Alexandria's fighting strength is off with Rick. Carol, Morgan, Maggie, Carl, and a few others mount a defense. But it's Carol who is the toughest, who by now knows exactly how to snap into action. One attacker barrels toward the town gate in a truck. Spencer Monroe, in the guard tower, shoots him dead before he arrives. He crashes into the wall, setting off the truck's air horn—the one that will attract the quarry herd. Now everything is a complete mess. The Wolves are hell-bent on murdering every living person in town. Carol kills one, and disguises herself as one of them. Coolly, she weaves in and out, killing them as mercilessly as they are killing. Morgan, meanwhile, will defend himself with his staff, but won't attack. Eventually, they drive off the invaders.

Out in the woods, Rick and the crew are trying to create new diversions for the walkers that peeled off from the main group. They try desperately in one nearby town to come up with something, to no avail. There are too many. Glenn and Nicholas want to set fire to a feed store, only to find it already burned. They are out in the street, surrounded by the dead. The sounds of gunfire from Alexandria can already be heard. They run into an alley only to find a fence. They are trapped, with dozens of walkers filling in behind them. They climb atop a Dumpster, but it's hopeless. Nicholas shoots himself in the head, and falling, drags Glenn down onto the ground with him. The walkers feast on Nicholas's body, while Glenn somehow manages to drag himself under the Dumpster without any walkers noticing him.

Rick gets back to Alexandria ahead of the herd, but just barely. Now they are trapped. There are hundreds of the undead outside the walls. Farther away Daryl, Sasha, and Abraham lead the zombies away, and then have their own troubles getting back. At one point, Daryl runs into three strangers, Dwight, Sherry, and

Tina, all on the run from the Saviors. They rob Daryl, who later reconnects with Sasha and Abraham. On the way back to Alexandria, they will have the first encounter with a group led by a man named Negan.

Inside the walls, the situation looks grim. The Alexandrians have never faced anything like this, and many are hopeless. They are even more despondent when the walkers overwhelm a wall, rupturing the town's only defense. They pour through, the deadliest of day-trippers. Everybody is forced to run and hide. Now people are actually trapped inside their houses. Deanna gets caught up in a fight, and is bitten by a walker. Rick takes her to Jessie's house, where others are also hiding. Rick wants to take Carl, Judith, Michonne, Gabriel, Jessie, Ron, and Sam out by wearing bedsheets covered in zombie guts. Deanna can't run with them. She sends them off, and waits for the inevitable. When walkers enter the house, she decides instead to go out in a proverbial blaze of glory, opening fire and screaming wildly. All things considered, it's a pretty good way to go.

Rick sends Gabriel off with Judith, and leads the others away. The plan is initially successful. They all get out, and are moving silently among the dead. It falters, though, when little Sam freaks out. The noise attracts the dead, who attack him. Jessie loses it and is also attacked. Ron loses it and takes a shot at Rick, missing and hitting Carl in the eye instead. Rick rushes his son to the infirmary and then goes back outside to single-handedly clear out the herd. He is soon joined by Michonne, and then everybody. The entire town finds its strength, comes together, and fights off the herd in an epic battle.

Months later, the town is being rebuilt and restocked. Carl is healing. Life is getting back to normal. Rick and Daryl go on a supply run. While out there, they come across a pesky newcomer. He robs them, so they track him down and capture him. But they don't kill him. Turns out this stranger, named Paul "Jesus" Rovia, comes from another community, called Hilltop. Brought back to Alexandria, he explains everything to the townspeople, and says that he was also looking for supplies and trading partners. Curious, a group goes with him to Hilltop. It's a thriving community with tall walls, old FEMA shelters, and in the center a grand antebellum mansion, Barrington House. Gregory is the man in charge here, a man who is not particularly brave and is particularly vain. He is more than willing to cut a deal to save himself, and that's essentially what he's done with the Saviors. But it's a bad deal, and getting worse. Rick and his crew agree to kill the Saviors in exchange for supplies. They find an outpost, and murder everybody in it, probably more than two dozen people. What they don't know, however, is that they did not kill Negan. Or the whole group. They hit only one outpost. Soon they will be brought face-to-face with the full power of what they've put themselves up against.

Daryl, Denise, and Rosita go on a supply run for medicine. Abraham and Eugene go to a spot that Eugene thinks he can turn into a bullet-making shop. Carol slips out of town, too distraught at all the killing. The first group tragically runs into Dwight and a contingent of Saviors. Denise is killed by a bolt from Daryl's crossbow, fired by Dwight. Daryl and Rosita fight off the Saviors with help from Eugene and Abraham, and return to town. Daryl has vengeance on his mind, and goes back to find Dwight. Glenn, Michonne, and Rosita follow him, hoping to bring him back. They will all be captured by the Saviors. Carol also encounters Saviors, whom she wipes out. Rick and Morgan go looking for Carol, then Rick turns back and Morgan goes on. Back in Alexandria, Maggie is having complications from her pregnancy, and the decision is made to try to get her to Hilltop, which has a proper doctor, medical facilities, and medicine.

They find several roads blocked by the Saviors. The group is toying with the Grimes clan, redirecting them, terrifying them. Eventually, they try splitting off, creating their own diversion. Eugene drives off in the truck, and the rest try to literally carry Maggie to Hilltop. It doesn't work. It's nightfall, and they are all—Rick, Michonne, Carl, Abraham, Sasha, Eugene, Aaron, Daryl, Rosita, Maggie, and Glenn—captured by the Saviors, who herd them into a clearing in the woods. There are dozens of Saviors, maybe a hundred. The group is far, far more powerful, well equipped, and capable than Rick or anybody else realized. Then their leader emerges. Negan. He's the king of the apocalypse. He struts and gloats over them, carrying that baseball bat wrapped in barbed wire. "It's gonna be pee-pee pants city real soon," he says, smiling. Negan almost always smiles. He balances theatrics with brutality, and clearly enjoys the fantastic pain he metes out. One of them, he explains, must die, punishment for the attack on his outpost. After that, they will work for him, under the same terms as all his other minions: half of everything goes to him (and he determines what constitutes half). He plays a game of "eenie, meenie, miney, mo" to select the sacrificial lamb. He brings the bat crashing down on a head—we do not see whose it is. "Taking it like a champ!" Negan crows triumphantly, raining down more blows.

The screen goes black.

CHAPTER 11

DISSECTION

"I GOTTA GO. GOOD LUCK, DUMBASS."

—GLENN RHEE

(SEASON 6, EPISODE 3, "THANK YOU")

In the season 6 episode cited above, Glenn Rhee stands on top of a Dumpster at the back end of an alley, with no escape except for the way he came in. That route is blocked by dozens, maybe a hundred of the undead. He is out of bullets. His only companion is Nicholas, a man who once tried to kill him, a man who has barely been able to survive in the post–zombie apocalypse world, and a man who at this exact moment has given up on the possibility of surviving even one more minute.

A series of unfortunate, unforeseeable developments led Glenn to that Dumpster. The Wolves attacked Alexandria at the same time that the walkers were being led out of the quarry. Rick's plan is wrecked, and Glenn is trying to redirect the walkers away from home. He and Nicholas are in another town, looking for some way to do this, when they get trapped in that alley.

Glenn has survived for a long time on his smarts and his determination. He is trying to employ both of those qualities now. Nicholas, however, knows it's all over, and what is going to happen to them. Unlike Glenn, he has one round left in his pistol. "Thank you," he says to Glenn. He puts the gun to his temple and pulls the trigger. Blood splatters across Glenn's shocked face. Nicholas's suddenly limp body falls into Glenn, and both go tumbling down to the ground, set upon immediately by dozens of flesh-craving zombies. (If you watch this scene enough times, as I sadly have, you'll realize there are some absolutely great zombies in that scrum, really some wonderful makeup jobs; watch really closely and you'll also see director Greg Nicotero, in full zombie costume. He directed the scene from inside that herd of walkers.)

This scene in the alley was the crescendo of the episode. Forget for a moment what you know about what happens later, about how Glenn survives, and simply consider the action in the scene: Glenn is on the ground, surrounded by a couple dozen walkers. Dozens more are behind them. They have descended upon him and Nicholas and are in a feeding frenzy. There is literally no space between him and the undead. And yet . . .

I know people who were crestfallen when they thought Glenn was dead, and elated when he showed up alive four episodes later. They didn't care about story logic or anything else. They just wanted Glenn back. But the only way you can achieve that level of engagement is if the stakes are real. Which means people gotta die. This is something the show understands. Characters are put in peril all the time, and sometimes it looks especially grim for them. Most of the time they find a credible way out. Glenn's escape from the alley was not credible, though, and it certainly made the stakes less real.

Look, we all know this is a television show, and one based on another fictional medium—the comic—so there is a willing suspension of disbelief involved, which allows you to overlook a number of things that would ruin the illusion. For starters, zombies aren't real. But it even goes beyond that. There are smaller points that we are willing to overlook, too. Here are a few examples:

GRASS. I've seen this one mentioned myriad times by the nitpickers. You'd think that with most of humanity having been wiped out by a zombie plague, there wouldn't be anybody left to cut the grass. But the grass in the prison is cut, as is the grass in the abandoned towns. The show's production staff does a tremendous job of creating the illusion of an apocalyptic world, but it's just hard to find locations where nobody's cut the grass for a couple of years.

GAS. If you've ever left gas in the tank of your lawnmower over the winter, you know that it's unusable gunk by spring. That's because gasoline, a product refined from crude oil, lasts only a few months. So, if you're living in a collapsed society where nobody's refining any more gasoline, your car isn't going anywhere. In other words, none of the cars you see on *The Walking Dead* should be running.

SKULL STABBING. This is one I'd always wondered about. It is far, far more difficult to get a knife through a skull than you may think (I don't know from practicing it). Unless you aim for the ears or eyes, chances are you won't be able to do it. Yet time and time again on *The Walking Dead,* we see virtually everybody braining zombies and making it look easy. I consulted a couple of weapons experts on this one. In general, it takes a specific kind of knife—a big one like a medieval Saxon seax or modern bowie knife—a significant amount of strength, and a lot of training. Without that, you're more likely to have the blade bounce off the skull than penetrate (even zombie bones don't decompose that fast). "While something from seax size up can smash or punch through a skull," said weapons expert Marc MacYoung, "most of the time what you would be hearing is 'dink, dink,' followed by screams of the person being eaten alive by zombies."

Every show and movie has these kinds of things. As viewers, we're willing to let them go, so long as the story being told is good enough that we forget about them. Only the nitpickers take it too seriously. But in writing Glenn's incredibly improbable survival, showrunner Scott Gimple and his writers broke a cardinal rule of storytelling: they defied their own story's internal logic. In doing so, they exposed the entire magic trick that is a television show.

Glenn had gotten out of tight scrapes before. But trapped in the alley, he had no way out. He was lying on the ground, surrounded by dozens of flesh eaters. Glenn was dead; had to be. The credits rolled, and immediately the Internet erupted in pure shock and confusion. *The Walking Dead* always killed off characters, and not just the proverbial "red shirts." This was different, though. Not only could you not have seen this one coming—not even the comic book fans who knew the story lines—it seemed so utterly final. There was no way, *no way,* Glenn could have survived that. Right? Nah, couldn't be.

And then . . .

A grave-looking Chris Hardwick appeared next, to introduce his show, *The Talking Dead,* and tried to ease people through what they'd just seen. It had already become something of a running joke that when a character on the show dies, the actor comes on the talk show and sits at the far right on the couch, next to Hardwick. Yet Steven Yeun was not on the set. Not only was Yeun not there, nobody from the show was. The guests were actress and *Walking Dead* superfan Yvette Nicole Brown and writer Damon Lindelof. Moreover, Hardwick read a cryptic statement from Gimple, which suggested at the least that Glenn's story was not yet complete. "In some way we will see Glenn again." Then, to top this whole thing off, Glenn was not included in the show's "in memoriam" segment.

Oh. Oh, *really*? The wheels started turning. People started to sense something afoot. It didn't take long for fans to go back to the episode and start analyzing it, frame by frame. On first viewing, it seemed clear that Glenn was getting eaten alive. On second viewing, to some people at least, it wasn't so. Chatter started bouncing around on Twitter; fan videos started cropping up on YouTube. Exhibit A: You don't see *Glenn's* body getting ripped apart. You see *a* body. The camera angle is low and tilted. All we see are blood spurts, and intestines being pulled out, but from whose torso we're not sure. Exhibit B: If those intestines are coming from Glenn's body, given the angle, they'd have to be coming from his chest, and your chest isn't full of intestines (the fact that we've started getting into a debate about what is physically possible on a fictional TV show about a zombie apocalypse shows how far this thing went). Exhibit C: There appears to be a definite physical gap between where Glenn's head and neck are and the body cavity from where those guts appear to be coming out. They're too high, too far from his own visible neck. Glenn, the obsessives said, was not dead.

Pfft, this obsessive said. *That dude's dead.*

I was so convinced Glenn was dead that I wrote a separate post about it the next day—in hindsight a relatively arrogant post—explaining all the reasons that I thought added up to his being dead. In retrospect, of course, I was dead wrong. Sure, I re-watched the scene, too. Myriad times. But it just seemed inconceivable to me that Glenn could have survived that. "It can't possibly be true," I wrote flatly. Should Glenn have died there? Of course Glenn should have died there! He was lying on the ground, surrounded by zombies. From the behavior of these beasts we have seen for six seasons, it's impossible to believe that not even one sees Glenn and attacks him. Not even one!

Four episodes later, in "Heads Up," the story goes back to the alley, and we all get to see for ourselves how he managed to survive. He's able to crawl out from under Nicholas's body, drag himself over to the Dumpster, and then squeeze himself *under* the Dumpster, all without being noticed by any one of the two dozen or so zombies that are literally inches away from him. Watching it, I felt like Annie Wilkes in *Misery,* complaining about the cliff-hangers in the serials she used to watch as a kid. "He didn't get out of the cock-a-doodie car!" she screams. Glenn didn't get out of the cock-a-doodie alley. How quickly could he have possibly dragged his entire body underneath that Dumpster? Could he have done it so fast that not one of those undead flesh eaters noticed the movement of an entire warm-blooded body? Glenn's a skinny guy, but is it realistic to believe he could even squeeze his body underneath that Dumpster without at least having some part of him exposed long enough to attract some biters? I spent way too much time on Google looking at pictures of Dumpsters, and I just don't think it'd be that easy to crawl under one.

The problem with Glenn surviving is that to achieve it, the writers had to break the rules of a fictional universe that they'd spent five years developing. "If they're going to build the walkers up to be dangerous," said Adam Carlson, who started the fan website Undead Walking three years ago, "you gotta make it kind of consistent. They're either deadly or they're not."

When I asked Carlson about this incident, he just sighed. "Oh, man," he said. He didn't like the monthlong cliff-hanger, but beyond that, he questioned what the point of it was anyhow. In the comics, Glenn's death at Negan's hands is such an iconic moment that even people who didn't read the comics (like me) knew it was coming. So what, Carlson asked, did this cliff-hanger in the alley prove? "What was the point in that fake-out?" he said. "All they had to do was build that up, have him with Maggie, taking care of her, talking about the baby. That would've been a much better buildup."

Keep in mind, Carlson and I are both fans of the show. What's doubly frustrating about this whole Glenn in the Alley thing, to me at least, is that it ruins what could have been the best three-episode, self-contained story the show has ever told. Those three episodes, "First Time Again," "JSS," and "Thank You"—written by, respectively, Gimple and Matthew Negrete, Seth Hoffman, and Angela Kang, and directed by Nicotero, Jennifer Lynch, and Michael Slovis—display some phenomenal storytelling. At certain points, the events appear to be occurring in real time. There isn't any fancy flipping between tales, no establishing shots to show a passage of time. The attack of the Wolves happens just after Carol puts a casserole in the oven, setting the timer for forty-five minutes, and ends before the timer goes off; Glenn's desperate attempt to redirect the walkers happens in the same afternoon. After three and a half hours of airtime for the first three episodes, barely more than that had passed in show time. By the time Glenn gets trapped in that alley, the sense of heightened anxiety and dread is palpable. From the quarry-walkers incident, to the attack of the Wolves, to the terrible aftermath, it's a story about impossible odds, unpredictable mistakes, unforeseeable calamities, and death. It's everything *The Walking Dead* is about, and it's brilliant and gripping and you are dragged kicking and screaming into that alley with Glenn and Nicholas. I absolutely loved where those three episodes took me, even as Glenn and Nicholas tumbled off that Dumpster to an almost certain death. These episodes were a gripping example of just how far the odds are stacked against these survivors. By having Glenn die—and not just a bunch of people we didn't know—the show would have *reinforced* rather than broken the rules.

There is a story, possibly embellished, about one of the very first movies ever shown publicly. It's a one-minute-long film, *L'Arrivée d'un train en gare de La Ciotat,* made by two brothers, Auguste and Louis Lumière, which was shown in Paris in 1895. It's a fixed shot of a train arriving at a station, coming toward the camera, and people getting off. Simple, right? Go watch it on YouTube. It seems like nothing to us modern viewers. Well, the story is that the local Parisians, having never seen a film like this before, thought the train was actually coming into the theater, and freaked out. Talk about a magic trick! I've heard the same story told about the end of *The Great Train Robbery,* the 1903 movie that ends with the robber firing his gun directly into the camera. Did people know the train wasn't real? Did they know the robber wasn't real? Of course. Were they scared all the same? Probably.

I'll tell you another story. Some years ago, Radio City Music Hall was running a movie festival, which was great, because you'd get to see all these classic movies in one of the largest theaters in the country. I went to see *Jaws,* among many other films. Now, I've seen *Jaws* probably a hundred times, but never in a theater. When it came out my mother saw it in a theater and came back so terrified, like everybody else, she refused to let me go. So I'd seen it only on television. There is one scene, where Roy Scheider's Chief Brody is throwing out the chum line, when the shark comes out of the water for the first time, and you see how big it really is. I've seen that scene a hundred times; I knew exactly what was coming, at exactly what moment; I even knew the angle of the cigarette hanging from Brody's mouth. I knew *exactly what to expect.* When that shark came out of the water on a seventy-by-thirty-foot screen, those massive jaws, those razor-sharp teeth, those black doll's eyes, you know what I did?

I jumped back in my seat. Swear to God, I recoiled. I couldn't believe it myself. Now *that's* a magic trick. And the shark in that movie is notoriously unrealistic. But the story is so good, you are completely hooked (no pun intended). Look, the point I'm trying to make here is that all of this is very intricate, very complicated stagecraft, and when it's done well, it's a wonderful thing. *The Walking Dead* does it very well every single week, which is what makes it so special; but all of it is an illusion, every frame of it, and by blowing any aspect of it, you risk blowing the whole illusion.

CHAPTER 12

WAR AND PIECES

"THERE'S GOING TO BE A GOVERNMENT HERE ONE DAY."

—REP. DEANNA MONROE

(SEASON 5, EPISODE 13, "FORGET")

Given *The Walking Dead*'s subject matter, the end of the world and survival and all that, people can't help trying to discern the political message of the show. I had lunch with a friend just before I finished up this manuscript, and he argued, emphatically if not exactly convincingly, that *The Walking Dead* was a show with a liberal point of view. The way he saw it, there's far too much equivocating among the characters about the use of power and force. *Game of Thrones,* he said, where the whole point is the pursuit of raw power, is a more conservative show. Paradoxically, a 2016 study found that *The Walking Dead* was rated as the second-best show in a survey of Republicans, but only the sixth-best among Democrats. The top show for Democrats? *Game of Thrones*. Politicians themselves seem to have a sense of this, too. Jared Kushner, Donald Trump's son-in-law, told *Forbes* magazine that the Trump campaign's computer algorithms pegged *The Walking Dead*'s fan base as probably worried about immigration.

So they bought airtime during the show's fall 2016 season, assuming they were hitting their voters.

At Vulture, Sean T. Collins assailed the show for essentially being an apologist for fascism. "For years, both *TWD* and its spin-off series, *Fear the Walking Dead,* have portrayed survival in the post-apocalypse as a triumph of the will," he wrote, throwing in a reference to the notorious Nazi propaganda movie *Triumph of the Will.* At *National Review,* David French ripped liberals who like the show. In his mind, on this show, the characters "live by conservatism, die by liberalism, and the only way you give up your Smith & Wesson is if someone pries it from your rotting, zombified hand."

Personally, I don't think *The Walking Dead* has a political point of view, at least not one that easily fits into the liberal or conservative categories. *Star Trek* was a consciously political show, portraying a future in which classic liberal politics had emerged as the dominant form of class and political rule (even in space). *The Walking Dead* doesn't do that. What it does do, however, is portray all the elements that go into creating politics, and it starts at the absolute lowest level: individual survival. What makes it fascinating for poli-sci types and anybody with an interest in politics is that it shows the entire process of building up societies and governments, beginning with the "natural state" of man according to Thomas Hobbes, and moving right up through Maslow's Hierarchy of Needs. It's not espousing a political position, it's showing how politics come to exist in the first place.

Maslow's hierarchy is designed to explain human motivations in our civilized world, but it may just as easily be adapted to explain motivation in an uncivilized world. The hierarchy is often illustrated as a pyramid. On the bottom are physical needs, like food and water. Above that is safety. Next is "belongingness," forging relationships and networks of friends. Next is self-esteem, and above that, at the top of the pyramid, is self-actualization. For the first seven seasons of *The Walking Dead,* few have gotten past the third level.

At various points in the show, we get to see many of these characters on their own. When we first meet Rick Grimes, he is at the very bottom of the pyramid, alone in a broken world. Morgan Jones was protecting his wife and son. Then just his son. Then just himself. Bob Stookey bounced around from group to group, watching all of them eventually fail. After that he just wandered by himself, building little secure spaces where he could safely get drunk. Abraham Ford, too, was protecting his family, failed at that, and was ready to give up until he came across one pathetic survivor who needed his help: Eugene Porter. Father Gabriel saved himself by locking himself in his church, condemning all his parishioners to death outside. When we first see him, he's a scurrying figure who's barely able to fend off walkers. Tara is holed up with her sister, nephew, and father. Eventually she, too, is left alone in the world. All these single, lost people will come across each other's paths. Through seven full seasons, we watch this group search for safety and security, and build those bonds of love and friendship that will form the glue of their community.

"You said you were a family," Deanna Monroe says to Rick when they first meet (season 5, episode 12, "Remember"). "That's what you said. Absolutely amazing to me how people with completely different backgrounds and with nothing in common can become that." It's interesting that Deanna recognizes Rick as someone who can connect with other people, because she knows that it's a necessary ingredient to building a lasting, stable society. The Grimes clan has the key ingredients any group needs to survive in this world: a decisive leader, capable followers, and that bond. Alexandria lacks what they have, but Alexandria has something else that's valuable: walls and security. It won't be a seamless merger, but both groups do need each other.

The sense of family that the Grimes clan has is perhaps the most important element in trying to rebuild the world. "To Rick Grimes, the faith he places in his family, friends, and his job as leader and protector of his group, is his 'God,'" write professors Erika Engstrom and Joseph Valenzano, whom I referenced earlier when we were talking about religion. In the show, faith in religion and those old institutions is largely gone, since the institutions themselves are gone. If society is going to be revived, new institutions must be built, and the first building block is that bond among people. Without that, every person would just be in the kind of "natural state" described by Thomas Hobbes in his masterwork, *Leviathan*. Hobbes argues that the natural state of man, as in a state without the collar of a central government, is one where every man is at war with every other man. There is no industry or security, no artistic pursuits, just the "continual fear and danger of violent death, and the life of man, solitary, poor, nasty, brutish, and short," Hobbes writes. The Leviathan of the title is the defense of the idea of a central government as the one thing that can keep man from living in the conditions described above. In Hobbes's argument, people enter a social contract and surrender some of their personal freedoms in exchange for the kind of security and permanence that will release them from the terror of that brutish life in the wild.

The exchange of liberty for personal security is vividly portrayed in *The Walking Dead*. Rick's group is just a nomadic clan on the lowest rung of society when we first find them. At this point, there aren't even enough people to form any kind of real social contract. They are in a pre-political state, where the "family" unit is the only social bond. Now, that isn't to be dismissed on its own. Remember where we started, with Deanna Monroe deeply impressed by the bonds of love and fidelity this small band of survivors had forged. The people inside Rick's group will do anything for each other, including even dying for one another. That is a powerful glue to hold a group together. But in the world of the walking dead, it will get you only so far. "People are the best protection against walkers, and people," Rick tells poor, doomed Clara, the woman he meets in the woods outside the prison (season 4, episode 1, "30 Days Without an Accident"). He realizes, eventually, that numbers bring security.

The Grimes clan tries to make a safe home for themselves in the prison. Before the Governor shows up with a tank and army and lays waste to it, the prison is on its way to becoming a viable, secure outpost for survivors. There's a fledgling ruling body in the governing council; they can grow crops, raise livestock, and even fall in love and try to reach some of those higher levels of Maslow's hierarchy (it is a constant mystery to me how Carol and Daryl never end up together, but that's another story). The attack on the prison and its destruction wreck all that, scatter everybody, and send them right back to step one (season 4, episode 8, "Too Far Gone"). Years of effort blown to hell because of one lunatic.

From our vantage point, that episode is especially interesting. It's the forty-third episode overall, but as the season 4 "midseason finale" it's also the midpoint of the show through the first seven seasons, cleanly marking a midpoint in the story so far. Looked at in this way, the first half was all about the forging of the Grimes clan. The second half is about realizing that it might be possible to re-create civil society, and actually trying to do so. Each half has one main antagonist: the Governor in the first, and Negan in the second.

In this second half, the Grimes clan becomes part of Alexandria, a walled community outside of the capital, run by an ex-congresswoman, Deanna Monroe (the fifteenth district of Ohio, she explains, though she never gets around to party affiliation). Alexandria is a sort of Peyton Place of the post–zombie apocalypse. It was a planned community before the Turn, with solar power, big houses, a man-made lake, gazebos, very top-of-the-line. After the clan settles in—and that's a whole process in itself—we start being introduced to other colonies, and their governance styles. Here is a brief rundown:

HILLTOP. *Type of government: weak central authority.* Hilltop first appears in season 6. Another walled compound, Hilltop is a stable but small community with a weak central government, in the form of Gregory (Xander Berkeley), a man who lives to calculate his odds, and appears to have simply fallen into his role. But Hilltop has many advantages. It's situated high on a hill (good sight lines), with thick wooden walls. Most of the housing is old FEMA shelters, and at the center is a sturdy old antebellum mansion, Barrington House (when Hilltop first appeared on the show, Barrington House looked so real to me, I asked AMC where they found the old mansion for filming. It's not real, it's a set).

THE KINGDOM. *Type of government: monarchy.* The Kingdom is introduced in season 7. It's a community that appears to be thriving, built on the grounds of an old school campus. It's well armed and protected, and has crops and plenty of food. It's a place where people can grasp after those higher needs on Maslow's hierarchy. In the Kingdom, people play music and read. All of this is overseen by King Ezekiel (Khary Payton), a leader in the mold of the Platonic ideal of a philosopher-king. It's an act—Ezekiel was a community theater actor before the Turn—but it's a good act. People believe in Ezekiel, and they believe in the Kingdom.

OCEANSIDE. *Type of government: collective.* This is a strictly isolationist community of virtually all women, run as a collective, though one older woman, Natania, is the leader. Operating inside an old roadside motel, the Oceanside Cabin Motor Court, this community does not have strong walls to protect them, though they are very well armed (where they got the guns, we don't know). The site is isolated enough, seemingly, that they are safe from both humans and walkers, but they have a general rule of shooting anybody they encounter on sight. Just to be safe. This community's extreme measures are a result of their disastrous experience with the Saviors, who slaughtered all the men and boys.

TAKERS. *Type of government: tribal, and very weird.* The Takers (at least, that's what I call them; others call them Scavengers, and Negan calls them the "filthy garbage people") are an odd group of scroungers Rick finds while out looking for Father Gabriel. They live in a massive junkyard, have their own bizarre cadence and mannerisms, and march and move on silent commands. They appear to have a leader, Jadis, and one governing ethos, as Jadis explains: "We take, we don't bother." In other words, they don't go out of their way to acquire things, they just take whatever they can—whether it's stuff or deals with other groups. They also have no loyalty whatsoever, as Rick painfully discovers.

THE SAVIORS. *Type of government: the worst.* These are evil, vile, murderous bastards, part of the ironfisted totalitarian state run by the hellish dictator Negan. They are also, ironically, the most organized, successful group of survivors we've met so far. They've got a leadership structure in place, and a system for apportioning the group's material wealth, and a set of rules that everybody understands. If you look at it from the point of view of, say, Eugene

Porter, it works incredibly well. Negan's home base, called the Sanctuary, is a relatively well-protected old factory complex. The people living inside this complex live surprisingly decent lives. If they weren't such horrible, murderous oppressors, they'd be a real beacon of mankind.

What seems to matter most is that a leader in the post–zombie apocalypse is *decisive*. Even in our real world, we do not expect our leaders to be perfect, especially in the face of disaster (Americans know no shortage of this outcome). Yes, voters will "throw the bums out" if the economy should falter, but studies have shown that politicians who respond decisively to disasters will be rewarded by voters—whether or not the decision is the right one and even if those same politicians did not do enough to prepare for those very disasters in the first place. Negan and the Governor are homicidal and suicidal, but they are also decisive. Negan may be as liable to throw you into an oven as feed you a spaghetti dinner, but in his decisiveness, he can bring some sense of comfort—so long as you don't cross him.

Negan is a far more capable leader than the Governor, though just as bloodthirsty. We don't know anything about his pre-plague life, but he seems to understand power politics. He builds an empire based on one simple principle: half. Half of everything you own, he owns. In exchange for that, you get to live. It works to a shocking degree. Negan attracts people who are either too afraid of being alone anymore or just as deranged as he is. He builds a cult of Negan that is hundreds strong, and the preeminent power in the greater Washington, D.C., area.

The Saviors rule through raw power as opposed to political cunning. One of Negan's lieutenants, Gavin (Jayson Warner

Smith), perfectly sums up the difference (season 7, episode 13, "Bury Me Here"): "Ezekiel, there aren't any kings, presidents, or prime ministers, and all that was a fairy tale, too. Don't bring that 'your highness' shit our way." In his view, politics is an illusion, a mental construct that's been erased by apocalypse.

Gavin, perhaps ironically, is a perfect political philosopher for the post–zombie apocalypse. He understands exactly what he is doing. "I didn't go this route for stress; no, just the opposite." You might call this realpolitik. Gavin does not appear on any level to be taken in by the cult of Negan. In fact, he goes to some lengths to bend Negan's rules in order to keep things relatively civil. Where a good beat down would be called for, he lets Ezekiel and his men off with a warning. It isn't until Richard (Karl Makinen) forces a confrontation that Gavin's toady Jared (Joshua Mikel) gets to kill somebody—and when he kills the young kid Benjamin (Logan Miller) instead of Richard, Gavin is furious. Gavin acts with complete resignation and weariness about his circumstances. He's just trying to do the best things he can to make it through another day.

After the season 7 finale ("The First Day of the Rest of Your Life"), more than one Monday-morning quarterback questioned why Rick would have ever trusted the Takers, the army of oddball scavengers. In retrospect, it was a mistake to trust them, given that they turned on him when Negan made them a better deal. Sure, it was a bad decision. He went against one of his own cardinal rules—he took a chance. But he needed to take it. Rick isn't afraid to decide, and that's one reason people follow him, but decisive isn't the same thing as right. Rick has made enough mistakes to fill a book. In the world of *The Walking Dead,* virtually every person who has taken on a leadership role in any form has made mistakes that cost lives. Sometimes many lives. Here is a partial list of Rick's bad decisions:

- He trusted the Takers (season 7).
- He brought Randall back to the Greene farm (season 2).
- He didn't kill Andrew, one of the inmates they found in the prison, who wanted to kill him (season 3, episode 2, "Sick"). Rather, Rick just chased him off. Andrew returned and in retaliation set off the prison's alarm, stirring up a huge pack of walkers. This led directly to the death of T-Dog; Lori, who went into labor while fleeing, forced Maggie to give her an emergency caesarean, and then made Carl mercy-kill her. This one left a lot of welts.
- He did not shoot the Governor when he had a perfect chance (season 3, episode 13, "Arrow on the Doorpost"), during their sit-down. Had he, the subsequent destruction of the prison wouldn't have happened. The above two decisions end up sitting very heavily with Carl, who at one point comes to hate his father.
- He unilaterally threw Carol out of the prison (season 4, episode 4, "Indifference"). Was she wrong to kill two people in cold blood on the rationale of trying to contain a raging pig virus that was making everybody sick? Well, she could've at least asked. But Rick wasn't in charge anymore; Carol was. So who was he to throw her out? Moreover, Carol had become one of the group's most capable survivors, as she later proves by saving all of them after the Termites capture them. Bad decision to exile Carol Peletier.

Now, I don't have a problem with Rick making mistakes. It wouldn't be realistic for him to make the right choice every single time. Rick's greatest quality, apart from an uncanny survival instinct, is the ability to simply choose. In a world where life is measured in hours and days rather than decades, that is an essential quality to have. What will be interesting will be to see whether Rick can pivot into becoming a more nuanced leader of a large network of communities—assuming he survives the coming war with Negan, and that he wins that war. (Yeah, yeah, of course he will, right? Hey, you never know.)

Also, every leader makes bad, terrible decisions in this world, which should really be a reminder that all these people were just average nobodies before the Turn. The Governor is a terrible leader. He takes a relatively thriving community at Woodbury and mindlessly plunges it into a fight that leads to its annihilation. He then comes into another community and destroys that one in his insane lust to kill everybody at the prison. Negan's one great mistake—not wiping out the Alexandrians when he had the chance—will, I predict, eventually lead to his downfall.

In the Hobbesian worldview, this natural state of man, without the presence of the Leviathan—government—leads to perpetual war. "It is manifest, that during the time men live without a common power to keep them all in awe, they are in that condition which is called war; and such a war, as is of every man, against every man," Hobbes wrote. He outlined three prime reasons for why people fight: distrust, competition for resources, and glory. This is the world of *The Walking Dead* through seven seasons, a state of constant distrust and competition. Indeed, the most powerful force so far has been Negan and his voracious appetite for tribute and violence. Within this world there is no way to build a lasting society. Indeed, why would you even bother, if you were constantly being attacked, your crops plundered, your homes destroyed?

The greatest political decision, when living under a repressive regime like that of the Saviors, is simple, and it's something Gavin—again, the great political philosopher of the post–zombie apocalypse—explains succinctly to Ezekiel: "Well, you got a choice. Same one that's been there since the beginning, I guess. You can give up your guns, or you can try to use them." Submit and collaborate, or resist. This dilemma has always faced the occupied. For myriad reasons, most have chosen appeasement: Gregory, because he's a coward; Ezekiel, because he believes he can balance the Saviors' demands with his people's freedom (without the latter ever knowing about the former); Rick, because his will was shattered by Negan.

This dynamic is encapsulated in an exchange between Dwight and Gordon (Michael Scialabba), a guy who tries to escape the Sanctuary (season 7, episode 3, "The Cell"). Gordon got fed up with life under Negan and ran. It's something Dwight himself did at one point, before turning back after he and his wife, Sherry (Christine Evangelista), couldn't hack it on the outside. Dwight, Gordon, Sherry, Gavin, even Eugene, everybody in the Sanctuary has at one point had to decide to be with Negan or not. "Thug swoops in with a baseball bat and a smile and we're so scared we gave up everything," Gordon says. "But there's only one of him and all of us, so why are we living like this?" Dwight makes it clear why: he not only threatens to kill Gordon, he threatens to kill every person Gordon ever knew. He threatens to dig up Gordon's dead wife and feed her body to zombies. Dwight is well versed in Negan's coercive techniques, and of course they work.

Gordon surrenders. Dwight kills Gordon, and doesn't do any of the things he threatened. These tactics have worked well for Negan and his Saviors. They have built up a sturdy little empire by preying on the weak.

When season 8 begins in October 2017, that is going to change. The Saviors are not pushing their thumbs down anymore on scattered, weak, frightened colonies. Among the last images shown in the season 7 finale, "The First Day of the Rest of Your Life," is one in which Rick Grimes, King Ezekiel, and Maggie Rhee stand on a hastily constructed stage in Alexandria and address people. The signal is clear: there is now a war alliance between Alexandria, the Kingdom, and Hilltop. There is going to be a war for control of the apocalypse, and in a world where there are no rules to begin with, you can expect a particularly savage and brutalizing struggle.

It seems improbable that the Saviors will win this war. As grand a job as Jeffrey Dean Morgan does portraying Negan, one season of watching Rick and everybody else under Negan's brutal rule was quite enough. I'm guessing he'll be defeated, at which point the survivors can start building a world that, in some respects, resembles the one they used to know. Can they make it work? Have they lived in this natural state for too long? If the show's seven seasons can be split between before and after the Governor's attack on the prison, almost like volume 1 (survival) and volume 2 (family), then this new season, and the all-out war that's coming, marks the beginning of volume 3 (union), and it is in this new story that all these strands of politics are going to come to the fore.

What might the world of a grand confederation of post-Saviors look like? The world that Rick and Michonne discussed over a candlelit dinner of army rations ("mac and cheese *and* chili")? You can imagine a network of trading and shared security, and without the Saviors gobbling up half of everything, there should be plenty for the citizens of this new political union. After all, how many people are there in these communities? Growing enough food for everyone really should not be a problem. Security is an ongoing issue, of course. Reliable communications are a challenge. It seems like the countryside has been pretty well scavenged by these groups, but is there more out there to be found? Scavenging is likely to be a major occupation in this new world. Of course, another issue is, how much damage will this coming war cause? What will be left? *Who* will be left? It seems that these survivors are on the verge of escaping that natural state, that constant war of man against man. Will they survive long enough to be able to build a new world?

RECAP

SEASON SEVEN

- **SAFE HAVENS:** Alexandria Safe Zone, Hilltop, the Kingdom
- **SURVIVORS LOST:** Abraham, Glenn, Olivia, Spencer, Sasha
- **ANTAGONISTS KILLED:** Many "Negans." But not Negan.
- **NOTABLE WALKERS:** Winslow, Sasha

THE PREMIERE OF SEASON SEVEN TOOK ITS TIME RE-vealing who exactly was killed by Negan, but I'll dispense with that windup: he killed Abraham Ford. When Daryl loses his cool and jumps up to slug him, Negan dishes out swift punishment. "I will shut that shit down," he barks. He doesn't kill Daryl, but chooses somebody else, at random, to suffer the punishment: Glenn, whom he bludgeons with pornographic glee.

Rick kneels, blood from his dead comrade streaked across his face. Still, he is defiant. "I'm gonna kill you," he tells Negan. Which the top dog of the apocalypse takes as a challenge. His earlier point made, Negan embarks on his next mission, which is to break this group's leader. He throws Rick in the RV and drives off in what encompasses a private session of Negan-ism. When they return, it's daylight. Rick is ordered to cut off Carl's arm. If he doesn't, Negan will kill everybody else in the woods. Then everybody in Alexandria. Then Carl. It's a horrible choice. Negan is breaking Rick the way a cowboy breaks a horse. Finally, when Rick is actually about to do it, wailing and crying in agony, Negan stops him, at the last moment. It was the ultimate test, and Rick passed.

"You answer to me. You provide for me. You belong to me. Right?!" That's the new arrangement, the only one that will keep people alive.

"Right," Rick whispers. Rick Grimes is a broken man, and the occupation of Alexandria has begun.

After the killings of Abraham and Glenn, Negan takes his men, and Daryl, and leaves. Sasha takes Maggie to Hilltop, their original destination, where there's a doctor. They bring Glenn's and Abraham's bodies, too. Maggie, even in her weakened state, is already talking about fighting. She won't be the only one.

Meanwhile, Morgan has found Carol in the wilds. She was nearly killed by a random Savior, and indeed wanted to be killed. She wanted out. It's why she left Alexandria in the first place. But Morgan saves her, breaking his own oath by shooting the assailant dead. They meet two men on horseback and are taken back to these strangers' home: the Kingdom, a thriving walled community inside an old school campus ruled by a philosopher-king of the post–zombie apocalypse, Ezekiel, an imposing man who has a tiger for a pet.

Back in Negan's lair, an old factory complex known as the Sanctuary, Daryl is locked in a small windowless cell, forced to eat dog food sandwiches and listen all day to the same chipper, upbeat tune on repeat ("We're on Easy Street, and it feels so sweet, 'cause the world is but a treat when you're on Easy Street"). But Negan's squad can't break him, no matter how hard they try. "What's your name?" Negan asks him, sure that he's made another convert.

"Daryl," his captive replies. Back in the cell he goes.

Returned to Alexandria, Rick tries to make the new arrangement work. He sees that there is no other choice. The Saviors are far more powerful than he'd expected. The fact that Negan didn't just wipe them all out to begin with is a gift, of sorts. So now Alexandria will pay tribute to Negan, and get to exist. When Negan calls, Rick grits his teeth and tries to satisfy the man. Carl gets fired up and pulls a gun on a Savior, which prompts Negan to demand all their guns, every last one. Rick is so emasculated, he follows Negan around town, even carrying Negan's bat, Lucille. Negan is taunting him with it, almost begging Rick to use it against him. But Rick doesn't do so.

He does go out on scavenger runs, trying to scrape up enough tribute to placate his madman overlord. While he's out on one, Carl does a typically impulsive Carl thing: he stows away on a truck bound for the Sanctuary and tries to kill Negan. He doesn't go through with it, of course. (Indeed, one of the more amazing things is how many people want to kill Negan, and have a chance to kill Negan, but somehow don't do it.)

Meanwhile, Tara is still out on a scavenger mission with Heath. They left after the first attack on the outpost and have no idea what's happened since. Tara doesn't know about Negan, nor about her girlfriend's death. She and Heath are attacked by walkers on a bridge and get split up, and Tara ends up on a beach, where she is discovered by a young girl, Cyndie. This girl is from a group of survivors that have made a home in the Oceanside Cabin Motor Court. The Oceansiders are very well armed, but have a strict no-outsiders rule. Tara barely makes it out alive, saved by Cyndie and sworn to secrecy about their home.

Negan comes back to Alexandria with Carl and makes himself at home, waiting for Rick. He forces Olivia to cook a spaghetti dinner and sits down at Rick's table to eat it. When Rick arrives, tensions rise. Negan has a pool table brought out into the street, and plays a game with Spencer Monroe. Spencer, who never did like Rick much, is trying to convince Negan to kill Rick and turn the place over to him. Negan humors him for a little while, then, with a crowd watching the exchange, he pulls out a knife and guts Spencer, ripping his intestines out. This infuriates Rosita, who convinced Eugene to make her a bullet for a semi she found. Rosita aims at Negan and pulls the trigger—only to hit his bat. Negan orders one of his goons, Arat, to exact some punishment. She swings around and just shoots at the first person she locks on: Olivia, who falls dead on Rick's porch. The oppressors leave—with Eugene as their captive (Negan pieced that one together)—but the terrible incident only sends Rick into a 180. He is now ready to fight again.

But how? They need weapons, and they need allies. At Hilltop there is a power struggle going on. Jesus, Maggie, and Sasha are like a shadow triumvirate, but Gregory is still the ostensible head, and he is absolutely against fighting; he'd just as soon be rid of the three of them altogether. Jesus introduces Rick to the Kingdom, where they find Morgan, but Ezekiel is also afraid of going up against the Saviors, hoping to maintain his fragile state of affairs—they pay tribute to the Saviors, but the Saviors agreed to never enter the Kingdom. Richard, one of Ezekiel's trusted lieutenants, understands that eventually the Saviors' appetites will destroy the Kingdom. He is trying every way he can to convince Ezekiel to fight.

Inside the Sanctuary, Eugene's terror is quickly replaced by something quite different. Negan wants to make use of Eugene's mind. In Alexandria, Eugene was mainly a burden; here he is an asset. He realizes that he can make himself safe here, and he dives in enthusiastically. "I'm utterly, completely, stone-cold Negan," he says. "I was Negan before I even met you." Negan rewards him with a night of partying with three of his wives. The women convince Eugene to make them a suicide pill, saying it's for one of them. It's for Negan, and Eugene realizes it. He makes the pill but doesn't give it to them.

Back in the Kingdom, Carol is itching to leave. She doesn't want to be around anybody anymore. She simply can't continue being the person she was, nor can she stand the efficiency of her killing. Ezekiel talks her into settling in a small house just outside the Kingdom. She can go, he explains, but not go. So she sets up there, trying to live a life of solitude. Ezekiel, Morgan, and even Daryl (after he escapes) at various points come to visit her. Eventually, she pieces together that the fight with Negan did not go well, and that people she cared about are dead. At that point, Carol Peletier comes back.

Relations get worse between the Kingdom and the Saviors. Richard tries to sabotage one of the drops, a delivery of fresh cantaloupes, expecting he will be shot and that it will galvanize Ezekiel. Instead, the Saviors kill a young fighter named Benjamin. Richard, horrified at how his plan got screwed up, confesses to Morgan; at the next drop, Morgan loses his marbles and simply beats Richard to death, in front of the Saviors and Ezekiel. Even the King understands now: war is at his doorstep.

The Alexandrians eventually come across another group, the Takers, an odd assortment who live in a massive junkyard and speak in a peculiar, clipped cadence. Rick tries to convince them to fight on his side. They do, after a test. They throw Rick down a mountain of junk into a sealed cavity, which contains one of the gnarliest walkers of all time. It's got a steel helmet on, studded with spikes, and stakes through and sticking out of its chest—a virtually unkillable undead monster. Its name, we will later learn, is Winslow. Rick pulls a wall of garbage on top of it and then manages to cut its head off. Proof of his bona fides in order, the Takers agree to fight—if he can meet their demands, which are basically guns. Lots and lots of guns, the leader, Jadis, tells him. So the Alexandrians go out and find guns. Rick and Michonne come across what was once an army camp for survivors, now overrun with the dead but bristling with guns and other supplies like army rations. Tara finally confesses about Oceanside, breaking her pledge to Cyndie, and they go and raid that armory.

Rosita, thought, can't wait for all this planning. She swipes a sniper rifle and goes to Hilltop, knowing she'll be able to talk Sasha into a virtual suicide mission: going to the Sanctuary to kill Negan. Sasha's been taking care of Maggie but is still burning over Abraham's death. She jumps at the chance to end Negan's life. It's an odd couple, to be sure, two women who shared the same man, and who don't particularly like each other very much. But both are capable soldiers, and Sasha is a great shot. Plan A is to hole up in an outer building and try for a long-distance shot. When that gets scotched, they go for plan B: breaking in at night. They have a brief chance to rescue Eugene, who for some reason ends up outside at night, but to their great surprise, he doesn't want to go. In fact, he runs back inside. Sasha cuts a hole in the fence while Rosita is otherwise occupied, and then locks it back up. This will be a solo mission after all.

We never see the assault itself, but we see the aftermath: Sasha in the cell once used for Daryl. And Negan is of course still alive. He makes her the same offer he made Daryl, Eugene, and everybody: join or die. Eugene is sent in, and he explains that he took Negan's offer because he simply doesn't want to live in terror. (All things considered, it's a terrible reason for turning on your people.) Negan has a plan, because he knows what Rick's up to; Sasha doesn't know exactly what it is, but she knows it will involve using her against her own people, and she won't allow it. She talks Eugene into giving her the suicide pill he made. Inside the casket, on the long trip to Alexandria, she takes it, and dies.

All the elements for a major showdown at Alexandria's gate are now in place.

CHAPTER 13

SANITY AND MORALITY

"IF YOU KILL PEOPLE, DO YOU TURN INTO ONE OF THE MONSTERS?"

—SAM ANDERSON

(SEASON 6, EPISODE 7, "HEADS UP")

One of the more frequent answers I get when asking people why they like the show is a variation on this: "It allows me to play What Would I Do?" How would you respond if all of society collapsed, and flesh-craving undead were crawling all over the countryside?

Excuse the language, but . . . you'd shit your pants.

Nobody is prepared for the end of the world. I'll bet that even your average doomsday prepper isn't actually ready for it. Even with all the horrible things that have happened in this century alone, none of them are as catastrophic as the collapse of society portrayed in *The Walking Dead*. It would be akin to the Black Death, the plague that spread across Europe in the fourteenth century, with estimates that it killed a third to half of the population. All institutions failed. Priests, nobles, the courts, anybody in authority fled in an attempt to save themselves. Farmers abandoned their fields and their livestock. For a population where religion was literal and science fantasy, it seemed like God himself had abandoned the world. It was the Book of Revelation come to pass.

In this world, the reactions of the survivors varied. Some doubled down on their religious morality, thinking a reapplication of faith might save them. They cordoned themselves off from the rest of the survivors and attempted to live a life of temperance, hoping this would work. Others took the complete opposite approach, believing that since the world had gone to hell, why not act like it? They threw their morality to the winds, drinking and carousing. They drank in the bars, invaded homes, and did whatever they wanted. "This they could easily do because everyone felt doomed and had abandoned his property," the Italian poet Giovanni Boccaccio wrote in his account of the plague, *The Decameron,* "so that most houses became common property and any stranger who went in made use of them as if he had owned them. And with all this bestial behaviour, they avoided the sick as much as possible."

Boccaccio wrote, "In this suffering and misery of our city, the authority of human and divine laws almost disappeared, for, like other men, the ministers and the executors of the laws were all dead or sick or shut up with their families, so that no duties were carried out. Every man was therefore able to do as he pleased."

Sound like any place you know? It's hard to imagine the intense psychological damage living through something like that would do to you, and in our tale of a zombie apocalypse, we get a fictional stand-in for those very real horrors (if any producers out there want to do a show about the Black Death, ping me). From Shane taking his best friend's wife, to the Governor of Woodbury, to the cannibals of Terminus, to a roaming gang that actually call themselves the Claimers, to the vicious Negan, the world of *The Walking Dead* is very much like the plague-ravaged landscape of fourteenth-century Europe, wherein all norms of human behavior disappear. Right, wrong, morality, ethics. Throughout the show's run, there's friction between trying to do the "right" thing according to the old morals and rules and the "right" thing according to the new rules. In the beginning, Rick is noble to a fault. He risks his life to save Merle Dixon, despite knowing Merle is a bad man and a danger to the group. By the time he reaches Alexandria's walls, that old Rick is long gone. "I don't take chances anymore," he tells Morgan.

I've often thought that if you were to be plunged into a zombie apocalypse, the reality of it would be so overwhelming as to be beyond the mind's ability to process it. If *The Walking Dead* as a show were incredibly realistic, it would actually be unwatchable—a world of zombies and completely insane people doing completely insane things. There wouldn't be any "show"; no narrative, no characters, certainly no character development. Remember Jim, from the first survivors' camp outside Atlanta? His backstory, told very briefly, is horrific: His wife and son were literally ripped out of his hands by zombies when their home was overrun. He escaped only because the zombies were too busy eating his family to notice him. That is far too much trauma for a mind to bear, and Jim loses his. He starts randomly digging graves. It makes no sense, and it freaks out the other survivors. Imagine a show full of Jims, doing insane things for no remotely rationale reason.

Instead, thankfully, we get a show where people do maintain their sanity—some of them. The biggest key to survival, really, is how quickly you can shed your old morality and discover a new one. This is something Dale can't do. "The world we knew is gone," he tells Andrea back on the Greene farm, when they're debating what to do with their prisoner, Randall (season 2, episode 11, "Judge, Jury, Executioner"), "but keeping our humanity? That's a choice." This is a major flash point. The kid, Randall, was part of a larger group of desperados, and it was Rick's lingering humanity that made him decide to save the boy in the first place. But now they're stuck with him, and since Randall knows the Greene family from before the Turn and could bring his gang back to the farm, releasing him could later threaten the group. So what to do? Kill him in cold blood? Set him free? Try to make him part of the clan? Shane wants to kill the kid, and has no compunction about it. Others are fearful but don't want to make a choice. Rick is conflicted but leans toward killing him. Dale, though, is completely against murder. Killing the boy will change them, he argues. It will make them something they weren't before.

The entire group meets in Hershel's living room to discuss this conflict. Dale is the only one passionately opposed to it, but he's losing the argument. Even if he's right, there's no good alternative. That is becoming clear, even to Dale, who is now breaking his heart open to try to talk them out of it.

"If we do this, the people that we were, the world that we knew is dead. And this new world is ugly, it's harsh, it's survival of the fittest. And that's a world I don't want to live in," he says, tears streaming down his face. Even the ones who aren't totally for killing Randall have no viable alternatives. Overcome, Dale walks out. "This group is broken," he says to Daryl. Dale is right, but he is also wrong. He's right about this new harsh and ugly world, and how it is Hobbesian to a degree probably even Hobbes never imagined; after all, when Hobbes wrote about his "natural state," he was envisioning just a sort of pre-politicized society. He wasn't talking about a collapsed, wrecked society where people are chased, killed, and eaten by shambling, ravenous monsters. Classic "Hobbesian," in fact, is tame compared to the world of *The Walking Dead*.

Where Dale is wrong is in saying that the group is broken. It isn't broken, it's just adjusting to the new rules. The choice that keeps you alive is the right one. The choice that gets you killed is the wrong one. Those are the simple rules, and they are rules the group is already getting used to, as evidenced by how little support Dale gets after his big speech. In fact, not only do these survivors adopt these rules, they will master them as well as any of their enemies.

Adapting to this reality is the key to survival, something we see starkly in Carol Peletier. During that debate in Hershel's living room, as they are fighting and yelling, Carol pipes up, for once. "I didn't ask for this," she says. "You can't ask us to decide something like this." Now, Carol is still mourning her daughter, Sophia, but her statement is also a reflection of where she stands as a character: She is simply incapable of dealing with the situation—she hasn't adopted the new rules, but applying the old rules clearly doesn't work. So Carol, for now, is stuck. She will, of course, change and accept the new world for what it is. When the pig virus spreads through the prison (season 4, episode 2, "Infected"), Carol not only is in favor of killing two sick people to try to stop the flu from spreading but does the deed herself, without so much as asking one other person what they think. Later, when it becomes clear that the young girl Lizzie—a girl Carol essentially adopted—is dangerously deranged and can't be around people (season 4, episode 14, "The Grove"), it is again Carol who makes a decision she previously would have been incapable of making. She takes Lizzie out into a clearing, tells her to "look at the flowers," and shoots her dead.

The characters who quickly figure out that the old code is gone are the ones with the better chance of survival. As people start to band into small groups of survivors, they start developing their own codes, a reflection of the new world. There are the Claimers, the group that finds Daryl sitting in the middle of the road after he loses Beth (season 4, episode 13, "Alone"). The Claimers have a pretty simple code: you see something, you say the word "claimed" aloud, it's yours. You have to admit, it has a certain simple beauty to it.

No group reflects the complete adoption of a new code for a new world quite so fully as the residents of Terminus (the Termites, as I liked to call them) who show up at the end of season 4. They were once like any other group of survivors, we eventually learn. They found a safe haven in an old rail yard, literally a terminus, where they tried to attract others. They made signs and posted them along the rails, and had a radio broadcast. "Sanctuary . . . those who arrive, survive." By the time Rick and all the other scattered residents of the prison arrive, it has been transformed from a sanctuary to a circle of hell.

In a brief flashback, we see that Terminus itself was overrun by some other group of marauders, who locked up Gareth; his mother, Mary; and the rest, and tortured them, raped them, killed them, made them prisoners in their own home. Gareth and his crew turned the tables, took the place back, and imprisoned their captors. But the experience changed them. As Mary explains later to Carol: "We heard the message. You're the butcher, or you're the cattle." There is no better description of the only morality left in this world. In a world like that, murder isn't wrong, robbery isn't wrong, rape is . . . well, rape is still wrong. Even Negan says so. Then again, Negan has a stable of captive women he calls his wives, so his actual views on this are cloudy.

The question of course is once you cross this boundary, once you shed your old skin and slip on the new one, what do you become? Negan, of all people, calls out Rick and the other Alexandrians (season 7, episode 16, "The First Day of the Rest of Your Life") because they were going to blow up not only him and his men, but Eugene Porter as well. "He's one of you," Negan says, feigning astonishment. On the one hand, it's the height of irony.

On the other . . . they were going to blow up Eugene. "You people," Negan says, "are animals."

"In a world where people have unlimited freedom to choose their own behavior, we should expect that more people will descend into the abyss," Greg Garrett writes in the book *Living with the Living Dead*. Some of the people who are villains in the show, after all, were innocuous before the Turn. The Governor was nothing more than a middle-class family man and office worker; Shane Walsh was a sheriff's deputy; Dawn Lerner, who will come to run Grady Memorial Hospital in Atlanta with a despot's touch, was also a cop; contrarily, while Merle Dixon was a bad apple from the minute we met him, he goes from reprobate to hero as time goes on.

Again going back to Hobbes, most of the conventions of society are artificial constructs that lift us out of that natural state of perpetual war, one against the other. We create laws and rights and obligations, and agree to give up a small sliver of our own liberty for the greater good. What happens when those liberties are taken away? When morals are gone? We fall back into "a condition of war of every one against every one," Hobbes writes in *The Leviathan*, "in which case every one is governed by his own reason, and there is nothing he can make use of that may not be a help unto him in preserving his life against his enemies; it followed that in such a condition every man has a right to every thing, even to another one's body." There were two immediate parallels that jumped out to me reading that statement: "Every man has a right to every thing" sounds exactly like the philosophy of the Claimers. The next clause, about having the right "even to another one's body," sounds quite literally like the philosophy of the Termites, who after all take other people's bodies, carve them up, and eat them. It also harkens back to the Saviors, too, who go around taking whatever they want or can by brute force. In the season 7 finale, we even catch a glimpse of Negan and Jadis, the leader of the Takers, talking about the terms of their deal. It involved a certain number of bodies. They were haggling only over the number.

What amazes me about this world is that everybody isn't driven stark, raving mad by these conditions. Granted, that would make for a far less coherent, narrative-driven show, but it would be realistic. There are glimpses of insanity. Rick goes to "crazytown," as Glenn puts it, in the prison. Rick meets a woman, Clara, outside the prison walls who is clearly insane. When Glenn demands, during their escape from Terminus, that they rescue other prisoners, the person they rescue turns out to be—and you had to watch fairly closely to catch this—from the group that previously overthrew and terrorized Terminus. Gareth and his people captured their tormentor, locked him away, and drove him completely insane. Rather than insanity, what we get are people struggling with the realities of life in a world without rules.

You will often hear people complaining about violence in the movies or on TV, but while the violence can be excessive, it usually fits within a moral, ethical framework. Now, what if the story is one about a world where morals and ethics simply don't exist anymore? Rick Grimes kills out of vengeance. Rick Grimes kills in cold blood. I've already said—and I do believe it—that the show's ultimate message is one of extreme Stoicism in the face of the world's horrors, and I think ultimately that's a positive message. But in playing within the boundless landscape of this zombie world, the writers can push all kinds of things, and do.

Is Rick Grimes really a good guy? In the real world, questions of good and evil carry weight. In Rick's world, the question is meaningless. "The will to power motivates many villains in the zombie apocalypse," Greg Garrett writes. "They believe that by exercising power ruthlessly, they are giving themselves and those who follow them the best possible chance for survival. Never mind that for those of us sitting out the zombie apocalypse their actions seem sociopathic or even insane." It's notable that most of the people in *The Walking Dead* who do awful things, apart from Rick Grimes, are portrayed as sociopathic or worse. Negan, and Rick, really, walk the line the closest.

After Rick and Michonne lead a party into Woodbury to rescue Glenn and Maggie (season 3, episode 8, "Made to Suffer"), and Michonne nearly kills the Governor in a brutal fight, the Governor gathers his people into a dark courtyard. He's battered and bloody, with a bandage over his eye where Michonne gouged him. The town has seemingly just been attacked. People are scared. The Governor delivers a speech that plays off everything his people are feeling:

> What can I say? Hasn't been a night like this since the walls were completed. And I thought we were past it. Past the days when we all sat, huddled, scared in front of the TV during the early days of the outbreak. The fear we all felt then, we felt it again tonight. I failed you. I promised to keep you safe. Hell, look at me. You know, I should tell you that we'll be okay, that we're safe, that tomorrow we'll bury our dead and endure. But I won't. 'Cause I can't. 'Cause I'm afraid. That's right. I'm afraid of terrorists who want what we have. Want to destroy us!

Is he lying to his people or telling the truth? You may think that he's obviously lying, trying to rile up his group over a fight that he began, but think about it for a minute. Yes, he is aggressive from the start. His policy is to kill any potential competitors to Woodbury, and it is he who starts the entire conflict. But if he's doing it to protect the town, then maybe it is justified. How is he to know what the people in the prison really want or are really there for? If you've learned the rules of this new world, like the Claimers and the Termites, you know it is kill or be killed. So why not employ an aggressive foreign policy? This is something that even Rick Grimes will later adopt to an extent, and he learns it through painful experience. "I don't take chances anymore," he tells Morgan after the two are reunited. Taking chances can get you killed. The Governor may be telling the truth. He may actually be afraid.

Okay, I'm not going to take this too far, because in the end the Governor is a psychotic who guns down his own people and burns his own town to the ground. He's insane. But his speech is very persuasive and portrays him in a very different light. Playing off people's fears, and fears of the unknown, is a rather effective strategy in any world, and the Governor uses that to his advantage. And he's not entirely wrong to be immediately distrustful of the Grimes clan. Who knows what other groups have come in contact with Woodbury? Everybody is dangerous. "Force and fraud are in war the two cardinal virtues," Hobbes writes. "Justice and injustice are none of the faculties neither of the body nor mind." You're the butcher or you're the cattle, and the quicker you learn that lesson, the better your chances for survival.

While *The Walking Dead* does a stellar job of making its villains as likable as its heroes, the people we root for are almost always good. Daryl Dixon, for instance, is as shining-star heroic as it gets. Here is a man whose pre-Turn history—like his brother's—would lead you to think he'd be an absolutely unleashed animal in the aftermath of societal collapse. And given his superior skills, he'd be really frighteningly good at it. But it's quite the opposite. Daryl may growl and scream and lunge and threaten, but he rarely does anything morally questionable, and when he does he has a good reason to. Daryl is a more upstanding citizen in the zombie world than he ever was in the old world. Hell makes Daryl a *better* man, not a worse one. He risks his life to find Sophia after she runs off the highway in season 2, and nearly gets himself killed in doing so. In season 6, episode 6, "Always Accountable," he comes across Dwight in the woods, and even after he's taken captive by him and his companions, Daryl's noble spirit wins out. He escapes with a bag of supplies but goes back because the bag has insulin in it, which diabetic Tina needs. He even helps them flee after the Saviors arrive (and it costs him, of course, down the road); Daryl is so good, so noble, he never even has sex. In the entire run of the show, he's never been with anybody. You'd think he'd find somebody, right? He's extremely close with Carol, but nothing ever happens (much to the chagrin of the Carol-Daryl "shippers"). He never finds anybody at the prison, where seemingly everyone is shacking up, and he doesn't find anybody in Woodbury, either. Even Lancelot of Camelot wasn't free from his own human emotions and desires.

The first attack on the Saviors is the one big caveat to Daryl's nobility, and everybody else's, for that matter. Rick leads a group to a Saviors outpost, thinking they are going to kill the entire gang and rid Hilltop of their oppression. It's a valuable deal to them: Hilltop has food and supplies that Alexandria needs, and all Alexandria has to offer in exchange is their ability to kill. It is not a skill set they've ever used for anything but defense, and the decision weighs on them, but they need what Hilltop has. So Rick, Daryl, Michonne, Glenn, Jesus, Sasha, Tara, Carol, Maggie, Heath, Aaron, Abraham, Rosita, even Father Gabriel, slip into a Savior outpost in the dead of night and kill everybody in cold blood.

Father Gabriel waits outside the building, guarding against anybody fleeing. He finds one, and takes him down with a rifle. "Let not your heart be troubled," he says as the Savior lies on the ground, writhing in pain. "In my Father's house are many mansions. If it were not so, I would have told you. I go to prepare a place for you." This is something Jesus told his disciples to comfort them at the Last Supper, after he explained exactly how he would be betrayed and crucified. Now, though, a proverbial man of the cloth, dressed in priestly garb, who is executing a man who calls himself a Savior, is speaking the words.

Several Alexandrians struggle with the implications. Glenn, who used to deliver pizzas and lead a normal life, is shaken. In all the years he's been with Rick, he has never killed somebody—worse, he's doing this in cold blood, too, slipping into somebody's bedroom in the dark and plunging a knife into their skull. Heath is shaken, too. Aaron is just trying to stay alive, though when the time comes, he stabs a guy right in his gut. "If it wasn't us, it was going to be you," Aaron says, justifying the attack. He's right, of course. The reality is that when the world falls apart, when all the artificial props are removed and the institutions fail, you will do what you must do to live. Or you will die.

CHAPTER 14

THE FIRST DAY OF THE REST OF YOUR LIFE

"YOU SUCK ASS, RICK. YOU REALLY DO."

—NEGAN

(SEASON 7, EPISODE 16, "THE FIRST DAY OF THE REST OF YOUR LIFE")

Rick Grimes kneels in a clearing, his son by his side, once again about to experience Negan's idea of punishment. This time, Negan is going to kill Carl, *really kill him*. Rick seethes with defiance, a defiance that astounds the strongman. "Wow, Rick," Negan whispers. Then he gets up, picks Rick's hat off Carl's head, and rears back with that baseball bat. "You said I could do it." He's about to swing when out of nowhere Ezekiel's huge tiger, Shiva, comes leaping in, shocking absolutely everyone, even Negan.

"The First Day of the Rest of Your Life," the final episode of *The Walking Dead* so far, is such an epic battle, we need to break it out and talk about it on its own for a moment. It is the climax to a story that's been building since Daryl, Abraham, and Sasha first tussled with Negan's goons (season 6, episode 9, "No Way Out"), and it's an episode that weaves both action and themes. This isn't only about a dramatic fight, though it is about that. It's also about the bonds of family that we've been talking about finally flowering and pulling together three different communities to resist the vile Saviors. It's also the climax to a story that began all the way back in the pilot episode, the culmination of everything that began when Glenn Rhee decided to help a stranger he saw trapped inside a tank on a city street in Atlanta.

You know the setup: Rick and the Alexandrians are finally ready, and armed, to fight Negan. The Kingdom has come to this decision on its own, too, and is marching to the fight. Rick has specifically asked Hilltop to stay out, wanting to have some reserve in case the fight goes poorly. This doesn't sit well with Maggie, who has become the de facto leader of the colony. Negan meanwhile knows exactly what is going on, because he made a deal with the Takers, who are going to turn on Rick from inside the walls. When Negan arrives at Alexandria, he appears as his smiling, taunting self. He's got everything ready, or so he thinks. He is going to put down this revolt, disarm Alexandria, and take a life to prove his point.

The episode itself is wonderfully cinematic, under the direction of Greg Nicotero working from a script that had a trio of writers: showrunner Scott Gimple and longtime writers Angela Kang and Matthew Negrete. Nicotero, who started out on this show as the special-effects guru, has come into his own as a director, and follows in the tradition that Darabont first set with this show, one that brings a big-screen cinematic feel to the small screen. When the Takers roll into Alexandria, Nicotero's camera is above the road and catches the action in one shot; we see the roof of the RV, then the bicyclists, then the big dump trucks. It's a somewhat disorienting image, but it's supposed to be—things are happening on the ground that are changing the world we see. This is an episode that, like the season 6 premiere (also directed by Nicotero), would play well in a theater. With the long running time (about an hour and twenty-five minutes, with commercials), it's practically a movie anyway.

The entire episode hinges on Sasha's plan to thwart Negan's plan, and in the process, she gets a memorable coda. I don't like to compare the show to the comics, but this time it's worth doing. In the comics, there is a character named Holly (not in the show) who gets captured by Negan. Negan shows up at Alexandria and "gives" her back, with a sack over her head. They bring her inside, and take off the sack to find—she's dead, and a zombie. Essentially, Negan plants a zombie bomb. Comic fans, therefore, may have had an inkling of where this was going, but the rest of us didn't. In the episode, Sasha is loaded into a casket on the back of a flatbed (Negan always with the theatrics.) Inside there, she takes the suicide pill Eugene gave her one episode prior ("Something They Need"). But he didn't expect Sasha to *turn herself* into a zombie bomb. Neither, of course, did Negan.

Sasha's story occupies a large part of the last few episodes of the season. After Abraham's death at the hands of Negan, she is obsessed with the idea of revenge. She dedicates herself to taking care of Maggie, but knows that at some point, she is going to go off on a mission to kill him. Her first attempt at killing Negan goes sour and she is captured, but she is still determined to make what's left of her life mean something. And she does not have to do what she ultimately chooses to do. Negan offers everybody a choice. She could have chosen to live, if she'd wanted. She chooses, instead, to sacrifice herself for her family, for her friends. It is a pristine example of *storge,* and Sasha feels it so strongly, she even manages to turn her death into something that benefits her family. Sasha's sacrifice may never reach the fame of Sydney Carton's in *A Tale of Two Cities,* but it is reminiscent of that sacrifice, and it is perhaps even more valuable. Carton took the guillotine to save an innocent man, and for his unrequited love of Lucie Manette. "It is a far, far better thing I do than I have ever done," Carton says. Sasha, though, sacrifices herself to save her entire community. Her surprise gives the Alexandrians an opening they need to start the fight. Sasha, who survived plague and apocalypse, love and heartbreak, pain and misery, goes to a far better rest than she has ever known. She swallows Eugene's suicide pill, turns on the old iPod he gave her, and listens to a song by Donny Hathaway: "Someday We'll All Be Free."

Indeed.

On the action side, the episode has several genuine well-timed and well-executed surprises: the Takers' betrayal (some guessed it beforehand, but I didn't); Sasha's suicide; and the arrival of the Kingdom, which comes announced by Shiva, the tiger that comes flying into the scene just as Negan is about to kill Carl. Even Negan seems genuinely frightened by the tiger, and the man who is a master of theatrics gets a painful lesson in them. Hot on the heels of that, the Hilltop fighters burst into town, led by Maggie, to join the fight. "That widow's alive, guns a-blazing," Negan says, the magnitude of the resistance finally clear to him. He's had enough. He flees in a truck, flipping Alexandria the bird as he does.

On just the level of entertainment, these surprises are perfectly executed. There'd been no giveaway to the viewer that the Takers were going to turn on the Alexandrians—there was even a fanciful exchange between the Takers' leader, Jadis, and Michonne, where Jadis tells Michonne she's going to sleep with Rick after this is all over. It's a red herring thrown at the viewer, but it works. Sasha's story is told through a series of flashbacks, and we know what's going to happen when Negan opens that casket, but the flashbacks wrap up her story and make her self-sacrifice self-evident. Even in death, she's a fully realized hero. Then, I mean, a tiger bursting across the screen is just pure spectacle, but the timing is so critical. You really do believe—at least, I really did believe—that Negan was going to murder Carl, and that would have been just a monstrous jolt to the entire story. The prospect of him getting killed ratchets up the drama to a high pitch, and director Nicotero lets it linger just long enough for you to sweat before unleashing Shiva.

All this action, all these twists and turns, though, serve a larger goal: they show these three colonies of survivors coming together, forging bonds in war that—hopefully—will see them through to a new peace somewhere down the road, and the establishment of something resembling the old world. This being *The Walking Dead,* you know that isn't going to come easy, or maybe at all. The defense of Alexandria and the birth of a new coalition, though, tie a neat bow on the arc of the entire story over the past seven years.

It started with a bunch of strangers trying to cope with something that was inherently beyond comprehension. Some were able to, some weren't. They became a small band of survivors without any permanent home, people scraping along looking for the barest elements of survival. They became adept at survival, and then had to meet a new challenge: forming a larger community. It wasn't easy. They had to overcome their own mistrust, their own fears, and balance out their own freedom to act against the benefits that come with the security of a larger group. At any point, it all could have gone sour. These people needed something to hold them together in this insane world, and they finally got it. At the end of the episode, there's a voiceover of Rick and Maggie speaking. They're talking about Sasha, and how she possibly could've planned that surprise. However it happened, that gave them a chance, Rick says, as did Maggie's decision to join the fight. "You made the right decision to come," he says. It wasn't her decision, she replies:

> The decision was made a long time ago, before any of us knew each other, when we were all strangers who would've just passed each other on the street, before the world ended. And now we mean everything to each other. You were in trouble, you were trapped, Glenn didn't know you but he helped you. He put himself in danger for you. And that started it all, from Atlanta, to my daddy's farm, to the prison, to here. To this moment now. Not as strangers, as family. Because Glenn chose to be there for you, that day a long time ago, that was the decision that changed everything. It started with both of you, and it just grew. All of this. To sacrifice for each other, to suffer, to stand, to grieve, to give, to love, to live, to fight for each other. Glenn made the decision, Rick. I was just following his lead.

It's of course a sentimental scene and speech, and it's meant as a coda to Glenn's story. While Maggie is speaking, we see scenes of the aftermath of the fight. Importantly, Maggie, Ezekiel, and Rick address the gathered people, a signal of the formal alliance of these three colonies. But the speech is about more than a sentimental send-off. She talks about sacrificing, suffering, grieving, and fighting, and doing it for each other. It's that call to action, to faith and works, to Stoically enduring no matter what's going on around you. To live like that is a choice, and if you make that choice enough times, you can help build something bigger than yourself. This group is a *family,* Maggie says. Family can be a saccharine cliché in a lot of stories, but here it represents something specific. It's that key ingredient that Deanna Monroe first saw in the Grimes clan. They have rediscovered in the remnants of humanity that *storge,* that brotherly love. And it was sparked by a choice made by the most moral of all these characters, Glenn, who never lost his faith in humanity.

It doesn't come without cost, of course. Glenn, for one, is dead, and it's not like he brought them to the edge of the promised land, either. Abraham, Sasha, Olivia, and others are all dead, and this new alliance is going to need all the bodies it can get. They've finally found each other, but their bonds will be tested immediately, because Negan is out to destroy them. One can only imagine (or read in a comic) what he has planned for these people. In fact, while the episode does come with a resolution, it is more a setup for the next chapter. Negan gets back to the Sanctuary, spends a few minutes trying to figure out how Sasha managed to kill herself, and then collects his people together and gives them a message: "We are going to war."

The episode folds in all the elements that make the show such a visceral experience for viewers, and it has only one zombie in it! (Sasha, of course.) If anything illustrates that this is more than just a zombie show, it's that. It's about rebuilding the world, and for the first time, you can see a path back for the survivors, out of the Turn, out of the horrors of a world overrun by zombies and madmen. They're not there yet—and unless Kirkman & Co. decide to wrap this show up, they'll never quite get there—but you can see that these aren't just careworn survivors anymore. These are people who belong to something bigger than themselves: an enduring and cooperating group, an association of fellows coming together for common ends.

AFTERWORD

THE END

"THIS IS A NIGHTMARE. AND NIGHTMARES END."

—BOB STOOKEY

(SEASON 5, EPISODE 2, "STRANGERS")

The inspiration for *The Walking Dead,* and all its guts and glory, began with an ending—George Romero's *Dead* movies, and, specifically, the endings of those movies. In Romero's first film, nobody survives a night among the dead. Romero's next two films end with a handful of straggling survivors making desperate escapes in helicopters as zombies overrun the world. Kirkman wanted to know what happened to those survivors after the last reel finished.

Zombie stories usually have one of two endings: mankind turns back the tide, or the zombies take over the world. In the original *Night of the Living Dead,* mankind wins, even if the individual men and women we meet in the movie all die. By the time Romero made *Dawn of the Dead,* humankind is on the run. In the remake, the zombies kill everybody and take over. In the UK's *Dead Set,* zombies overrun the world and no humans are left alive. In *28 Days Later* and its sequel, it seems that humanity has managed to keep the zombie apocalypse contained to England. In Max Brooks's great novel *World War Z,* mankind wins, after an epic, years-long struggle. The movie version, which seemingly ditched everything in the book but the title, hints at this outcome. Even Romero hasn't been able to let his endings stand. Since 1985's *Day of the Dead,* and after Kirkman began *The Walking Dead* comic in 2003, Romero has made three more *Dead* movies: *Land of the Dead* (2005), *Diary of the Dead* (2007), and *Survival of the Dead* (2009). In these movies, he expanded on the universe he'd begun back in 1968, and focused on more survivor stories.

The one thing all these stories have in common, though, is that they *do* end. And someday *The Walking Dead* will end, too. Probably. Most likely. Seemingly. How many prime-time shows run forever? *Lassie* ran seventeen seasons, *Gunsmoke* twenty, and *The Simpsons* is still showing us life in Springfield. But every show eventually does end. Even if *The Walking Dead* kept its rating up, and ran for another decade, eventually they'd have to turn the cast over, and eventually even the best creative team runs out of drive and gumption. An end seems inevitable.

While its popularity ensures that *The Walking Dead* has no end in sight, one person already knows the ending: Robert Kirkman. At least that's what he has said publicly. He has the entire story sketched out in his head, and has an ending in mind. This is important. Bonansinga, the horror novelist, teaches his students to have an ending in mind before they start writing. To him, it's critical that the writer know where the story is going. It's an essential element of writing. Deciding when to end a television show, though—assuming the choice is in the showrunner's hands—is tricky. Look, if *The Walking Dead* used season 8 as its finale—it isn't going to, but let's just play this game—if they picked a definitive end date, what they've produced through those eight seasons would stand on its own. They would have created a landmark show, introduced unforgettable, iconic characters, and changed the face of television. That's not a bad legacy. Is it better to cement that into place and walk away, or to keep going to some opaque end down the road? We're clearly headed for the latter, so it's worth pondering for a moment here two things: When should the end come? And what might it look like? Has *The Walking Dead* jumped the shark?

If you don't already know, the jump-the-shark moment is a reference to the moment in *Happy Days* (season 5, episode 3) when the Fonz gets on water skis and literally jumps over two sharks. It has become a metaphor for when a TV show stops caring about things like internal logic, continuity, drama, its characters, even its audience. It's when the writers start plugging in crazy stunts and gimmicks just for the sake of shock value, or even worse, ratings. I heard people saying it had happened after both the Glenn-in-the-alley cliff-hanger and the Negan-in-the-woods cliff-hanger. This is a dangerous moment that no true artist should ever want to reach.

I remember watching season 7, episode 12, "Say Yes," the one where Rick and Michonne find a survivors' camp in a carnival, and for the first time in a while, being on the edge of my seat. Every second, I was expecting something to pop out and threaten those two: a walker, a patrol of Saviors, some random desperado, anything. I was hooked. It was a feeling I hadn't had for a while with this show—not since before Glenn impossibly got out of that alley. I realized how badly that cliff-hanger had affected how I watched this show, and realized that somewhere along the line, somewhere after Negan killed Glenn and Abraham and before Negan's subjects began their revolt, the show had gotten me back. All the way back. I don't think *The Walking Dead* has jumped the shark. But that's me. Others will feel differently.

The Walking Dead's ratings are still otherworldly, and the current cast is deep and veteran; it has four or five actors after Andrew Lincoln who could step into the starring role, like Melissa McBride, Norman Reedus, Lennie James, Danai Gurira, or Lauren Cohan. In other words, there could be significant changes in the cast and the show likely wouldn't suffer. Kirkman certainly doesn't want to end it, and he's not about to run out of material. In a late 2016 issue of the comics, number 161, Kirkman touched on the show's future in the "letter hacks" column he writes. "It took us six seasons to get to [issue] 100. It won't take us six years to get to 200 and that will take us to season . . . twelve. And we'll still be ahead of the show at that point." In other words, the man's talking about at least five more seasons of the show. Moreover, Kirkman doesn't own the show, AMC does. Even with the dip in season 7's ratings, it's impossible to imagine AMC would willingly let the show go off the air.

Kirkman did provide one clue, on Marc Maron's popular *WTF* podcast. "I do hope that *The Walking Dead* goes on long enough that when it ends, they're like, 'Good thing we took care of those zombies.'" So, at the very least, you can see him leaning toward a happy ending. At the Charlotte Walker Stalker Con, Michael Rooker, who played Merle, gave his take on the ending. In his vision, there's an image of a set of railroad tracks, and a single person walking down them. You hear a voiceover, and soon enough realize it's Carl, grown, and that the entire show has been him recounting his past. Also, given that he's alone, "everyone on the show is dead. He's the only survivor, and he's on his own and walks off into the sunset." There's something beautifully majestic, and also very sad, about that image.

For my own part, I've thought about the ending many times. When I ran my version by Jay Bonansinga, he saw it slightly differently: He pictured the survivors walking over a sea of comatose zombies, like the last scene in *The Birds*. Are they really dead? Is it over? We never find out. That's a pretty good ending—and it's a very Jay Bonansinga ending, too, in the best way—but I'd go for something a bit more finite. Because you've read this book this far, indulge me a bit more:

It is some distant point in the future. Myriad challenges have been met, foes vanquished, zombies brained. The fledgling network of survivor camps have formed an alliance and carved out a true safe zone around the mid-Atlantic states. Law and order exist. People are doing the hard work of rebuilding the world. Michonne returns from some trip out in the hinterlands. She's back in Alexandria, back home. She meets Carl, who is out walking with an adolescent Judith. Carl is a young man now, and an up-and-coming leader in the community. There's persistent talk of him taking on the role that was meant for his father. Carl is asking Michonne about her trip, and she's telling him about what she's seen out there. "You know what I didn't see?" she says.

"Walkers," Carl answers.

"Walkers," she agrees. "Haven't seen one in months. Don't know that any are left."

"Well," Carl says, "that's a start."

"It sure is."

And off they walk, down the street, toward the setting sun. It's over. The humans have won. Society will be restored. It's a happy ending. Sort of. Because you know what you don't see here, besides walkers? Rick. Daryl. Carol. Morgan. Ezekiel. Dianne. Maggie. Eugene. Negan. Gregory. Rosita. Aaron. Tobin. Jesus. In my ending, the humans win, but only after suffering grievous losses. The only survivors from the current cast are Michonne, Judith, and Carl. Everybody else dies along the way, even Rick Grimes, which makes him kind of like the show's Moses, the shepherd who brings his people to the promised land but does not get to enter. The show's true center, then, is Carl, a child when the Turn hit, who was put through hell on his way to manhood.

We talked about the idea of "faith without works is dead" earlier, and another way to state that is "works give faith life." Pain and grief are human constants, and some of us get doled out more of that than others, and you just have to grind through it. Look, I've been there, and it stinks. Nobody wants pain. But like Marcus Aurelius and Abraham Ford understood, that's just the way it is. You do what you need to do, and then you get to live.

So all those characters will die over however many more seasons the show runs. They'll be replaced by other people—Michonne, Judith, and Carl aren't the last three people left on earth. The important point, after all, won't be that certain people survive, but that in their struggle they transmit the things that matter to this new world, like that humanity exemplified by Glenn. Carl, a kid who at various times himself seemed to succumb to his baser instincts, becomes everything his father tried so hard to be. Good does triumph over evil, mankind does endure. Works build faith. Ending it like this kind of gives it to you both ways. It's happy . . . well, happy-ish . . . but it's also brutally sad, because almost everybody you care about dies. And that's what usually happens in zombie stories. At least, the really good ones.

BIBLIOGRAPHY

INTRODUCTION: THE BEATING HEART OF *THE WALKING DEAD*

I was fortunate enough to be part of the crowd that night at Madison Square Garden, so the majority of this is firsthand accounting. Additional details on ratings here and later in the book come mostly from the website TV By the Numbers. And specifically:

Porter, Rick. "Sunday cable ratings: *The Walking Dead* takes a bigger-than-usual hit in episode 2." TV By the Numbers, Nov. 1, 2016.

Porter, Rick. "The 20 highest-rated shows of 2016: *The Walking Dead* and *The Big Bang Theory* win the year." TV By the Numbers, Dec. 26, 2016.

CHAPTER 1: THE GERM

I moderated one panel with Robert Kirkman, in 2015 at South by Southwest, and I've seen him speak at others, including another panel at that same conference and New York Comic Con. From that I pieced together a lot of his background story. Some factual information was confirmed by Skybound Entertainment, and much else is already in the public record.

Some of the details on Kirkman's early days are from a 2016 interview he gave at the New York Comic Con. There are two articles about the talk:

Pepose, David. "NYCC '16: *The Walking Dead* Panel." Newsarama, Oct. 8, 2016. http://www.newsarama.com/31379-nycc-16-the-walking-dead.html.

Kirkman, Robert. Interview with Brian Crecente, South by Southwest, March 14, 2015. https://www.youtube.com/watch?v=jJmkgqfGdIs.

Kirkman, Robert. Interview with Paul F. Tomkins, Made Man, Oct. 14, 2013. https://www.youtube.com/watch?v=ZW7v6SCAy1k.

Vigna, Paul. "New York Comic Con: *Walking Dead* Creator Robert Kirkman Talks Negan and Season 7." *Wall Street Journal,* Oct. 6, 2016.

I culled a lot of detail about the show's development from public documents related to Frank Darabont's lawsuit with AMC, which are accessible to the public on the New York State court system's website. The initial complaint, filed on Dec. 17, 2013, was especially helpful: https://iapps.courts.state.ny.us/fbem/DocumentDisplayServlet?documentId=iiWvL/9lhAAm0uZ93uv4jg==&system=prod.

All details about Cynthiana are from the town's website, http://www.cynthianaky.com/.

Juan Gabriel Pareja, Kerry Cahill, and Jay Bonansinga were all interviewed over the phone.

Additional select sources:

Brewer, James. "The cancellation of AMC series *Rubicon*: Too close to home?" World Socialist Web Site, Dec. 2, 2010. https://www.wsws.org/en/articles/2010/12/rubi-d02.html.

Bricker, Tierney. "Did You Spot Ashton Kutcher's Sister in *The*

Walking Dead Finale?" E! News, April 7, 2016. http://www.eonline.com/news/754813/did-you-spot-ashton-kutcher-s-sister-in-the-walking-dead-finale.

Clark, Kevin. "NFL Players' Weekly Challenge: Making It Home for *The Walking Dead.*" *Wall Street Journal,* Nov. 23, 2015.

Davis, Brandon. "Chris Daughtry Auditioned for *The Walking Dead.*" Comicbook, May 12, 2016. http://comicbook.com/thewalkingdead/2016/05/12/chris-daughtry-auditioned-for-the-walking-dead/.

Davis, Brandon. "John Cusack Wants to Appear on *The Walking Dead.*" Comicbook, May 31, 2016. http://comicbook.com/thewalkingdead/2016/05/31/john-cusack-wants-to-appear-on-the-walking-dead/.

DeWolf, Nancy. "Everything Old Is New Again." *Wall Street Journal,* Oct. 22, 2012.

Ebert, Roger. "*Night of the Living Dead.*" *Chicago Sun-Times,* Jan. 5, 1969 (originally). http://www.rogerebert.com/reviews/the-night-of-the-living-dead-1968.

Goodman, Tim. "*The Walking Dead*: TV Review." *Hollywood Reporter,* Oct. 30, 2010.

Harkness, Ryan. "Ronda Rousey Gets Geeky Over *Game of Thrones* and *The Walking Dead.*" Uproxx, April 20, 2016. http://uproxx.com/sports/ronda-rousey-odell-beckham-game-of-thrones-walking-dead-draftkings/.

Hibberd, James. "AMC sells overseas rights to *Walking Dead.*" *Hollywood Reporter,* June 9, 2010.

Hill, Jim. "Makeup Master Greg Nicotero Helps Make AMC's *The Walking Dead* a Gory Must-see." Huffington Post, Dec. 18, 2012. http://www.huffingtonpost.com/jim-hill/walking-dead-amc_b_1968726.html.

MacKenzie, Steven. "George A. Romero: *The Walking Dead* is a soap opera with occasional zombies." The Big Issue, Nov.

3, 2013. https://www.bigissue.com/interviews/george-romero-walking-dead-soap-opera-occasional-zombies/.

Moss, Linda. "What McEnroe Built at AMC." Multichannel News, June 22, 2003. http://www.multichannel.com/news/orphan-articles/what-mcenroe-built-amc/153762.

Peisner, David. "Robert Kirkman: I Can Do 1,000 Issues of *The Walking Dead*." *Rolling Stone*, Oct. 8, 2013.

Petski, Denise. "*The Walking Dead* Spanish-Dubbed Episodes to Air on NBC Universo." Deadline Hollywood, Oct. 20. 2015. http://deadline.com/2015/10/the-walking-dead-spanish-nbc-universo-1201588549/.

Reed, Patrick. "On This Day in 1992: The Start of the Image Comics Revolution." Comics Alliance, Feb. 1, 2016. http://comicsalliance.com/tribute-image-comics/.

Roxborough, Scott. "*Fear the Walking Dead* Sets Global Ratings Record for AMC." *Hollywood Reporter,* Aug. 28, 2015.

Ryan, Maureen. "*Mad Men*'s Matthew Weiner on the Clash with AMC and the Season 5 Premiere." March 15, 2012, HuffingtonPost. http://www.huffingtonpost.com/2012/03/15/mad-men-matthew-weiner_n_1347740.html.

Stetler, Brian. "Season 5 of *Mad Men* Is Delayed Until 2012." *New York Times,* March 29, 2011.

"*The Walking Dead* Continues to Break Records Worldwide." World Screen, Nov. 8, 2010. http://worldscreen.com/the-walking-dead-continues-to-break-records-worldwide/.

Ward, Kate. "*The Walking Dead* premiere attracts 5.3 million viewers." *Entertainment Weekly,* Nov. 1, 2010.

CHAPTER 2: THE MAGIC TRICK

Conversations with both Addy Miller and Tom Savini were integral in helping me understand the process of creating zombies and the special effects. Frank Renzulli helped me understand how the effects work within the story.

Additional select sources:

Lowe, Kevin. *Savage Continent: Europe in the Aftermath of World War II.* Picador, 2013.

Peisner, David. "Robert Kirkman: I Can Do 1,000 Issues of *The Walking Dead.*" *Rolling Stone,* Oct. 8, 2013.

CHAPTER 3: PATHOLOGY

Roger Ebert's 1969 article about going to see *Night of the Living Dead* at a Saturday matinee is a fantastic essay that every zombie fan should read.

The history of the genre and of George Romero has been covered extensively. Some details are from the 2008 documentary *One for the Fire: The Legacy of Night of the Living Dead,* but virtually all of the details are available in various forms, the oral histories having been told and retold.

Otto Penzler was gracious enough to sit down with me when I walked in unannounced to his lower Manhattan bookstore, the Mysterious Bookshop, and talk zombies and pulp fiction.

Sarah Wayne Callies was kind enough to point me in the direction of her 2013 speech at the University of Hawaii about zombies and Chekhov.

A lot of the early zombies movies, and I do mean a lot, are available on YouTube in full. *White Zombie, King of the Zombies, Revenge of the Zombies, Night of the Living Dead, Zombies of Mora Tau, Zombies of the Stratosphere* (not an easy watch, but educational to be sure), and others are out there, waiting to be watched late on a Saturday night.

To be honest, I don't remember exactly which rabbit hole led me to William of Newburgh and Walter Map, but a proper zombie history would not be complete without them. The translation I sourced of William's *Historia rerum Anglicarum* was prepared by Scott McLetchie, and was published on Fordham University's Internet History Sourcebooks Project, http://sourcebooks.fordham.edu/halsall/basis/williamofnewburgh-five.asp#22.

Two other key sources were:

Black, William-Henry. "A Descriptive Analytical and Critical Catalogue of the Manuscripts Bequeathed Unto the University of Oxford." 1845.

James, M.R. "How to read Walter Map." Mittellateinisches Jahrbuch, Vol. XXIII, 1988. http://people.bu.edu/bobl/map.htm.

Additional select sources:

Ebert, Roger. "*Night of the Living Dead.*" *Chicago Sun-Times*, Jan. 5, 1969 (originally). http://www.rogerebert.com/reviews/the-night-of-the-living-dead-1968.

Hartlaub, Peter. "Dead and Fred: George A. Romero's connection to Mr. Rogers." SFGate, May 13, 2010. http://blog.sfgate.com/parenting/2010/05/13/dead-and-fred-george-a-romeros-connection-to-mr-rogers/.

McConnell, Mariana. "Interview: George A. Romero on *Diary of the Dead.*" CinemaBlend, 2008. http://www.cinemablend.com/new/Interview-George-Romero-Diary-Dead-7818.html.

Phillips, Mary E. "Edgar Allen Poe: The Man," Part II, Section 6. The John C. Winston Co., 1926. http://www.eapoe.org/papers/misc1921/mep2cb06.htm.

Rodrique, Jean-Paul. "The Geography of Transport Systems."

Hofstra University, Department of Global Studies & Geography, 2017. https://people.hofstra.edu/geotrans/eng/ch1en/conc1en/telecomdiffusionUS.html.
Than, Ker. "Neanderthal Burials Confirmed as Ancient Ritual." *National Geographic,* Dec. 16, 2013.

CHAPTER 4: BRINGING THE DEAD TO LIFE

Much of the details about creating the zombie effects come from extras on *The Walking Dead* season 1 DVD, and an online short, "The Well Walker: Inside *The Walking Dead*" (https://www.youtube.com/watch?v=IoJW1hs967I).

In addition, Tom Savini was again integral in understanding the practical logistics of creating these effects, and I relied on additional thoughts from Juan Gabriel Pareja and Xander Berkeley.

Additional select sources:

Adams, Sam. "In Its Season Premiere, *The Walking Dead*'s Brutal Violence Finally Went Too Far." Slate, Oct. 24, 2016. http://www.slate.com/blogs/browbeat/2016/10/24/in_its_season_premiere_the_walking_dead_s_brutal_violence_finally_went_too.html.
DeFino, Dean J. *The HBO Effect.* Bloomsbury Academic, 2013.
Gerbner, George. "Cultural Indicators: The Case of Violence in Television Drama." *The Annals of the American Academy,* March 1, 1970. http://web.asc.upenn.edu/gerbner/Asset.aspx-?assetID=379.
Jaworski, Michelle. "Here are the complaints the FCC received after *The Walking Dead*'s season 7 premiere." The Daily Dot, Dec. 15, 2016. https://www.dailydot.com/parsec/walking-dead-fcc-complaints/.
Talbot, Margaret. "Stealing Life." *The New Yorker,* Oct. 22, 2007.

CHAPTER 5: HEART

Much of the material here was pulled from interviews with the cast both before and after I started writing this book. I talked to Melissa McBride in 2013, for instance, and Norman Reedus came through the newsroom for an interview in 2014. Robert Kirkman was in town for Comic Con in 2016. I interviewed Jay Bonansinga, Xander Berkeley, and Andrew Lincoln in 2017.

Additional select sources:

Ho, Rodney. "Atlanta actress Melissa McBride transforms Carol, her *Walking Dead* character." *Atlanta-Journal Constitution,* Oct. 8, 2014.

Peisner, David. "Melissa McBride: Carol Represents *The Walking Dead* Viewers." *Rolling Stone,* Oct. 15, 2013.

Ross, Dalton. "*The Walking Dead*: How Sarah Wayne Callies saved Carol." *Entertainment Weekly,* Feb. 10, 2016.

Vigna, Paul. "Full Interview: *Walking Dead* Star Norman Reedus." *Wall Street Journal,* March 2, 2014.

Vigna, Paul. "*The Walking Dead* Season 7 Preview: 'The Show Itself Changes.'" *Wall Street Journal,* Oct. 20, 2016.

Vigna, Paul. "Why *The Walking Dead* Speaks to Scary Economic Times." *Wall Street Journal,* Oct. 11, 2013.

CHAPTER 6: RUPTURE

Most of the details in this chapter are sourced from various filings in the lawsuit Frank Darabont filed against AMC which are available online via the New York State court system website.

The initial complaint can be found here: https://iapps.courts.state.ny.us/fbem/DocumentDisplayServlet?documentId=iiWvL/9lhAAm0uZ93uv4jg==&system=prod.

The case's documents can be found here: http://iapps.courts.state.ny.us/iscroll/SQLData.jsp?IndexNo=654328-2013&Page=151.

Additional select sources:

AMC year-end and fourth-quarter 2015 financial statement, Feb. 25, 2016. http://investors.amcnetworks.com/releasedetail.cfm?ReleaseID=957113.

Gardner, Eriq. "*Walking Dead* Creator Hit with Second Lawsuit Claiming Co-Ownership." *Hollywood Reporter,* Aug. 8, 2012.

Masters, Kim. "*The Walking Dead*: What Really Happened to Fired Showrunner Frank Darabont." *Hollywood Reporter,* Aug. 10, 2011.

McMillan, Graeme. "*The Walking Dead* Behind-the-Scenes Battle That Almost Doubled the Zombie Count." *Time,* Oct. 10, 2012.

Sloan, Scott. "*The Walking Dead* Day brings the zombie apocalypse, and its artists, to Cynthiana." *Lexington Herald Leader,* Aug. 4, 2016, http://www.kentucky.com/entertainment/tv/article93677227.html.

Yeoman, Kevin. "Frank Darabont Steps Down as *The Walking Dead* Showrunner." ScreenRant, July 26, 2011. http://screenrant.com/frank-darabont-the-walking-dead-showrunner/.

CHAPTER 7: EXPANSION

The factual information for this chapter is all available online. Additional commentary came from interviews with Cliff Curtis, Jay Bonansinga, and Joanne Christopherson, who provided stats related to the course and additional documents that were helpful in other chapters as well.

The initial episode of *Talking Dead* has several web-only segments available on AMC's website, that are pretty entertaining in their own right.

For what it's worth, my hometown has a sturdy brick library that would make a great safe haven in the event of a zombie apocalypse, and also happened to be a good writing space.

Additional select sources:

Adalain, Josef. "AMC Is Mulling a Talk Show About Its Own Dramas." Vulture, Aug. 29, 2011. http://www.vulture.com/2011/08/amc_is_mulling_a_post-game_tal.html.

Meslow, Scott. "Don't Waste Your Time with Shows Like *Talking Dead*." *GQ*, July 20, 2016.

Porter, Rick. "*Walking Dead, Monday Night Football* go 1-2 again in cable top 25 for Dec. 5011." Screener, Dec. 13, 2016. http://tvbythenumbers.zap2it.com/weekly-ratings/cable-top-25-for-dec-5-11-2016/.

CHAPTER 8: MARCUS AURELIUS AND ZOMBIES

This chapter was both a rabbit hole and a starting point. Long before the idea of a book about this show was hatched, I'd written an article in 2013 for the *Wall Street Journal* that represented my first attempt to glean the deeper meaning of the show. It's something that's been on my mind since then, and trying to answer that question is really the main point of this entire book.

There were several people I talked to whose insights ended up in this chapter, including Sonya Iryna from Undead Walking. Ann Mahoney was generous enough to talk about her religious take on the show.

The paper about religion on the show written by Erika Engstrom and Joseph Valenzano was great on its own, but the bibliography of that paper, and all the sources they cited, was a treasure trove of additional information for me. I'm indebted to them for sharing it.

Additional select sources:

"America's Changing Religious Landscape." Pew Research Center, May 12, 2015. http://www.pewforum.org/2015/05/12/americas-changing-religious-landscape/.

Aurelius, Marcus. *Meditations* in *Marcus Aurelius and His Times,* translated from the Greek by George Long. Walter J. Black Inc., 1943.

The Bible (King James Version), public domain.

Engstrom, Erika, and Joseph Valenzano. "Religion and the Representative Anecdote: Replacement and Revenge in AMC's *The Walking Dead.*" *Journal of Media and Religion,* Aug. 11, 2016.

Hall, Stuart. "Encoding and decoding in the television discourse." University of Birmingham, 1973.

Vigna, Paul. "Full Interview: *Walking Dead* Star Norman Reedus." *Wall Street Journal,* March 2, 2014.

Vigna, Paul. "Why *The Walking Dead* Speaks to Scary Economic Times." *Wall Street Journal,* Oct. 11, 2013.

Winston, Diane. *Small Screen, Big Picture: Television and Lived Religion.* Baylor University Press, 2009.

CHAPTER 9: *THE WALKING DEAD'S* GREATEST MOMENT

This chapter simply would not have been possible without the help of Ann Mahoney, who patiently walked me through the entire one-night production.

The concept of *storge* was introduced to me by Engstrom and Valenzano, and indeed there is a reason chapters 8 and 9 are grouped together; the concepts introduced in chapter 8 by Engstrom, Valenzano, and others are largely abstractions of what is perfectly illustrated in the epic Alexandria fight.

Incidentally, if you're interested in knowing the order in which the Alexandrians are shown in that final quick-cut sequence, I watched it on DVD, pausing at each cut, and finally came up with this order: Glenn brains a walker, Morgan swings his staff, Daryl waves his knife around. After that, it's Maggie, Sasha, Eugene, Father Gabriel, Tobin, Carol, Michonne, Abraham, Aaron, Rosita, Bruce, Kent, Francine, Kent, Bruce, Michonne, Eugene, Aaron, Sasha, Gabriel, Sasha, Barbara, Morgan, Tobin, Carol, Eugene, Francine, and, finally, Rick Grimes.

CHAPTER 10: FOUR WALLS AND A ROOF IN CHARLOTTE, NC

Most of the details in this chapter come firsthand from the Charlotte, NC, Walker Stalker Convention, including interviews with participants and actors.

Weapons

I was already planning on doing a short section on weapons, but it was Kerry Cahill's comment about her character's bow, and how it was designed to amplify her character, that made me realize how much the weapons meant to the individual characters.

The Walking Dead Wiki site and the Internet Movie Firearms Database were indispensable sources for this section.

Additional select sources:

Baker, Chris. "The Colt Python—An Ideal Zombie Gun?" Lucky Gunner, Feb. 5, 2013. http://www.luckygunner.com/labs/colt-python/.

Stenudd, Stefan. "Aikido in *The Walking Dead.*" Aikido, Art, Writing, Philosophy and More, Nov. 3, 2015. http://www.stenudd.com/aikido/aikido-walking-dead-s06e04.htm.

CHAPTER 11: DISSECTION

Adam Carlson and I had a good long chat about Glenn in the alley, and Frank Renzulli helped me think through the issues from a writer's perspective.

I really have wondered for a long time about how easy it would be to actually get a knife through a skull. Marc MacYoung and Gary Harper were both kind enough to lend their expertise.

Additional select sources:

Vigna, Paul. "Sorry, *Walking Dead* Fans, That Death Was Real." *Wall Street Journal,* Oct. 26, 2015.

CHAPTER 12: WAR AND PIECES

Some of the ideas for this chapter came from Joanne Christopherson's online course, especially the concept of applying Maslow's Hierarchy of Needs to *The Walking Dead*, and of course some of it is an expansion of concepts that were explored earlier in the book. Though I didn't mention it by name, Daniel Drezner's *Theories of International Politics and Zombies* was also an inspiration for the ideas in this chapter.

It turns out that the politics of *The Walking Dead* is actually a pretty popular topic. There was no end to the articles on this topic, and the list below is just a sampling of what's out there on the show.

Collins, Sean T. "The Fascism of *The Walking Dead.*" Vulture, Dec. 13, 2016. http://www.vulture.com/2016/12/the-walking-deads-fascism.html.

Drezner, Daniel W. *Theories of International Politics and Zombies*. Princeton University Press, 2011.

French, David. "In the Zombie World, Only the Conservative Survive." *National Review,* Oct. 3, 2015.

Healy, Andrew, and Neil Malhorta. "Myopic Voters and Natural Disaster Policy." *American Political Science Review,* Vol. 103, No. 3, August 2009.

Hobbes, Thomas. *Leviathan*. Updated by Prof. Jonathan Bennett, July 2004, http://www.earlymoderntexts.com/authors/hobbes.

CHAPTER 13: SANITY AND MORALITY

This is another topic that you could write a book about, and in fact others have. A preview copy of Greg Garrett's *Living with the Living Dead* (Oxford University Press, 2017) showed up on my desk and provided valuable insights into the effects of zombies and apocalypse on the mind.

Hobbes ends up making another appearance in this chapter, but it seemed to me the best historical analogue to the world portrayed in *The Walking Dead* is the Black Death of the fourteenth century. It captures both the mystery plague, the rampant, random death, and the collapse of society. There are obviously countless volumes on the topic, but I had time enough to consult only a few. The best contemporary account is probably Giovanni Boccaccio's *The Decameron*, published in 1353. The Italian poet Petrarch also wrote about it, and a take on that can be found in George Deaux's 1969 history, *The Black Death, 1347,* published by Weybright and Talley.

ACKNOWLEDGMENTS

There are some people without whom this book would not have been realized.

First is my agent, Gillian McKenzie. This book didn't exist before Gillian asked me one day, "Do you think there's a book to be done about *The Walking Dead*?" It was an "I could have had a V8" moment. *Of course* there's a book to do, I replied, and we started sketching out the ideas for it. Gillian was an energetic supporter of the book and worked hard to find the best editor for it.

Matthew Daddona, my editor at Dey Street, did a superb job of working under a really tight deadline and making sure we got this book done, and done well. He was full of suggestions and encouragement, and was not afraid to break out the proverbial red pen. This would have been a far less focused book without his efforts. In fact, the entire team at Dey Street, including publisher Lynn Grady, publicist Caroline Perny, marketing director Kendra Newton, marketing manager Kell Wilson, and senior production editor David Palmer, jumped into action to make sure this book stayed on track and got done. William Ruoto did the great interior design, and copyeditor Laura Cherkas saved me from more errors than I care to acknowledge. Tony Moore provided his iconic talents for the fantastically grisly and graphic cover. The anatomy of the walking dead, indeed.

My colleagues and editors at the *Wall Street Journal* have long supported my zombie habit, and were enthusiastic backers of this book as well. I'm grateful to editor in chief Gerry Baker, and ethics and standards editors Neal Lipschutz and Karen Pensiero for their blessing. Within the Business & Finance section, I want to thank the section's managing editor, Dennis K. Berman. Stephen Grocer, my editor on the Moneybeat blog, hired me to write about finance and stocks, and over the years has stoically endured my forays into bitcoin and zombies. He's been a good boss, a good friend, and a great proponent of my work. Thanks to Erik Holm for all the Monday morning post-show discussions. Lastly, Michael Rapoport was the one who suggested me for the recaps in the first place, so this really is all his fault. In the arts department, I'm grateful for Barbara Chai for giving me the opportunity to write the recaps, and to Lisa Bannon for continuing them. I'd also like to thank Michael Calia and Mike Ayers for their help over the years as we waded through zombies, dragons, robots, and Elliot Alderson's psychosis; we formed quite a geek squad.

Mike Casey, my coauthor and friend, brought me into this world of publishing, for which I will be ever grateful.

A number of people lent their time and expertise to this book, and any mistake or errors are mine, not theirs. Thank you to Otto Penzler, Dave Solo at Walker Nation LLC, the staff at Walker Stalker Con, Joanne Christopherson, and Erika Engstrom. Jay Bonansinga and Frank Renzulli were very generous with their time, and helped me understand the show from the writer's perspective. Xander Berkeley, Ann Mahoney, Juan Gabriel Pareja, Andrew Lincoln, and Kerry Cahill all had great insights into the show and gave me things to think about I hadn't even considered before. Thanks also to June Alian at Skybound, and at AMC, Jim Maiella, Olivia Dupuis, and Emily Hunter for their help over the years.

Lastly, but most importantly, I want to thank my family. You mean the world to me. I'm fortunate to come from a large, loving family and to have married into another equally wonderful one. I was blessed to have two encouraging parents, Michele and Joseph, who instilled in me very early a love of reading and fantastic stories about famous sailors and mystery-solving brothers. My mother-in-law, Sara Krisher, aunt JoAnn Kulpeksa, sister Jeanne-Michele, and brother-in-law Matt Anderson have all been great for post-episode, next-day debates.

I cannot say enough to thank my son, Robert, and my wife, Elizabeth. You inspire me to do better things, both of you. Before you came along, I was a guy who thought he could write books, and should write books, but never actually did. Liz is my supporter, sounding board, best friend, and TV-watching partner. This book involved a lot of nights and weekends away from them, and Liz kept everything running smoothly at home while I was hiding in the garret, banging away on the keyboard. I cannot thank you both enough for your support and love.

ABOUT THE AUTHOR

PAUL VIGNA is a reporter for the *Wall Street Journal* and also contributes to the popular MoneyBeat blog. He is the author (with Michael J. Casey) of the critically acclaimed *The Age of Cryptocurrency* and *The Truth Machine*. He lives in Verona, New Jersey, with his wife, Elizabeth, and their son.